Innocent Civilians

Also by Colm McKeogh

THE POLITICAL REALISM OF REINHOLD NIEBUHR

Innocent Civilians

The Morality of Killing in War

Colm McKeogh
Lecturer
University of Waikato
New Zealand

palgrave

© Colm McKeogh 2002

All rights reserved. No reproduction, copy or transmission of
this publication may be made without written permission.

No paragraph of this publication may be reproduced, copied or
transmitted save with written permission or in accordance with
the provisions of the Copyright, Designs and Patents Act 1988,
or under the terms of any licence permitting limited copying
issued by the Copyright Licensing Agency, 90 Tottenham Court Road,
London W1P 0LP.

Any person who does any unauthorized act in relation to this
publication may be liable to criminal prosecution and civil
claims for damages.

The author has asserted his right to be identified as the
author of this work in accordance with the
Copyright, Designs and Patents Act 1988.

First published 2002 by
PALGRAVE
Houndmills, Basingstoke, Hampshire RG21 6XS and
175 Fifth Avenue, New York, N.Y. 10010
Companies and representatives throughout the world

PALGRAVE is the new global academic imprint of
St. Martin's Press LLC Scholarly and Reference Division and
Palgrave Publishers Ltd (formerly Macmillan Press Ltd).

ISBN 0–333–97237–6

This book is printed on paper suitable for recycling and
made from fully managed and sustained forest sources.

A catalogue record for this book is available
from the British Library.

Library of Congress Cataloging-in-Publication Data

McKeogh, Colm, 1965–
Innocent civilians : the morality of killing in war / Colm McKeogh.
    p. cm.
  Includes bibliographical references and index.
  ISBN 0–333–97237–6
    1. War—protection of civilians. 2. Combatants and noncombatants
(International law). 3. War—Moral and ethical aspects. I. Title

KZ6515 .M35 2002
172'.42–dc21   2001054884

10   9   8   7   6   5   4   3   2   1
11   10 09 08 07 06 05 04 03 02

Printed and bound in Great Britain by
Antony Rowe Ltd, Chippenham, Wiltshire

For Caoimhe and Siobhán

Contents

Acknowledgments

Chapter 5 of this work was written while on sabbatical at the Department of International Politics, Aberystwyth, in 1999. I am grateful to the staff of the department for their hospitality. I am grateful too to my colleagues at the University of Waikato. Finally, my thanks are due to the anonymous reviewers for Palgrave whose comments were unfailingly informed and constructive.

1
Introduction

> *How senseless is everything that can ever be written, done, or*
> *thought when such things are possible. It must all be lies and of*
> *no account when the culture of a thousand years could not pre-*
> *vent this stream of blood being poured out ...*
>
> E. M. Remarque[1]

War is a purposeful act of lethal force on the group level. It causes, and
is intended to cause, death, misery and destruction. Whatever its ends,
war is fought using people as instruments: their suffering, incapacita-
tion and death are the means to its military and political ends. Yet not
all people are to be so treated. For many centuries in the Western
world, the targeting of some people has been deplored and it remains
the case in our own time that the harming and killing of 'innocent
civilians' in war is thought worse than the harming and killing of
soldiers. When NATO went to war against Serbia in 1999, US Secretary
of State William Cohen assured the world that 'we go to extraordinary
lengths to reduce the risks to innocent civilians' and British Prime
Minister Tony Blair boldly declared that 'we take every single measure we can to try to avoid civilian casualties'.[2] NATO did indeed make
efforts to avoid civilian casualties and Pentagon officials claimed that
the fear of civilian casualties was a key factor in virtually every aspect
of war planning. Instead of attacking 'area targets', it sought precision
in its bombing; when smoke or clouds obstructed laser-guided bombs,
strikes were cancelled. NATO's concerns to minimize civilian casualties
were matched by Serbian efforts to draw worldwide attention to inci-
dents where NATO air strikes had killed Kosovar or Serbian civilians.

The concern to limit the effects of war to the fighters themselves may be as old as war itself. There is evidence from earliest written testimonies of attempts to restrict the means permissible in war, to spare lives when possible, and to forego the spoiling of lands. Prior to the Christian era, the idea developed that some members of the enemy population ought not to be targeted in war: Celtic tribes spared bards and poets so that the history of the battle could be recorded; Hebrew, Greek and Roman philosophers, poets and prophets decried violence against women, children and prisoners.[3] From such beginnings developed the idea of immunity in war. This idea was supported by a diverse array of values. Ettiquette required respect for women. The Jewish scriptures taught that the innocent ought not to be punished for the crimes of the guilty. Christianity preached charity and mercy. Chivalric codes contributed the idea that one ought not to harm the unarmed and defenceless. Enlightenment rationalism deplored the waste and cruelty of war. And, finally, military professionalism focused on the skill of gaining victory over armed opponents without massacre and wanton destruction. Over time all of these values added weight to the notion of non-combatant immunity so that, by the end of the nineteenth century, there had evolved in Europe legal principles of restraint in war. At their core was the principle that non-combatants ought not to be the target of attacks in warfare; only military personnel and property may be targeted.

The prohibition on killing civilians was the first restriction on war to be founded in international law, predating prohibitions on weaponry. In the eighteenth century, this law or custom of war was embedded in the military tradition of every European power. It had the status of unwritten law and it rested on a consensus agreement among the European states. From the 1850s, the main branches of law of war were codified into formal treaty-registered international law around the principle of non-combatant immunity. The twentieth century began with the establishment of the principle in law by the Hague Conferences of 1899 and 1907 and the Land Warfare Regulations produced by the latter.

As the twentieth century progressed, the principle of non-combatant immunity (PNCI) came to be central to the Western justification and waging of war. The Charter of the International Military Tribunal (IMT) set up in 1945 at Nuremburg considered the conventional law of the Hague Convention's Land Warfare Regulations to have become customary law. Most of the war crimes prescribed in the IMT Charter are offences against the PNCI (the murder, ill-treatment or deportation of the civil population; the plunder of public or private property; the wanton destruction of cities, towns or villages; devastation not justified by military necessity); so too with its category of crimes against humanity (murder, extermination, enslavement, deportation and other inhumane acts committed against any civilian population, and persecutions on political, racial or religious grounds). In the latter half of the twentieth century, the principle of non-combatant immunity has been stated most forthrightly in the 1977 first Additional Protocol to the 1949 Geneva Conventions, articles 48 and 51 of which state:

In order to ensure respect for and protection of the civilian population and civilian objects, the Parties to the conflict shall at all times distinguish between the civilian population and combatants and between civilian objects and military objectives and accordingly shall direct their operations only against military objectives ... The civilian population as such, as well as individual citizens, shall not be the object of attack ...[4]

The principle has also been central to the prohibition of certain weapons. An example is the Convention on Anti-Personnel Mines signed in Oslo in 1997, the Preamble of which begins:

The State Parties
Determined to put an end to the suffering and casualties caused by anti-personnel mines that kill or maim hundreds of people every week, mostly innocent and defenceless civilians and especially children ...[5]

The PNCI may not yield to the notion of reprisals, nor may it be overridden by the principle of military necessity.[6]

The PNCI features not only in the modern law of war but also in thinking about the morality of war. The dominant Western tradition of thought on the limitation and legitimation of war has long been the 'just war' tradition. This tradition of thought is a rejection both of pacifism and of amoral realism; it seeks a middle path, as Grotius in his oft-quoted conviction expressed in the Preface to *De Jure Belli ac Pacis* put it, between 'those who believe that in war nothing is lawful, and ... those for whom all things in war are lawful'.[7] The 'just war' approach is divided into *ad bellum* and *in bello* components, the former looking at the morality of resort to war and the latter at the means that are morally permissible within war. *Jus in bello* is independent of *jus ad bellum* in that a war must be fought justly by both parties regardless of the relative justice of their causes. However, *jus ad bellum* is not independent of *jus in bello* in that a war which does not offer a reasonable chance of victory, if fought *justly*, must not be fought at all. The PNCI is pre-eminent among the *in bello* requirements and is described by the US Catholic Bishops in their pastoral letter on war and peace as 'one of the central principles for a Christian ethic of war'.[8] Those who write about the morality of war from a non-religious perspective also single out the principle that it is wrong to attack or kill non-combatants as the most important limit on warfare.[9] It is because it is a breach of the PNCI that terrorism is forthrightly condemned: its wrongness consists primarily in the fact that it targets, not military installations and personnel, but civilian ones. From its treatment by both religious and secular moralists, the PNCI emerges as an important moral principle. It is not merely a custom of war with no moral basis (like, for example, different treatment for prisoners of war who are officers in the enemy armed forces than for prisoners of war who are enlisted men). Rather the PNCI is a principle with a moral foundation: it is widely referred to as a moral principle and the killing of non-combatants is popularly seen as worse than the killing of combatants in war.

The PNCI is then widely perceived as a moral principle. But what is its moral basis? Why is it wrong to kill civilians? Why morally must non-combatants not be targeted? What is so morally pertinent about this division of people into the two categories of combatant and non-combatant? These questions about the non-combatant's immunity in war must be answered in conjunction with questions about the combatant's status in war: why is it legitimate (morally and legally) to kill combatants in war? Why is it that soldiers may kill other soldiers and not be guilty of murder? For the soldier is distinguished from the civilian by two attributes: he may kill without incurring guilt of murder and he may be killed without any claim that he was guilty or that he merited death. How is it that a person, fit and healthy and of conscriptible age, gains these two attributes on donning a military uniform in wartime? Once the legal and moral status of the soldier is clear, then that of the non-combatant will be clear too. A further set of questions concerns the strength of the principle. How absolute is the 'immunity' of non-combatants to be? How serious is a breach? Is the PNCI an exceptionless rule, one that is to be obeyed at all times? Is the killing of non-combatants something that is never to be done? Or does the ideal of not targeting non-combatants yield to the achievement of war aims? Are there circumstances in which it is defensible to kill civilians in war?

It might be thought that the answers to these questions are straightforward and non-problematic. There are many explanations of the moral basis of the PNCI that appear at first glance to be persuasive. There follow seven such answers commonly given to the question: why may non-combatants not be killed in war?

Why may non-combatants not be killed in war?

1. because they are innocent;
2. because they are not fighting;
3. because they are defenceless;
4. because killing them is unnecessary;
5. because it reduces the casualties of war;
6. because sparing women and children allows the species to survive; and
7. because killing them is against 'the rules of the game'.

Each of these seven suggestions appears to have some merit and all seven undoubtedly contribute to our strong feeling that civilians ought not to be targeted in war. All are attempts to defend the principle yet, on closer examination, none can give a fully satisfactory explanation for the difference we see between combatants and non-combatants in war. None can explain why all combatants may be targeted at any time in war and why no non-combatants may.

1. Because they are innocent. The first answer to the question 'Why may non-combatants not be killed in war?' is the one that appears

to be implicit in the phrase that is the title of this book. This answer says that non-combatants may not be targeted because they are innocent. They have done no wrong and they neither merit attack as a punishment nor have they, by their wrong-doing, waived their right to be treated as a person. Such a claim seems to be implicit in the widely-used term 'innocent civilians' but it is also made explicitly, for instance by the US Catholic Bishops when they relate non-combatant immunity directly to innocence: 'Nothing ... can justify direct attack on innocent human life in or out of warfare'.[10] Another Catholic writer openly connects innocence and non-combatancy when he writes of 'the innocence and consequent immunity of civil populations'.[11] The Oslo Treaty on landmines appears to imply the same reasoning when, as mentioned above, it refers to 'innocent and defenceless civilians'. If such a connection between non-combatancy and innocence exists, then this would explain the apparent moral force of the PNCI. To breach non-combatant immunity would be a serious act because it would involve attacks on innocent people, people who have done nothing to merit such attacks. This explanation connects the PNCI to the most fundamental principles of human justice: that human life be treated as an end in itself and never as a means, that no one may be punished except for their own crimes, that the life of an innocent human being may not be taken as a means to some end, and that an innocent person may not be killed no matter how advantageous it would be to his fellow human beings. This explanation would explain the moral outrage that occurs at deliberate attacks on civilians in war and by terrorists. However, difficulties arise when we ask the question: why may combatants be killed in war? For the claim that civilians may not be killed because they are innocent would seem to imply the corollary that combatants may legitimately be killed in war because they are guilty. But we must then ask: of what are civilians innocent? Of what are soldiers guilty, so guilty that they may legitimately be killed?

When applied to war, the concepts of guilt and innocence are normally applied at the *ad bellum* level and linked directly to the idea of 'just cause'. As we will see in the next chapter, such an ascription of *ad bellum* guilt to combatants was made by Augustine in his justification of war. For war to be justified, according to Augustine, one's enemy must have an unjust cause, that is, one's enemy must be doing something legally wrong (such as aggression or a breach of law or their legal obligations). In doing so, they are also committing a moral wrong. Soldiers on the enemy side are participating in this legal wrong and are thereby also committing a moral wrong. For this reason, they may be killed. Killing them in war may be seen as akin to punishment. So Augustine makes the guilt of combatants dependent on the unjust cause they are promoting through their combatancy. It may be that both parties to a conflict will be guilty, but never the case that both sides will be innocent. The usual case is for one side to be innocent and the other guilty. But this use of the term innocence cannot provide a moral basis for the PNCI as it exists today for two reasons. First, Augustine's reasoning points to one side to a conflict being guilty (both soldiers and civilians) and the other innocent. Only one side's combatants are (usually) participating in an injustice. Those soldiers fighting for the side with a just cause are morally worthy while the soldiers fighting for the side with an unjust cause can be said to be guilty (guilty of participation in the unjust cause). Those soldiers fighting for the side with a just cause may not legitimately be killed: to kill those combatants is to commit murder. This is very different to the distinction between non-combatant and combatant which is the basis of the PNCI today. The modern PNCI is built squarely on an idea of belligerent equality. The justice of their countries' *ad bellum* causes is irrelevant to the rights and responsibilities of combatants and non-combatants. All civilians on both sides have equal rights, regardless of the justice of their country's cause.[12] All soldiers, regardless of which side they are fighting for, have equal status. The idea that soldiers share in the guilt of their leaders is one which international law has been trying to avoid since its foundation in the seventeenth and eighteenth centuries by Grotius and Vattel.

A further problem with this attempt to explain the PNCI in terms of innocence is that it is not clear that soldiers fighting for an unjust cause could be described as 'guilty'. In the modern age, combatants, whether conscripts or professional soldiers, are acting under orders. They do not decide that the war should be fought or how. Those who carry a burden of guilt for an unjust war are political leaders who are often members of the civilian population. Determining legitimate and non-legitimate targets in war on the basis of guilt and innocence would seem to make civilian politicians the most legitimate targets in war. If guilt is our concern, we should target only the politicians who initiate the unjust war; yet, as civilians, they are to be granted immunity in war.[13] As we shall see, Augustine ascribed guilt to all (combatant and non-combatant) on the side without 'just cause' and he ascribed innocence to all on the side with 'just cause'. Augustine's successors, Vitoria and Suárez, attempted to align the combatancy/non-combatancy distinction with the guilt/innocence one but without success. Such an alignment would yield the most forceful justification for the immunity of non-combatants in war as well as the most convincing moral justification for the killing of combatants but, in sixteen centuries of trying, no theologian or lawyer has accomplished it. The concepts of guilt and innocence cannot both justify war and limit it.

2. Because they are not fighting. A second reason offered as to why non-combatants may not be killed is that they are not fighting. What makes them non-combatants is that they are not fighting and we may not kill those who do not resist us. The explanation of the PNCI in terms of innocence claimed immunity for non-combatants on the grounds that the justification of punitive killing does apply to them (they are innocent). This second explanation claims that non-combatants ought to be immune because the justification of preventative killing does not apply to them. As non-combatants are not killing, or about to kill, they themselves may not be killed.

At the root of this suggestion is the principle that lethal force may legitimately be used only against those who are themselves using such force. This line of reasoning points the way to the future development of the PNCI but it does not explain its present form. For it is not the case that combatants may be targeted in war only when they are fighting. Combatants are targeted in war even when they are not engaged at that moment in fighting.

The idea that non-combatants are immune because they are not fighting has, as its corollary, the notion that combatants may legitimately be killed *because they are fighting*. This would seem to imply that the use of force is wrong, so wrong that one may legitimately be killed for it. Once again, this does not appear to be a convincing moral basis for the PNCI as it runs counter to the 'just war' approach which, from its inception, saw killing as in certain circumstances justified or even morally obligatory.

3. Because they are defenceless. A third suggestion for the moral basis of the PNCI is that it is wrong to target non-combatants because they are defenceless. There is, claims this explanation, something unjust about the strong or armed attacking the weak or unarmed. This may be so but the defencelessness of the non-combatant is not the foundation of non-combatant immunity. For non-combatants may not be defenceless; they may be armed. Even non-combatants who possess weapons are to be immune in war. It is not that non-combatants are unarmed and unable to defend themselves which makes them immune but simply the fact that they are not combatants. The suggestion that the PNCI is based on the defencelessness of non-combatants is further undermined when the same reasoning is applied to combatants. For if we ought not attack defenceless people, then we should attack combatants only when they can defend themselves. It may once have been the case in Europe and elsewhere that armies clashed on the battlefield only after polite inquiries to confirm that both were indeed ready. But this is no longer the case. On the strategic level, wars are often no longer declared. On the tactical level, the advantage of surprise is not foregone by allowing the enemy to get ready to defend himself.

4. Because killing them is unnecessary. Another suggested explanation as to why it is wrong to target non-combatants is that it is not necessary. It claims that it is wrong to target non-combatants in war because it is not necessary for military victory to do so. If this were

the moral basis of the PNCI, then it would seem to provide a strong moral reason for not killing non-combatants. Killing would be permissible if it served some military purpose but *unnecessary* killing, pointless killing, would be reprehensible. However, whether or not it is militarily *necessary* to kill non-combatants to achieve the ends of war depends on the particular circumstances and cannot be decided in advance. It is only by looking at the circumstances of choice that we can decide whether the ends of the war are achievable without killing civilians. Thus this line of reasoning cannot provide a basis for a general principle that it is wrong to kill non-combatants. It can only ground the principle that it is wrong to kill non-combatants when it is not required for military success. The principle that non-combatants ought not to be targeted has persisted despite great changes in the nature of war. The PNCI was established in law in the age of limited wars between small professional armies from which civilians could easily be excluded. However, the principle did not fade away in the age of total war which began in Europe with the Napoleonic wars between revolutionary France and coalitions of its opponents. The principle persisted, and indeed was strengthened, in the twentieth century despite the fact that some military strategists saw city-busting, morale-shattering attacks on the civilian population as the only way to win a war.

5. Because it reduces casualties of war. A fifth explanation of the moral basis of the PNCI claims that civilians ought to be immune in war because such a practice will reduce the death and damage caused by war. The PNCI, this explanation suggests, is based on a desire to reduce the destruction done by war. Non-combatancy presents itself as a category which can be delineated relatively easily in theory, recognized easily in practice, and granted immunity from attack without denting military effectiveness too much. Non-combatancy may even appear to have some independent moral foundation, thus adding to its appeal in theory and to its force in practice. According to this explanation of the PNCI, though, non-combatants are not in a morally distinct category from combatants. There is no moral status of non-combatants that demands they be granted immunity, just a morally-driven concern to reduce the damage and destruction of life caused by war. Geoffrey Best, in *War and Law since 1945*, takes

this pragmatic approach and explains the ban on targeting non-combatants only in such pragmatic terms.[14] A blanket ban is easier in practice, he says, and small print should be eliminated as it would be open to too much interpretation and rule-stretching during hostilities.

6. Because sparing women and children allows the species to survive. This explanation of non-combatant immunity suggests that the principle is based on a biological motive, namely, that the sparing of women and children in war permits the survival of societies or civilization, a race or the species itself. The PNCI as it stands, however, gives protection to male as well as female non-combatants, and to the aged as well as the young. Also, the targeting of even a small number of civilians in war provokes condemnation which suggests that our concern is with the individual and not solely with the species.

7. Because killing them is against 'the rules of the game'. This explanation justifies the PNCI as simply one of the 'rules of the game'. These rules have been explained as follows:

> [O]nce the game has begun, all participants are subject to the same rules. These are thus: any participant is liable at any time to be attacked and killed by the other side, unless he has already surrendered or been captured or is wounded; no participant may attack a person who is not a participant in the game, even if such an attack would be strategically or psychologically beneficial to his side.[15]

This seventh suggestion has no problem in justifying the PNCI as it currently stands. No problems arise either from who precisely is a 'combatant' and who is not, or from what may be done to combatants and when. The current positions on both issues are simply the rules of the game as they stand. However, it also gives the weakest moral force to the PNCI. It says that civilians ought not to be targeted because war has its code of rules and players should abide by them.

The seventh suggestion fits with the characterization of the combatant from its establishment in law at the start of the modern international state system in the seventeenth century to the present day. Western culture accepts that, in the special circumstances of war, some people can have their human status suspended. Military personnel in war, and until such time as they become *hors de combat* through wounds, shipwreck or being taken prisoner, may be treated as non-persons, instruments, as means to a military or political objective. Their role as soldiers turns them into non-persons, instruments, things. Once in the role of combatant, it is accepted that a person's life can be treated as of instrumental value, both to his commanders and to the enemy. It has been accepted in Western culture that, in certain circumstances (war) soldiers (when not wounded or surrendered) may be treated not as humans but as things. They have given up their right to be treated as persons (their right to life, their right not to be killed as means to some end) *and* they have also been granted immunity from blame, been absolved of culpability for the killing they commit. So combatants are doubly depersonalized. They need not be guilty in order to be killed, and they do not incur guilt by killing. They are depersonalized when they are killed and also when they are not held responsible for the killing they commit.

This explains the strict dichotomy which the PNCI asserts between those in uniform and those not. It explains why any combatant may be killed at any time but non-combatants may not. It also gives the principle of non-combatant immunity the absoluteness and importance that is commonly ascribed to it. It *is* a terrible thing to kill non-combatants *because* they are people. They have not given up their fundamental human right to be treated like persons (and in return they have not acquired the freedom to kill without culpability for their acts: they cannot kill and be immune from blame). We can even apply the term 'innocence' to non-combatants and apply it to non-combatants on both sides regardless of the justice of their countries' causes. The wrongness of killing non-combatants can be equated with the wrongness of killing the innocent. The term 'innocent' is used here as short-hand for the principle that it is wrong to treat a person's life as means to an end unless they merit it as punishment or occupy a formal role in which they may be so treated. Accordingly, non-combatants on both sides are innocent persons and may not be killed as a means to an end.

But to describe civilians as innocent persons is not to imply that soldiers are guilty. Soldiers may be equally 'innocent' but they are not 'persons'. The reason why combatants may be killed is weak if it rests only upon a customary acceptance that, in war, those in uniform may be treated as other than human beings. One may or may not accept this convention. But the moral reason why civilians may not be killed remains strong. The moral reason why non-combatants may not be killed is that they are human beings and their lives may never be used as a means to an end. The prohibition on killing non-combatants is not simply customary. It retains a full moral force. Non-combatants have not given up their right not to have their lives treated as a means to an end.

The right and the good

We have outlined seven possible explanations for the moral basis of the PNCI. These seven may be divided into two types in accordance with the two ways in which we commonly think about ethical and moral issues: one on the basis of justice (what philosophers call 'the right') and the other on the basis of goals ('the good'). The first type of approach evaluates actions by referring to justice while the second judges some actions to be good or bad by referring to certain goals (an action is good if it contributes to goals such as health, freedom, wealth, the reduction of harm). We use both approaches in evaluating and judging courses of action but justice sets limits to the attainment of good outcomes. Good is to be maximized but only within the parameters set by justice. For example, economic wealth is a good but to increase wealth by enslaving some of the workforce is wrong because slavery is contrary to justice (it amounts to using the very life of another person as a means to an end). Health too is a human good but we ought never to maximize health by using (against their consent) a living person's heart and liver and kidneys to save four lives. It would be contrary to justice. It is good to maximize health but only within the parameters set by justice. To take an innocent person's life, even though it would permit four other people to live who would otherwise die, is unjust and must not be done.

Explanations of the PNCI in terms of civilians' innocence, defencelessness or non-combatancy are explanations in terms of justice. They claim that civilians are not to be targeted because it would be unjust to target these categories of people in war, because to target these people in war would not treat them in the way that justice demands they should be treated. In contrast, the explanations of the

PNCI on the grounds that it reduces the casualties of war or permits the species to survive present the principle as a moral rule justified on the basis of the good: civilians ought to be immune in war, not because justice demands it, but because good consequences would flow from it. The immunity of civilians in war would contribute to goals such as the reduction of harm, lessening the destructiveness of war, minimizing the number of lives lost.

A difficulty with the two explanations in terms of 'the good' is the outrage that occurs at even one breach of the PNCI. If the PNCI is not a rule of justice but only of the good (if there is nothing in itself wrong in killing non-combatants but a general rule against killing them would tend to have good effects) then the occasional deliberate killing of a few is no great crime. The overall aim of reducing as much as possible the destructiveness of war is not harmed much by the targeting of non-combatants now and again. Also, the deliberate killing of civilians would be defensible if it lessened the death and destruction of a war. Attempts are made to justify in this way the killing of civilians in war. For example, the killing of 100 000 Japanese civilians by atomic bombs may have saved the lives of an equal or greater number of lives of US servicemen by ending the war. If the basis of the PNCI is 'the good', then any moral outrage would be groundless (or at least the outrage must be, not at killing of non-combatants, but at the breaking of a rule). Yet moral outrage at the deliberate targeting of civilians in war is widespread; in the eyes of many, a great moral wrong was done at Hiroshima and Nagasaki.

How absolute is the PNCI?

The question of whether the PNCI is based on 'the good' or 'the right' is crucial for understanding the moral basis of the principle but it also has a bearing on the absoluteness of the principle in practice. For whether a rule is based on 'the good' or 'the right' may affect how strong a rule it is, and how clashes with other rules or values are dealt with. A rule justified on the basis of 'the good' has less potential to be exceptionless. The good that it aims for may be better achieved in some circumstances by breaking the rule. If this is so, then the rule is weakened. If the PNCI aims at lessening the destruction of war, for example, then there may be circumstances in which abiding by the prohibition on killing civilians may delay victory, lengthen the war, and lead to greater destruction. Perhaps the obliteration bombing of cities would shatter enemy morale and cause the war to end early and with reduced casualties. Geoffrey Best, who sees the moral basis of the PNCI as the maximization of 'the good', sees it as a weak rule which must give way to military demands. Civilians are to be spared only as the requirements of military success permit. The practice of restraint in war cannot impinge to any significant degree on achievement of military aims. Such an interpretation, however, makes no distinction between the lives of soldiers and civilians. The lives of soldiers are worth as much as civilians. All casualties to be mourned. As another holder of this position puts it, it is 'justifiable to carry out an action in wartime which may result in civilian casualties if more lives are saved by this action than are lost by it'.[16] Such an interpretation of the moral basis of the PNCI weakens the strength of the principle and makes the immunity of civilians in war conditional rather than absolute. The immunity of civilians is conditional on achievement of the *ad bellum* end: civilians are not to be targeted unless military victory requires it. Civilians may be killed only when necessary to secure the aims of the war.

This interpretation of the PNCI (which permits non-combatants to be killed when military victory requires it) does not eradicate entirely the distinction between combatants and non-combatants in war. A distinction may still be made between enemy combatants and enemy non-combatants: the former may be killed for any reason but the latter may be killed only to save the lives of one's own combatants. This interpretation does not give 'immunity' to non-combatants, but it gives them some weighting in the calculations of *in bello* proportionality while there is no such weighting on the lives of enemy combatants. There are inconsistencies with such a weak interpretation of the PNCI, however. It does not give true immunity to civilians and thus runs counter to the usage of the term 'principle of non-combatant immunity'.

If the moral basis of the PNCI is seen as one of justice, 'the right', then the principle is more likely to be an absolute and unbreakable rule. For justice takes priority over goals and sets limits to their achievement. Indeed, a rule of justice may well be exceptionless. If the PNCI is seen as a principle of justice, then it may operate as a just limitation on the maximizing of goals and may take priority in cases of clashes with other values. There may be some acts that must never be done regardless of consequences: even if they are the only means to right a wrong or to win a war, they still must never be done. It may be that to take the lives of innocents or of non-combatants as a means to the ends of the war is always wrong and must never be done. The status of civilians would then truly merit the description 'immune'.

Further support for such a strong interpretation of the PNCI comes from its status in 'just war' thought. For the PNCI is a central element of this dominant Western approach to morality of war. The PNCI stands as only one of two rules dictating the conduct of warfare (*jus in bello*). Whereas the *jus ad bellum* widely cited at the time of Desert Storm contained seven conditions of a just resort to war (just cause, legitimate authority, right intention, a reasonable chance of success, last resort, the end of restoring peace, and *ad bellum* or strategic proportionality), the *jus in bello* had only two rules for the proper conduct of war (*in bello* or tactical proportionality, and discrimination between combatants and non-combatants). The first *in bello* rule (tactical proportionality) requires an assessment, with regard to each act within war, of the good it is likely to achieve and the harm it is likely to inflict. Such an assessment of likely goods and likely harms can be flexible, imprecise and subject to wishful thinking. The second requirement, discrimination between combatants and non-combatants, has the potential to be a firmer restriction on conduct within war. Indeed, for the *jus in bello* to be strong, the PNCI must be absolute. The weaker the PNCI as a rule, then the closer is the 'just war' approach to Machiavellism or an amoral realism: all may be done that is necessary to achieve the *ad bellum* end.

In both justifying war and limiting it, 'just war' thinkers are fighting a two-front war against pacifists and realists. Against pacifists, they must justify the use of lethal force as a means to the promotion of rights, interests, security: they must argue that such ends as the protection of the innocent or promotion of rights are goods which can outweigh the harm done through the use of force. Against amoral realists, they must argue that there are limits to the permissible use of force, even if those limits mean that those rights, interests and security are thereby foregone.[17] 'Just war' thinkers argue that the protection of the innocent or the promotion of rights are goods of sufficient value to justify the taking of human life, but they are not the ultimate good. Not all acts, they claim, are permissible in the promotion of these ends. The non-accidental killing of civilians has the potential to be one of those acts that must never be done. The PNCI has, more than any other *ad bellum* or *in bello* requirement, the potential to distinguish clearly the 'just war' approach from a realism which will use all means to achieve its ends. The killing of civilians can be the line in the sand beyond which no war can go without losing its claim to justice.

Aims of this book

This book outlines the history of the PNCI in Western thought. It traces the development of the principle through the work of key figures in the 'just war' tradition of thought: Augustine, Aquinas, Vitoria, Suárez, Grotius and Vattel. It outlines the values and pressures which influenced the evolution of the principle and charts the principle's future development. This work argues that the PNCI can only be satisfactorily explained as a rule of justice, that the targeting of non-combatants in war is prohibited because it is thought unjust.[18] The PNCI gained support from many different values; indeed, the principle has become unchallenged as a central element of the laws of war, the ethics of war and the etiquette of war largely because it rests on many different supports. The exact form of the principle took many centuries to emerge and is changing still. In its earlier variants, the sources and supports for the idea of discrimination in war were diverse and included moral theology, canon law, international law, military custom and the 'law of arms'. In its modern form, codified into international law, it was not a deduction from moral principles but the outcome of negotiations and conferences, and the product of diplomatic pressure and military resistance. As part of the custom and practice of states, the moral basis for the principle of non-combatant immunity was never made explicit. The development of the PNCI continues today, as the circumstances in which combatants may be targeted are reduced to those in which they are actively engaged in killing or seriously harming others.

But, this work argues, the development of the PNCI has been driven by the most fundamental principles of human justice: that the innocent must not be punished for the crimes of the guilty, and that the life of an innocent person may not be taken as a means to any end, however noble or good. In the development of the principle in

Western thought over the past sixteen centuries, the paramount concern has been to apply the powerful moral concepts of guilt and innocence to the justification and limitation of war. For this reason, the history of the concept of civilian immunity in war cannot be separated from the history of the Western attempt to justify war. This book starts the search for the roots of the PNCI in what might seem an unlikely place: the *ad bellum* thought of a 'just war' thinker, Augustine, who had little to say about *jus in bello*. It then traces the evolution of this principle through later eras of Western thought by looking first at the changing *ad bellum* justification of war (each chapter will include sections on 'the combatant' as well as 'the noncombatant', outlining each thinker's reason why the former may be killed but not the latter). Augustine justified war by reference to guilt; those who came after him sought to limit war by reference to the innocence of civilians. This is unsurprising, perhaps, as guilt yields the most powerful justification of war and innocence the most compelling justification of civilian immunity. The attempt to justify war by reference to guilt while limiting it by reference to innocence has been vigorous and widespread. Indeed, it continues even today. Yet guilt cannot justify war while innocence limits it as long as war kills innocent civilians.

2
Guilt and Punitive War 1

It is as great presumption to send our passions upon God's errands as it is to palliate them with God's name.

William Penn[1]

There is no figure more influential in the development of the Western justification of war than St Augustine of Hippo. He was born Aurelius Augustinus in the year 354 at Thagaste, an inland city of the Roman province of Africa. The century of Augustine's birth was important for the Christian Church as it saw, in 312, the conversion of the Roman Emperor Constantine from persecutor to protector of Christianity. More important than the conversion of a Roman Emperor to Christianity was the conversion of Christianity to the Roman Empire and to the warfare by which that empire maintained itself. For the latter Augustine can take more credit than anyone else. It is the achievement of Augustine, more than of any other Christian authority, that the violence of war came to be seen, not as a complete negation of the Christian message of love and charity, but as at times a requirement of it.

The seat of the Empire had moved from Rome to Constantinople in 330 so the capture and sacking of Rome by Alaric and the Goths in 410 was the end neither of the city of Rome nor of Roman civilization. It was, though, a shock to the Roman world and it brought recriminations. Non-Christians blamed the new religion for weakening the

19

Empire and this accusation spurred Augustine to write his great work, *The City of God*:

> Those who worship a multitude of false gods, whom we usually call pagans, tried to lay the blame for this disaster on the Christian religion, and began to blaspheme the true God more fiercely and bitterly than before. This fired me with zeal for the house of God and I began to write the *City of God* to confute their blasphemies and falsehood.[2]

Begun in 413 and completed in 426, the work had as its intended readership the educated pagan. Three years after its completion, the Vandals overran the province of Africa; Hippo was besieged and its bishop, Augustine, died in 430 before the city fell. Through his thought and writings, he continued to exert great influence on Christianity as a father of the Church and as 'the Doctor of Grace'.

There was substance to the charge that Christianity had weakened Rome's military power as pacifism was widespread among the early followers of Jesus. The issue of war arose for Christians as a question of whether or not they should serve as soldiers in the imperial forces.[3] At first, not many Christians were faced with this problem as the Empire identified them with the Jews who were exempt from military service. Also, from before the birth of Jesus, the Roman army was a professional force, with the universal obligation to serve no longer in force. The Roman army recruited all of its soldiers by voluntary enlistment, with many of the volunteers being sons of soldiers.[4] Thus it was Christians who were the sons of soldiers, or soldiers who had converted to Christianity, who first faced the issue of Christianity and war. When the question of Christian service in the army is discussed by the early Church Fathers, the majority agree that soldiers must quit the army before baptism. No Christian author of the third century defends Christian participation in war and there is evidence of soldiers quitting the army on conversion from the second half of the second century. Tertullian considered this issue of whether a Christian could serve in the army in *De idololatria* and he was forthright that 'there is no agreement between ... the standard of Christ and the standard of the devil'.[5] A Christian could not serve as a soldier even in peacetime. In his later *De corona militis*, Tertullian again rejected war and military service and queried how a person, who is not to fight even for Christ himself, could do so for others.[6] The Church canonized many who wrote against war or who were martyred for their opposition to it: Maximilian was martyred in 295 at the age of 21 for his refusal to take up arms; St Gregory Nazianzen (329–89) and St John Chrysostom (347–407) wrote against military life as did Basilius the Great (330–79) who recommended that those who had shed blood should be denied holy communion for three years.

Augustine, however, took a different view. Far from embracing pacifism, he defended war as a Christian activity. His acceptance of war was not simply a reply to the charge that Christianity had been responsible for the downfall of the Roman Empire. The bedrock of Augustine's beliefs about force was the warfare of the Old Testament. He could point to the military feats of Abraham, Moses, Joshua, Samson, Jephta, Gideon, David and Judas Maccabeus and to the image of the God of hosts ordering war against the enemies of his people. That God himself had ordained wars as punishment of the enemies of his people was to Augustine a proof that war could be legitimate for Christians. This divine sanction was Augustine's strongest justification of the right to wage war.[7] His acceptance of war also had deep roots in his theology and political thought. As the *City of God* shows, Augustine was very much a 'realist' in his approach to politics: he saw coercion as indispensable to order. In Augustine's case, his political realism was derived from a pessimism about human nature. To Augustine, the biblical story of the Fall was an assertion of the imperfectible nature of human beings. He writes of the Fall that so 'great a sin was committed that by it the human nature was altered for the worse'. He goes on to ask: 'who can describe the number and severity of the punishments which afflict the human race, pains which are not only the accompaniment of the wickedness of Godless men but are part of the human condition and the common misery?' Augustine himself attempts such a description when he continues:

> That the whole human race has been condemned in its first origin, this life itself … bears witness by the host of cruel ills with which it is filled. Is not this proved by the profound and dreadful ignorance which produces all the errors that enfold the children of Adam, and from which no man can be delivered without toil, pain and fear? Is it not proved by man's love of so many vain and

hurtful things which produces gnawing cares, disquiet, griefs, fears, wild joys, quarrels, law suits, wars, treasons, angers, hatreds, deceit, flattery, fraud, theft, robbery, perfidy, pride, ambition, envy, murders, parricides, cruelty, ferocity, wickedness, luxury, insolence, impudences, shamelessness, fornications, adulteries, incests, and the numberless uncleannesses and unnatural acts of both sexes which it is shameful so much as to mention ... ? These are indeed the crimes of wicked men ...[8]

Augustine's pessimism about human nature translates into a pessimism about politics. The corruption of human nature by self-love means that political and social ideals cannot be implemented in this world. Instead, the most that can be aimed at is a basic order brought about by the threat and use of force. The twin themes of the necessity for order and the wickedness of human beings are the core of Augustine's attitude to war. It is because of the perennial selfishness of human beings that order can be achieved only through the threat and use of force. Yet this order is of benefit to Christians while they sojourn on earth. It allows them to maintain their lives while they wait for that mortal condition to pass away. But peace and order are also of benefit to those who are not yet part of the City of God; peace and order are, indeed, in the common interest of all.

Augustine's justification of war

When Augustine turns to the conditions under which warfare by Christians could be justified, he starts from the Roman notion of justified war. The Romans, Augustine writes, fought justified wars when 'the pressure of their enemies forced them to resist, so that they were compelled to fight, not by any greed of human applause, but by the necessity of protecting life and liberty'.[9] He adopts the Roman list of just causes for which war may be waged and extends it:

> Just wars are usually defined as those which *avenge injuries*, when the nation or city against which warlike action is to be directed had neglected either to *punish wrongs* committed by its own citizens or to restore what has been *unjustly taken* by it.[10]

To the two just causes developed in Roman law (the return of seized property and the repulsion of attackers), Augustine has here added a third with a crucial moral implication: the avenging of injuries. For a Roman such as Cicero, the aim of a just war had been to achieve restitution for a hurt through the recovery of lost goods (*res repetitus*) and a return to *status quo ante bellum*.[11] Cicero had required a clear violation of pre-existing rights of the injured party and stipulated that the ensuing war was to be limited to redress and compensation. This was not the case for Augustine.

Augustine's new 'just cause' introduced a moral and distinctively biblical flavour to his treatment of the right to wage war. There is a crucial moral implication to this avenging of injuries: the *legal* wrong done by the adversary is the just cause of the war, but this legal wrong is also proof of a *moral* wrong. It is the moral wrong which compels the Christian to wage war as a punishment. This new moral dimension to a just war is more apparent when Augustine writes that:

> it is the wrong-doing of the opposing party which compels the wise man to wage just wars; and this wrong-doing, *even though it gave rise to no war*, would still be a matter of grief to man because it is man's wrongdoing.[12]

Thus, to a Christian, war is almost to be welcomed as an opportunity to punish wrongdoers who might otherwise escape punishment. Punishment is again to the fore when Augustine writes:

> The real evils in war are love of violence, revengeful cruelty, fierce and implacable enmity, wild resistance, and the lust of power, and such like; and it is generally to punish these things, when force is required to inflict the punishment, that, in obedience to God or some lawful authority, good men undertake wars ...[13]

Also made clear here is the second of Augustine's conditions for a just war: as well as being fought for a just cause, it must be waged with the right intention.

To Augustine, then, war has a dual purpose and character. It both protects the moral order by protecting the legal order and it also punishes the guilty for their wickedness. This connection between crime and sin is crucial to Augustine's Christian justification of war. There exists for Augustine such an intimate connection between the juridical and moral orders that a breach of the former necessarily involves a breach of the latter.[14] A nation which violates the legal rights of another also breaks the moral law. Thus, the aggressor is always morally guilty (and the Christian has a duty to punish the wicked on God's behalf). The inclusion of punishment as a new just cause yielded the first new definition of a just war since Cicero: *justa bella ulciscuntur injurias* (just wars avenge injuries). Augustine built on the Roman concept of a just war but ends up describing war in terms the Romans certainly never used: loving punishment of the wrongdoer. It is just to punish the wicked for the wrong they have done, and it is charitable to stop them doing further evil. War can be an act, not only of justice, but also of Christian charity when it aims to prevent wrongdoers from doing further wrong.[15] This notion of war as punishment still relies on divine as well as human authority. For one of the props to Augustine's punishment model is the doctrine of the divine right of kings.[16] In Augustine's model, the ruler inflicts punishment as God's minister. It is God's punishment that is inflicted on the wicked through war. This idea of the ruler as the agent of God came to the fore after the conversion of Constantine and served to bolster the authority of both Church and State.[17] This condition of 'proper authority' was the third of Augustine's three requirements of a just war.

One can draw modern parallels to Augustine's descriptions of war as loving punishment of a wrongdoer and as prevention of further wrongs. The first is to euthanasia (killing in war can be an act of love and charity towards the killed) and the second is to capital punishment (killing in war can be a just punishment for wrongs committed). Augustine himself did not talk in these terms but they serve as useful illustrations of his views. In both euthanasia and capital punishment, the reason for the killing is very much connected with the person being killed. In both instances, it is some act or attribute of that person which is the reason we kill them. So a case can coherently be made that the person, though killed, has not been treated as a means to an end (as long as the execution is a punishment and not a deterrent to others; as long as the euthanasia is genuinely to ease the pain of the patient and not the financial burden on the public health service). However dubious (and even absurd) Augustine's defence of war in those terms may seem, it had very worthy aims: to permit the punishment and killing only of those who deserve it and to condemn the punishment or killing of the innocent.

Augustine sought a justification of war that was not in terms of the consequences of the act. As a Christian, Augustine believed that he could not accept a justification of war simply on the grounds that it brings about a better state of affairs. It is easy to see why Augustine sought to avoid relying solely on an argument of the greater good in his defence of war. To do so would be to admit that we kill because we like the consequences of it; we kill because it makes the world a better place. That would entail an implicit admission that we kill people who do not deserve to die, people who have done nothing that merits punishment or death. All we can say about the people we kill is that they were in an unfortunate place at an unfortunate time. That is not an admission Augustine could permit himself to make. Augustine sought to justify, not simply war, but every act of killing in war by reference to the person killed. The justification of killing in war which Augustine sought was one in which the person at whom the act of killing is directed, their attributes and actions, form part of the reason for the commission of the act. It is for this reason that Augustine tried to justify the death of every person killed in war on the basis of their guilt. By so doing, Augustine could also claim that a just war is for the good of everyone. Even those warred against benefit from the punishment of their past wrongs and prevention of further wrongs.

In all, Augustine established authoritatively three requirements of *jus ad bellum*. These were proper authority (only the holder of the divinely-sanctioned office of ruler could declare war), just cause (the cause of war must be the repulsion of attackers, the return of property wrongly taken, or punishment) and right intention (the motive must be charity, justice and love of neighbour, not vengeful cruelty, implacable enmity or love of violence). These three conditions were to be repeated by all authorities on war until the modern era.

Simultaneous just cause

The question of whether both sides to a war could have a just cause is a very significant one in the Augustinian justification of war. Any claim that both parties to a war might have a just cause would have serious implications for Augustine's connection between crime and wickedness. In his writings on war, Augustine does not deal directly with this issue. Russell suggests that the Doctor of Grace came close to recognizing that both belligerents could have some measure of justice in their respective causes despite its implications for the characterization and justification of war as punishment.[18] But Augustine only hinted at the possibility and no more. Any judgment that both sides can have a just cause would undermine his characterization of a just war and thus his justification of war. For if there is *ad bellum* justice on both sides, then neither side is legally guilty, morally wicked and in need of loving punishment. To be coherent, Augustine's model allows only one side in a just war to have justice. Any acceptance of the possibility of simultaneous just cause would generate a fundamental inconsistency in his defence of war.

The combatant

Augustine offers two answers to the question: why may combatants be killed in war? The first is that they are guilty and may justly be punished; the second is that it is loving and charitable to prevent them from committing further wickedness (by killing them if necessary). His justification of war points to these two answers. Augustine's principal moral justification of war is that it is loving and charitable to punish the wicked, those who do evil. The enemies of the just warrior are wicked and merit punishment. Augustine's defence of war as the punishment of wickedness implies that those whom the just warrior harms and kills in war merit this treatment as a just punishment for their personal guilt. All soldiers who fight on the unjust side share in the legal wrong and in the moral wrong. And this guilt is the reason why each person on the enemy side can be killed.

Augustine, in his justification of war, never directly addresses the issue of innocence and guilt on the personal level. His concern is with the justice and injustice of causes for which the combatants are fighting. He does not explicitly derive this implication of personal guilt from his assertion of collective guilt (Russell suggests that innocence or guilt on the personal level were simply of no concern to Augustine).[19] But no other construction can save Augustine from the serious charge of justifying the taking of innocent life as a means to other ends. Augustine does claim that (just as Lot's family was an exceptional innocent few in the city of Sodom) so there will rarely be just people in an unjust nation. This claim is an admission that there will, at times, be some innocents among the enemy and that they are nonetheless killed in war.[20] Augustine's defence to this charge that innocent people are killed in 'just wars' is multi-faceted. First, he points out that innocence or guilt is an internal spiritual condition which it is impossible to ascribe with certainty to individuals. Secondly, he reminds us that death is merely a physical evil and not as bad as bad motivation.[21] Thirdly, he takes refuge in the doctrine of original sin. To Augustine, this doctrine guarantees that all are wicked and deserving of punishment for past sins. Even those who wage war for the just cause deserve to be punished and chastised by God (this is also Augustine's answer to the question why, if war is God's punishment of the wicked, the just are not always victorious: war is God's way of punishing the wicked but also of chastising the just).[22] He does not use these claims as a justification for war but as an excuse when his justification of war fails to fit reality. In war, the killing and harm cannot be restricted to those who deserve them. Augustine's ultimate reliance on original sin to excuse killing the innocent amounts to an admission of defeat for his attempt to justify war in the moral manner he demands.

Conscientious objection

Augustine condemns all on the side without just cause for their participation in a legal and moral wrong. Given this, one might expect to find in his writings support for selective conscientious objection and a plea to all subjects to consider the justice of their ruler's cause before participating in war. In fact, this is far from the case. Though Augustine admits selective conscientious objection in extreme cases, his general advice to subjects is to obey their ruler. If a soldier disagrees with his prince over the justice of the cause, but is not absolutely certain, he is advised by Augustine to obey and to fight even an apparently unjust war. It is only if his ruler orders deeds that clearly contravene divine precepts that the subject should refuse.[23] Augustine's primary concern is to condemn disobedience and individual wilfulness. To this end, he absolves the individual in the role of soldier of moral responsibility for his actions in that capacity. He claims that those in the role of soldier and executioner who kill the innocent are not themselves guilty of murder: 'one who owes a duty of obedience to the giver of the command does not himself "kill" – he is an instrument, a sword in its user's hand'.[24] Thus, a soldier who kills unjustly under orders is not guilty of murder but one who refuses an order to kill is guilty of treason. Clearly, the morally safe course of action for soldiers is to kill even on the orders of a sacrilegious king fighting an unjust war.

This treatment of the issue of selective conscientious objection is unsatisfactory given the Augustinian model's characterization of the unjust party's combatants as guilty and of war as punishment of wickedness. A just cause is required to make fighting morally permissible yet those called on to do the fighting may not agree that such a just cause exists. It is the fact that they are fighting for a party without just cause that allows those soldiers to be killed without murder being done, yet they are not encouraged to investigate the justice of their cause. Augustine would rather they simply followed orders and participated in the act which makes it morally permissible, even obligatory, for others to kill them. This raises huge problems for Augustine's justification of war. Augustine deals at length with the issue of the innocence of the just warrior: he is concerned to show that a soldier can kill without incurring guilt and without being motivated by malice (and that therefore Christians can serve as soldiers). With regard to those warriors fighting for the side with just cause, Augustine holds that their outward act does not reflect their inward state: their violence need not be an expression of malice but can be an expression of love. With respect to soldiers fighting for the side without just cause, however, Augustine holds that their outward act (their participation in aggression) does constitute proof of their personal wickedness and guilt. Clearly, the claim that killing can be motivated by love can be applied also to the soldier on the side without just cause. If the just warrior's act is not necessarily a manifestation of his inward disposition, then why is his enemy's? Where is the wickedness, where is the intentional evildoing, which war is to punish? Augustine's claim that the act of killing is not necessarily a reflection of an inward disposition of malice does not sit easily with his claim that the enemy soldier is being punished for his sinning. This incongruity is significant as it renders unstable the very foundations of Augustine's justification of war.

The non-combatant

What is the position of the non-combatant in Augustine's model of a just war? The answer is that no distinction between combatant and non-combatant is made by Augustine. In his justification of war based on national guilt, Augustine establishes no moral difference between soldiers and civilians. One might think that there should be discrimination, not between soldiers and civilians, but between the guilty and the innocent. For the justification of war on the basis of guilt had the implication, ignored by all who applied it, that the innocent ought not to be harmed in war. This went unacknowledged as any requirement that the innocent should not be killed would make all wars unjustifiable. Instead, Augustine was content either to ascribe guilt to all in the enemy nation (all on the side without just cause are guilty) or to none (for he seems also to acknowledge that soldiers are as innocent of commitment to injustice as civilians: they are but a sword in the hand of him who gives the orders.)

Augustine does not restrict targeting in war to combatants only nor does he place any other significant restrictions on the conduct of war. Warfare can be limited by its *ad bellum* end or by a separate set of *in bello* rules. The Romans had no separate *jus in bello* limiting permissible means yet they saw war as limited by its nature as a legal instrument and by its *ad bellum* end. The end for which war is fought (recovery of goods or repulsing of attackers) limits the duration and scope of war. Once goods are recovered or the attackers repulsed, war must end. In the war, acts that do not contribute to these ends are not justified. But this was not the case with Augustine. For, though Augustine adopted the Roman legal notion of a just war, the new *ad bellum* end he added no longer limited war. No longer was war limited to the recovery of goods or the repulsion of attackers. The aggression was seen, not simply as a crime for which redress must be limited, but also as a sin, for which much greater punishment may be appropriate. The emphasis on punishing wrongs rather than repelling attackers or recovering lost goods opened the way to unlimited wars whose aim was the punishment of wickedness and vice.[25] Augustine's moral emphasis on the guilt of the enemy population could justify violence against the whole population. It made difficult any restrictions on the means of warfare employed or merciful dealings with the enemy people.

Augustine's punitive model of war did yield some restrictions on conduct in war. Augustine stipulates that war is never to be fought in a spirit of passion or vengeance. War is an act of retributive justice; glory and revenge are impermissible ends of war and acts of vengeance, cruelty and malice are prohibited within war. Retributive justice and loving punishment are to be the motivation of the Christian warrior and war is to be waged in a spirit of love and charity. In a passage from *Ad bonifacium* that was to be repeated centuries later by both Gratian and Thomas Aquinas, Augustine writes:

> For peace is not sought in order to be the kindling of war, but war is waged in order that peace may be obtained. Therefore, even in

waging war, cherish the spirit of the peacemaker that, by conquering those whom you attack, you may lead them back to the advantages of peace ...[26]

This requirement of 'right intention' has some implications about how the war may be waged. For Augustine there were certain acts which, even though they occur in a just war, were to be considered blameworthy. These were acts such as needless killing and wanton destruction which are contrary to the required motivation of love and justice. Augustine writes:

> The desire to harm, cruelty in vengeance, an implacable spirit, unquenched ferocity in revolt, the desire to dominate and other similar attitudes ... this is what the law condemns in warfare.[27]

But this early limitation on the conduct of war says nothing specifically about non-combatants. It may be that much killing of non-combatants in war could be needless killing (and therefore motivated only by malice or vengeance) or it may not. It may be the case that, in the particular circumstances of a war, the killing of non-combatants contributes something to military victory. All Augustine's prohibition of vengeance and malice can do is to prohibit the killing of people (soldier and civilian) when this adds nothing to the chances of military success. But all categories of people in the enemy population may be killed if their deaths would improve the chances of military success.

Clerical participation in war

There was, however, one category of non-combatant which, from the time of Augustine, was granted immunity in war. Clerics were neither to fight in war nor to be targeted in war. As early as 400 the Council of Toledo had ruled that 'if anyone after baptism wages war dressed in a chlamys or a baldric, even if he has not committed the most serious offences, if he has been admitted as a cleric, he should not accept the dignity of deacon'.[28] In 451 the Council of Chalcedon prohibited clerics and monks from joining the army. From the fifth century, the objection to clerical participation in war was unanimous.[29] This prohibition was restated in the first general collection of ordinances of Charlemagne, issued around 769: 'We absolutely prohibit clerics to bear arms and to go to war, except for those who have been chosen because of their duties to celebrate Mass and to carry the relics of the saints'.[30] This ban on clerical fighting was part of a general prohibition on the clerical use of weapons which extended to hunting as well as warfare. Clerics could not shed blood, either human or animal. The ban on clerical participation in war was not simply an implication of the advice to those who served God not to be concerned with the things of this world. Nor was it based on the difficulties in attempting to serve two masters. Rather, it was the act of killing which was thought to sully (as the ban on clerical hunting clearly shows). The ban on clerical participation in war is an acknowledgment that the most Christian thing to do is to forgo all killing.

It came to be universally accepted in Western Christendom that military service, though permissible for the laity, was improper for the clergy. The established reasoning was to be based on the idea of the two levels of Christian vocation put forward by Eusebius of Caesaria in the fourth century. Eusebius held that Christians of the higher level (the clergy and religious) were to aim at the highest Christian ideals; they were bound by the 'counsels of perfection', the revealed truth as to how the human person is to achieve their true end and perfection in this world. Such higher Christians are not to fight in war but to remain dedicated to God.[31] Other Christians (the laity) need not aim so high; they took on all the duties of citizenship, including the waging of just wars. This differentiation between lay and clerical morality is not firmly grounded and there is certainly no biblical basis for it. It is odd to interpret Jesus' command of non-resistance strictly for those Christians who desired to attain perfection (equated with clerics) and to hold that, for others, it rules out only killing motivated by vengeance or lust for killing.[32] In requiring pacifism of those who sought spiritual perfection, Eusebius came astonishingly close to an outright prohibition on war for all Christians.[33] That something is not to be done by the most perfect Christians, because they are the most perfect Christians, is almost an acknowledgment that it ought not be done by any Christian.

Augustine's authoritative doctrine of the just war could place no restrictions on either war's combatants or victims. The implication of guilt on the part of all people on the side without just cause meant that all could be killed if it contributed to the victory of the side with just cause. Despite this, the principle of clerical non-participation in war became firmly established in the culture of Western Christendom in the seven centuries following Augustine. Towards the end of this period, there were also attempts at entrenching limitations on targets.

The 'Peace of God'

As the end of the first millennium approached, there came a comprehensive attempt within Christendom to limit and restrict warfare. Between the 970s and 1030s, the bishops of the Frankish realm (part of modern France) convened peace councils which attempted to limit targeting in war. These innovative peace movements, known to us collectively as the *pax Dei* or 'Peace of God', granted a protected status to certain categories of person and property. This attempt was not the product of one unified, coherent movement with a fixed ideology. Rather there were various movements and phases to the phenomenon, each with its own geographic centre. The first period of activity arose as the thousandth anniversary of the birth of Jesus approached. A lull occurred in the Peace activity during the first two decades of the new millennium and there was a revival in the 1020s and 1030s as the one-thousandth anniversary of the crucifixion drew near.[34]

There was a variety of social, economic, political, religious, popular and ideological forces in tenth- and eleventh-century Europe which all fed into the Peace of God movement. There were profound social changes brought on by devolution of power. Also, by the late tenth and eleventh centuries, Western Europe no longer experienced foreign invasion: the incursions of Saracens, Vikings and Magyars into Carolingian Europe from the mid-ninth century to the middle of the tenth century were over. But over too was the dynasty founded by Charlemagne, for in 987 the West Frankish nobility passed over claims of the last Carolingian and instead elected Hugh Capet to the throne.[35] The gradual collapse of traditional authority of the Holy Roman Empire led local lords to institute exactions and pillages, to usurp the authority of their overlords, and to try to establish personal authority in their own areas. A symbol of the collapse of central authority was the great increase in castle building from 970 to 1030. The weakening of public power gave rise to intensified warfare among princes, dukes and knights fighting for land, peasants and power.[36] This disorder and feuding often impacted on the Church and peasantry and on their property. Walled towns had once been a refuge for the common people; the new castles were seen by them as a threat.[37] This increased disorder and incidence of warfare were key motives for the peace movements.

As well as the political and social changes, there were also apocalyptic fears of the proximity of the Last Judgment which led to changes in the practice of Christianity. An impulse for reform grew, motivated by anxiety about the purity of the clergy and of Christian society as a whole. The period saw a renewed building of churches and a reform of monastic life. Most importantly, there was a disciplining of clerical behaviour. The prohibition on the clerical use of arms which dated back to the fifth century had become widely ignored. By the tenth century, clergy commonly engaged in hunting and warfare. It has even been argued that armed clerics formed the backbone of Carolingian military might when, in the late ninth and tenth centuries, bishops and abbots acted as military leaders against the invasions of Saracens, Vikings and Magyars.[38] One achievement of the Peace of God councils was to reinstate the ban on clerical arms. Clerics had to forego their weapons in the face of demands for religious purity; in return they and their property would be safe from injury and theft. They also had to forego their wives (the practice of having wives and concubines was condemned by more than one council) and the sale of ecclesiastical offices and services (such as baptism) was also condemned.[39] The fact that killing was condemned alongside simony and sex is evidence that the concern was a moral one. It was the spiritual pollution caused by clerical sex, simony and the shedding of blood that was of concern. It was the perceived moral wrong of killing that motivated the renewed ban on clerical participation in war.[40]

The first manifestation of the peace movements was the council summoned by Bishop Guy of Le Puy at Laprade-Saint-Germain in 975 in order to deal with pillagers of his church and to secure the return of lands and revenues usurped from it.[41] With this council there began a quest to limit political violence which was to last into the 1030s. The earliest meeting from which peace canons survive was the council held at Charroux in 989:

(1) If anyone attacks the holy church, or takes anything from it by force, and compensation is not provided, let him be anathema.
(2) If anyone takes as booty sheep, oxen, asses, cows, female goats,

male goats or pigs from peasants or from other poor people –
unless it is due to the fault of the victim – and if that person
neglects to make reparation for everything, let him be anathema.
(3) If anyone robs or seizes or strikes a priest, or a deacon or any
man of the clergy who is not bearing arms (that is, a shield,
a sword, a breastplate or a helmet) ... let him then be held to be
excluded from the holy church of God.[42]

These canons decree that three crimes were to be punished by
excommunication: theft of church property, assaults on clergy, and
theft of animals from peasants. These three categories were later
extended by further peace councils and are present in all subsequent
Peace declarations of the period. They are, writes Goetz, typical of the
early Peace movement.[43]

These canons can be seen as an early manifestation of the pressures
which led to the development of the principle of non-combatant
immunity. The fact that the first canon concerns the protection of
the Church and its property leads some commentators to see the
Church's desire to protect itself and its property as a strong motive
behind the early Peace movement. Early councils sought to protect
churches from burglary and theft. Later councils extended the protection of church property to churchyards, domestic buildings and
storehouses. Finally, this protection was sought for all houses within
thirty steps of a church.[44] The usurpation of ecclesiastical and monastic lands was prohibited and the rights and revenues of the church
were to be secured. The protection of the church and its resources, at
a time of social and political upheaval and violence, was clearly a
central theme of the Peace movement. The second and third canons,
though, are more relevant to the PNCI as they seek to grant immunity
to certain categories of non-combatant person. The second canon of
Charroux condemns the theft of farm animals from peasants and the
poor. This was repeated in all peace statutes of which copies exist
today.[45] Peasants were protected indirectly through the protection
both of their food animals and of their draught animals. The intention seems to have been a desire to protect food production, an
explanation backed up by oaths which gave similar protection to
vineyards, mills, granaries, bees, carts transporting harvests and peasants' tools. Peasants were thus protected, it would seem, not so much
because they were defenceless persons but because their work was

vital to the provision of the necessities of life. Some councils extended this protection to merchants for the same reason.

Goetz suggests that the self-interest of the Church is sufficient to explain any immunity extended to non-combatants. Peasants were protected indirectly, he claims; the concern was not for them but for the fruits of their labour. However, even Goetz has to concede that, even in this early Peace, the restrictions on warfare exceed those motivated by the self-interest of the Church. 'Occasionally', he allows, 'the measures taken exceeded the strict framework of ecclesiastical protection'.[46] That the seeds of the PNCI are present in the Peace canons is evident when one looks at the third canon from Charroux and its successors. The third canon from Charroux prohibits the assault and arrest of unarmed clergy. This protection was extended to monks, later to nuns and then to unarmed companions of clergymen, and even to widows and noblewomen travelling without their husbands. The protection of clergy can be understood as an extension of the protection of the Church, its property and its resources but the categories of protected person grew until far more than churchmen and women were included. Later councils extended the principle until it encompassed all unarmed and non-combatant persons and some early-eleventh-century peace oaths gave protection to unarmed knights during Lent.

Even in this early council, then, the limitation of violence cannot be explained away as self-protection of the Church. The principle expanded until it became a general principle of immunity from attack applying to all unarmed and defenceless people. The concept of the 'civilian' was developing as laity and clergy were granted protection from warrior violence and as a more precise social delineation of the combatant occurred. One social effect of the Peace was to contribute to the emergence of the knight as a distinct group within the society of the time and to the creation of the new ideal of Christian knighthood, the *milite Christi*. From its foundation, the Peace movement sought to separate the armed and mounted horsemen from the unarmed peasants and clergy. Towards the end of *pax Dei* activity, in the 1020s and 1030s, knights were formed into an *ordo* of Christian society. These new *milites Christi* were given a holy purpose, defence of Christendom (and later liberation of the Holy Land).[47] In separating churchmen and laity from knights, the Peace played a part in the division of Western society into the three orders – *oratores, bellatores, laboratores* – that were the foundation of the feudal order for the following centuries.[48]

The Peace of God can be seen, then, as an early step towards a PNCI in European culture. Although Augustine's justification of war still dominated, the Middle Ages saw a renewed Christian abhorrence of killing. The rejection of killing as something the most perfect Christians should never do led to a ban on clerical fighting and the converse of that ban on clerical fighting was clerical immunity in war. It was not charity or mercy which demanded that the non-combatant clerics be spared but justice. It was not the business or function or social role or class of clerics which gave them a claim to immunity but their non-involvement in war. This was important as it was a reasoning which could be expanded unproblematically in order to grant immunity to other groups too. The nascent principle of non-combatant immunity was certainly aided by ideas of knightly chivalry, military professionalism and even class snobbery (M. H. Keen points to a kind of snobbishness among knights which led them to want to fight only those of their class). The idea of non-combatant immunity fitted too with the sense of what was chivalrous, which made at least some knights conceive themselves as protectors of the innocent.[49] The conflation of women and children (excluded from war by the Romans in the name of honour) and clergy and monks (excluded by the Church from fighting wars) was the first step along the road towards a general principle of non-combatant immunity. A more general principle of non-combatant immunity came another step closer when those engaged in agriculture were added to the category of the immune (when cultivating the soil: peasants serving in the army of their feudal lord counted as combatants). As the category of protected people expanded, so the category of legitimate targets shrank towards combatants and combatants alone.

3
Guilt and Punitive War 2

> *It may seem puzzling that the Decretalists seldom even mentioned the most obvious consequence of war, death. It was as if they felt that wars could be fought without killing …*
>
> F. H. Russell[1]

The early steps towards non-combatant immunity taken by the Peace of God movement occurred over five and a half centuries after Augustine's death. Nevertheless, Augustine's punitive model of war continued to dominate Western thought for many centuries. This chapter shows how theologians and canon lawyers of the medieval period continued to rely on and to promote Augustine's model of a just war. Indeed, it will be seen that they presented the Bishop of Hippo's characterization of war as punishment, with its implication of the guilt of combatants, even more clearly than did Augustine himself. Augustine's just war doctrine was firmly re-established in the twelfth century by a Carmaldulensian monk and jurist of Bologna, called Franciscus Gratianus (known now as Gratian). Between 1139 and 1150, Gratian compiled a comprehensive collection of canon law known as the *Decretum Gratiani* (canon law is the administrative, civil, jurisdictional, procedural and penal law of the Catholic Church). Gratian's work, which became the basic text for subsequent studies of canon law, was an important vehicle by which Augustine's approach to war continued to dominate Church thinking. Over 700 years after the death of the Bishop of Hippo, Gratian's compilation of canon law reaffirmed Augustine's model as the frame of reference for the theologians and canonists of the twelfth and thirteenth centuries who examined the moral and legal problems raised by war. Russell goes so far as to credit Gratian as the link between Roman law, the early medieval ecclesiastics and modern International Humanitarian Law.[2] It was Gratian, he says, who introduced the concept of the just war into modern international jurisprudence. Without him there would have been no modern legal development of just war thought, and no connection between modern international humanitarian law and Augustine's moral defence of war to Christians.

Justification of war

In the *Decretum*, Augustine's justification of war was accepted wholesale. Gratian follows Augustine in focusing almost exclusively on *jus ad bellum* and the Bolognese monk's legacy was to be his authoritative restatement of Augustine's three requirements for a just war: just cause, proper authority and right intention. In Causa 23, Gratian examines six main questions: whether it is a sin to make war; which kind of war is just; whether one should by force of arms avenge a wrong suffered by one's allies; whether an act of vindication is permissible; whether heretics can be converted by such a method; and whether clerics should fight.[3] Using the scholastic method, Gratian lists the objections to the points in question, quotes the traditional answers, mostly from Augustine, and often adds some conclusions of his own. Gratian's restatement of the requirement of 'just cause' confirms that punishment for guilt was indeed central to Augustine's justification of killing in war. Gratian's starting point is his total acceptance of the Augustinian claim that Christian charity can be the motive for waging war. Love and patience, he declares, do not prohibit warfare and killing; indeed, they may require it. This connection between love and killing was central to Augustine's justification of war, and Russell writes that it was thanks to Gratian's *Decretum* that this connection between love and killing became 'the cornerstone of ... the medieval jurisprudential analysis of warfare'.[4] Also in Causa 23 comes Gratian's acceptance of the Augustinian implication that those who war for an unjust side are sinning. Thus, like Augustine, Gratian seeks to justify the punishment of an evildoer as an act of benevolence performed against his will but in his best interests (he observes that the mutilation of pirates and thieves prevents them from further wickedness and that execution frees a criminal from his sin).[5]

Proper authority, one of the props to Augustine's punitive model, also features in the *Decretum* as one of the three principles of *jus ad bellum*. In the punitive model, it is crucial that the punishment which the ruler inflicts on the unjust through war is seen as God's punishment. Augustine had claimed this and Gratian follows suit. The just war of a proper authority is a divinely-ordained war in that it is God's punishment which the ruler inflicts on his unjust (and therefore wicked) enemies. The requirement of proper authority also supports the requirement of the charitable inward disposition of soldiers. That the war is waged on proper authority increases confidence that public officials are genuinely motivated by the quest for justice and not by private hatred, cruelty or revenge. Making officials responsible for the infliction of punishment and the execution of justice distances war from unrestrained violence and brutality. However, a serious difficulty in Gratian's work is the lack of precision in identifying those institutions that possessed the proper authority to wage a just war. The Emperor had such authority, so too had kings, but even lowly vassals were not explicitly excluded by Gratian. As 'proper authority' is crucial to making a war divinely ordained and therefore just, so the failure to identify clearly where this authority lies constitutes a fundamental deficiency in Gratian's approach.

Later writers working within the Augustinian framework provided by Gratian's *Decretum* are also clear about the assumption of guilt in war. Rufinus followed the Augustinian model of war, seeing war both as the defence of order and legality and as punishment of the criminal and wicked. As Russell interprets Rufinus' position: 'the adversary must deserve the war that was waged against him'; it is a punishment for having disturbed the peace and order.[6] Augustine's opinion on the punitive function of war is also restated very bluntly by Huguccio, a leading twelfth-century canonist. He is straightforward about the assumption of wickedness on the part of soldiers fighting for the party without just cause and goes so far as to claim that the guilty party would in fact realize that he deserved to become the target of the war.[7] Huguccio, like Augustine, saw a legal wrong or crime as implying moral wickedness or sin. He held the legal wrongdoers (and their agents) to be knowingly doing a legal wrong and therefore committing also a moral wrong. It is for this reason that they, individually, deserve to be attacked.

Huguccio also restates what might be called Augustine's fall-back position in his justification of war. This is that no human beings are innocent, so all deserve punishment. Augustine wished to justify killing in war as a punishment of the enemy for their sin (of promoting an unjust cause) but ultimately he could claim that all human beings merit punishment (so if war kills people other than the wilful and wicked perpetrators of a crime, justice of a sort is still done). This peculiar exculpation of killing in war resurfaces in Huguccio when, on the eve of the Third Crusade, he claims that the wars waged by Christians punished Saracens for their sins, while Saracen attacks punished Christian sins.[8] Even though the Christians were the side with just cause, he claims, they could not complain about injuries inflicted on them. Unable to limit killing to those who deserve it for a legal wrong and moral wickedness, Augustine had taken shelter behind the notion of original sin and the guilt of all human beings. Huguccio also found it necessary to retreat to the same refuge, as did his contemporary, the theologian Peter the Chanter, who describes warfare as one of God's punishments of a sinful humankind.[9] It should be mentioned though, that in the twelfth century, as Huguccio was airing the Augustinian view that a war's just cause was the wickedness of the adversary, the anonymous *Summa Coloniensis* of the Rhenish School justified princely authority over war by reference to human law without invoking divine or ecclesiastical laws.[10] Thus, at the very same time that other writers were restating the old Augustinian moral formula for a just war, the first steps were being taken towards a legal approach to war, from which moral criteria for the determination of a just war had been expunged.

Simultaneous just cause

It was an implication of Augustine's justification of war as punishment that only one party to a conflict (at most) could have justice on their side. To have a 'just cause' meant to confront an adversary who had an unjust one, so clearly both sides to a conflict could not have a just cause. Such a rejection of simultaneous just cause is an assumption of Gratian's work and nowhere in the *Decretum* is there consideration of the possibility of both parties to war having a measure of justice on their side. Indeed, almost nowhere in the canonical writings of this period does one find a claim that both parties to a war may have just cause. It is true that some members of the Bolognese

School claimed that a war might be just on both sides, as well as unjust on both sides. Stephen of Tournai appeared to break from the punitive model when he claimed that a war may be justly waged against an enemy who does not deserve punishment and, conversely, that a war might be unjustly waged against someone who deserved punishment by war.[11] But what Stephen is highlighting here is a mismatch between the status of the person warred against (their desert of punishment) and the motivation of the person warring (malice rather than a love of justice). His example of the converse case (a war justly waged against a people undeserving of it) is also a mismatch of the motivation of attacker and the desert of the attacked – this time on the basis of false information of the latter's desert provided to the former. A war could also be unjust on both scores – for example, a war waged for reasons of envy against a people undeserving of such persecution. But, in the main, twelfth-century writers reject the claim that each belligerent can have a partial claim to justice. With the one exception posed by Stephen of Tournai of a war waged on false premises taken in good faith, the consensus opinion among canonists was that one side had a monopoly of justice in a just war. As regards the theologians of this period, Russell reports that 'no ... theologian challenged the general opinion that a war could only be just on one side'.[12]

The clerical ban

In the twelfth century, the ban on clerical participation in war (with its implication that killing, even in a just war, is not something the most perfect Christian should ever do) still held. Gratian prohibited clerical participation in military activities but, convinced of the need to defend the faith by every available means, he was open to their participation in wars in defence of the Church. The canonists of the twelfth century had been unanimous in restricting military service to laymen, though they did not rule out occasional armed violence by clerics in other circumstances. Some permitted clerics to fight in wars against pagans but not against Christians. The principle of clerical non-participation in war was sometimes qualified by the type of cleric as well as the type of war. For some, what mattered was whether a cleric was in a sacred order, or a minor one, whether the members of minor orders were ordained as priests or whether they were living under a rule. Others, however, still held to the blanket prohibition on the bearing of arms by clerics.[13]

The combatant

'Right intention' was one of the three *ad bellum* requirements upheld by Gratian. As in Augustine's writings, 'right intention' provides some precursors to a *jus in bello*. Gratian, following Augustine, condemns certain acts in war and all his condemnations are to do with the just warriors' motivation for war. Killing must be motivated by love; therefore cruelty, lust for doing harm, savagery, lust for domination, greed, rapacity, and ferocity in war are outlawed as they could not be so motivated. Later canonists commenting on Gratian's *Decretum* diluted even these restrictions and allowed the waging of war by all means necessary to gain victory, provided that the cause was just. Ruses, ambushes, and deceptions were permitted by them. One enduring restriction, however, was the requirement to observe promises made to the enemy, as long as the enemy observes them. But even this restriction was qualified by canonists later in the same century who held that fidelity need not be promised to adversaries who were enemies of the Emperor or the Pope.[14] Theologians of the time, in discussing the question of ambushes and promises made to the enemy followed the canonists. None challenged the legitimacy of ambushes in a just war; as regards promises made to the enemy, most followed Augustine and required faith to be kept even with an enemy.[15]

Penance

Augustine's forceful justification of war, backed by his own eminence and authority as a father of the Church, established beyond question for medieval Christianity that war could be Christian. Gratian's *Decretum* served to reaffirm, not only that war could be just and Christian, but that war could be justified as punishment of legal and moral wrongdoers. Yet, though Augustine's own justification of war as punishment dominated Western Christian thought on war for over 800 years, there persisted, through the very same period of time, a phenomenon which casts a very different light on Christianity's attitude to killing in war. This was the practice of penance for all soldiers which is found in Western Christendom from the fourth century to the twelfth. The use of private penitentials through the Middle Ages, though they did not receive the official stamp of the Church, represented the common feeling of Christians for many centuries.[16] Underlying the system of penitence was the idea that killing, even in a just and public war, was sinful. It was a defilement from which it was necessary to purify oneself and for which it was necessary to gain absolution.[17]

The practice of penance predates Augustine's forthright defence of war and all its necessary means. Basil the Great (330–79), a father of the Church and the bishop of Caesarea, required a strict penance of 11 years for homicide and 3 for killing in war. As the system of penance developed, distinction was made between participation in just and unjust wars, and a lesser penance was imposed for the former. That penance was required even of soldiers fighting a just war contrasts markedly with Augustine's view of killing. To Augustine, soldiers fighting for the side with just cause do not incur guilt by their killing (unless they fight and kill with the wrong intention or attitude). The practice of penance, in contrast, sees every soldier as defiled by the very act of killing regardless of intention and disposition.

An Anglo-Saxon penitential dating from the seventh century was less severe than Basil's:

> If the king within the kingdom leads an army against insurgents or rebels and, being roused, wages war for royal authority or ecclesiastical justice, whoever commits homicide in carrying out the task for him shall be without grave fault but, because of the shedding of blood, let him keep away from church for forty days and let him practise fasting for some weeks, let him be received by the bishop for the sake of humility and, when reconciled after 40 days, let him take communion. Wherefore if an invasion of pagans overruns the country, lays churches waste, and arouses Christian people to war, whoever slays someone shall be without grave fault but let him merely keep away from entering the church for seven or fourteen or forty days and, when purified in this way, let him come to church.[18]

For killing in a public war, the usual penance was for 40 days, consisting of fasting, prayer, charitable works, and perhaps isolation from the church. The same penance and the same duration are to be found in many penitentials of the eighth and tenth centuries.

Four years after the Norman army of William the Conqueror achieved victory over the Saxon army of Harold at Hastings in 1066, a council of Norman bishops imposed a penance on the soldiers of the Conqueror. William had gone to great lengths to gain Rome's acceptance of his claim to the English throne and, before his invasion, had received a banner blessed by the Pope. Nevertheless, there was held in 1070 in Normandy a council of bishops to impose penances on all ranks of his army. Soldiers were to do a year's penance for each man killed and 40 days for each man struck. If the extent of a soldier's killing and maiming was unknown, penance was at the discretion of the bishop, one day a week for the rest of the man's life. In the eleventh century, Pope Gregory VII held kings responsible for the deaths incurred in wars waged with the end of gaining earthly powers. In 1078, he went so far as to declare military service to be incompatible with Christianity. Knights, unable to pursue their profession without sin, were to be excluded from penance until they set aside their arms. Gregory's purpose was not to deny a legitimate purpose to all warfare but only to purely secular war (he still wished to use soldiers in the wars of the Church against its enemies and heretics).[19] By this time, though, the system of penitence and repentance was already yielding to a different attitude to the combatant. The practice of penance faded as a new characterization of the combatant came into being with the ideal of the Christian knight and the code of chivalry which will be looked at in the next chapter.

Conclusion: punitive war and non-combatant immunity

Augustine's most lasting contribution to the debate on the ethics of war was not to provide a coherent or convincing justification of war but instead to highlight the standard that any justification of war must meet. In requiring that those killed in war merit death as a punishment, Augustine established a standard for the justification of war which neither he nor any of his successors could reach yet which none could ignore. This standard is also Augustine's contribution to the development of the PNCI. For the idea of non-combatant immunity is supported, not only by Augustine's requirement of right intention and a merciful loving warrior, but also by his *ad bellum* justification of war on the basis of fault and guilt. Augustine's treatment of 'just cause' (and not simply of 'right intention') contributed to the idea of non-combatant immunity by establishing the relevance of guilt and innocence to the justification of killing in war. Killing in war had to be a just treatment of the person killed. But the *in bello* implications of his *ad bellum* justification of war were not acknowledged by Augustine himself. Though he required that those killed in war merit death as a punishment, he was himself content that all in the enemy population were guilty – if not legally (for participation in an unjust cause) then morally (for other sins).

Augustine's model of a just war had obvious benefits as a theory (it added a moral and biblical air to the legal and pagan concept of a just war) but it can hardly be said to fit the reality of war, even in Augustine's own time. For, in reality, few if any wars could be characterized as punishment of the guilty (if guilt is taken as legal guilt and not as a general moral guilt). One area of the state use of force which could, however, be said to fit Augustine's punitive model is that of policing and law enforcement. The legal process protects the innocent and punishes the guilty. At times, the state will use lethal force to maintain law and order. In these instances, the use of lethal force must be precisely targeted. In contrast to war, minimum force is used to make an arrest and guilt is established in a court of law before punishment is inflicted. If this is impossible, then lethal force may be used as a last resort only against those individuals who are committing, or are immediately about to commit, a serious crime. Whereas Augustine's model of war holds entire countries to merit punishment, it has become a basic principle of Western law that no individual may be punished except for his or her own crime. The parallels between Augustine's punitive model and the law enforcement process may be significant given the fact that the military performed the function of police in the ancient and medieval world. The Roman army encountered by Jesus operated as Palestine's police force. Paul too knew the Roman soldiery as a police force when he approved of it. Writing before the persecution of Christians began in AD 64, he had experience of the Roman army only as the keepers of law and order. Though his teaching of Christian obedience to the state was to be used to justify conscription for war, Paul knew nothing of warfare.

The warfare of Augustine's time differed from modern war in important respects. To Augustine, the defence of the legal order against assault was also the defence of the moral order. His argument that an attack on political order is attack on the moral order made more sense in the case of the Roman Empire than at any time since. On only one of its borders (the Euphrates) was this civilization contiguous to another. Elsewhere, the Roman Empire was coterminous with civilization itself; it extended as far south as the Sahara desert, as far north as the sparsely populated German forests. Furthermore, the Roman legal order was fast intertwining itself with the moral order of the Christian Church. Thus, wars between the Empire and barbarian invaders could be seen, not as wars between competing orders, but as a struggle between order itself and anarchy. Even so, it is difficult to justify the Roman defence against the barbarians as punishment of individual sin. That characterization would require collective legal guilt to be ascribed to the members of the barbarian tribes. It would require that members of these tribes be seen as constituting a single entity in the way that the citizens and inhabitants of the Roman Empire did not.

Augustine's justification of war, which treats all combatants as accountable for the political ends they were fighting for, did not fit the warfare of Augustine's own era. It did, however, fit the wars of subsequent feudal societies slightly better. For these wars were characterized by a new type of combatant: the knight. When Augustine put forward his doctrine of a just war, the Roman army was no longer conscript and it had also abandoned its reliance on infantry. The success of the mounted Goths and Germans forced a change on the Romans: a Roman army under Emperor Valens was almost annihilated by the mailed cavalry of the Goths at Adrianople in 378.[20] Valens' successor Theodosius dispensed with an infantry arm and brought the Gothic cavalry into imperial service. Warfare in Europe was entering an age of cavalry which was to last for almost a thousand years. When Gratian was compiling his *Decretum*, 700 years after Augustine, warfare in Europe was even more centred on cavalry. The stirrup and the saddle had come to Europe and were in widespread use by the second half of the ninth century. Together, they gave the firmly seated horseman the capacity to deliver more powerful blows by sword or by lance.[21] The saddle and stirrup also made it possible for him to remain in the saddle during a rapid charge while the horseshoe permitted faster and further travel.[22] In all, these innovations permitted the use of charging horsemen as a shock tactic against foot soldiers.

By the tenth century, these knights (*miles*) not only dominated warfare but had become an aristocratic group second to *nobiles*.[23] The cost of the horse, weapons, shield and armour of the knight were far beyond the resources of the individual freeman.[24] The result was a great narrowing of social groups from which the fighter was drawn. Lords and towns provided the cavalry and, from the eleventh century, the infantry declined as the military obligations of the rest of the population lessened. One historian describes infantry of the twelfth century as 'absolutely insignificant' and continues:

> [F]oot soldiers accompanied the army for no better purpose than to perform the menial duties of the camp or to assist in the numerous sieges of the period. Occasionally they were employed as light troops, to open the battle by their ineffective remonstrations ... At Bouvines, the Count of Boulogne could find no better use for his infantry than to form them into a great circle inside which he and his horsemen took shelter when their chargers were fatigued and needed a short rest.[25]

Protected by leather tunics with iron rings or plates and later by the hauberk or mail shirt, the number of knights killed in war was small. Their armour provided protection against infantry weapons, and the stirrup meant they could no longer be toppled from the saddle so easily. Casualty figures from the twelfth century show the resulting low rates of mortality. At the battle of Tinchebray in 1106, not a single knight was killed on the French side. Of the battle of Brémule in 1119, a commentator of the time wrote:

> I have been told that in the battle of the two kings, in which about nine hundred knights were engaged, only three were killed. They were all clad in mail and spared each other on both sides, out of fear of God and fellowship in arms; they were more concerned to capture than to kill the fugitives. As Christian soldiers they did not thirst for the blood of their brothers, but rejoiced in a just victory given by God for the good of the holy Church and the peace of the faithful.[26]

Following the murder of Count Charles the Good in 1127, war was waged throughout Flanders for more than a year yet, of the thousand knights involved, only five were killed. At Lincoln in 1217, the victors lost one knight and the vanquished two (these figures are for knights, who were usually ransomed when captured; captured foot soldiers were put to death). These low mortality rates make less puzzling the phenomenon, noted by F. H. Russell, that the twelfth-century canonists seldom mentioned death and wrote as if wars could be fought without killing.[27] When one looks at the wars of the time, one finds that (as regards the principal combatants at least) this was almost the case. And non-combatants, as long as they were not inhabitants of a town under siege, could remain apart from hostilities.

More important than the low mortality rates in the wars of Gratian's era was the nature of the combatants themselves. It was to knightly warfare that Gratian applied the Augustinian justification and such warfare fitted the punitive model better than the warfare of Augustine's time. This was so because the knightly wars of feudal societies were wars waged by combatants who had some share in political power. Because of this share in political power, knights could be thought to bear some responsibility for the decision to wage war and for the cause for which they fought. Augustine's notion of personal guilt for the unjust cause of one's side was thus more coherent when applied to knights than to the foot soldiers of the Roman Empire.

As the Middle Ages progressed, though, the Augustinian characterization and justification of war became increasingly untenable as war and society changed and as the individualism of Western justice asserted itself. Christianity could not withdraw its support for war in defence of the political order nor could it restrict warfare to the type justifiable by the Augustinian model. An acknowledgment of the *in bello* implications of the Augustinian model – that some combatants and non-combatants on the side without just cause were not guilty and ought not to be killed – could only lead to a rejection of war. This road was not taken. Instead a new characterization of the combatant and a new justification of killing in war were sought to suit the new forms of warfare. These made their first appearance with the reintroduction of Aristotelian philosophy to the Western world.

4
Social Roles and Feudal War

The fifth method, the most refined, most popular and most powerful one, consists in begging the question, in making it appear that the question had long ago been decided by someone in an absolutely clear and satisfactory manner, and as though it were not worth while to speak of it.

Leo Tolstoy[1]

Thomas Aquinas was born in 1225 in the castle of Roccasecca near Naples, the seventh son of Count Landulf of Aquino.[2] At the age of five, he was sent to the great Benedictine monastery of Monte Cassino with an expectation of later joining the monastic order whose respectability and wealth appealed to aristocratic families of the thirteenth century. However, a teenage Thomas was to incur the wrath of his family by opting to join, not the Benedictine monks, but the new mendicant Order of Friars Preachers (Dominicans), established 20 years before. Kept under house arrest by his family for more than 12 months, he never wavered in his commitment to the Dominicans (even his brothers' sending of a prostitute to his cell did not break his resolve; the 19-year-old Thomas spent the night on his knees praying). After his release from Roccasecca, Thomas went to study with the Dominicans at Cologne. In his lifetime, he was given the nickname 'the Dumb Ox' because of his reluctance to speak and his great girth (it is said that a semi-circle had to be cut from the refectory table to allow friars sharing the same bench as him to reach their suppers) but after his death he was called the 'Angelic Doctor' on account of his piety and the purity of his intellect.

By the thirteenth century, there had been an intellectual renaissance which resulted in the founding of universities in Oxford, Cambridge, Cologne and Paris. In the same century, the works of Aristotle (384–322 BC), hitherto lost to Western civilization, had become available again as Arabic translations of the great philosopher's works were translated into Hebrew and then into Latin (at first by Jewish scholars who were less antagonistic to Islam than Christians). Aristotle's highly systematic and rigorous writings on almost all areas of human knowledge were seen by Church authorities as a threat to the Christian foundations of Western civilization. Aquinas, however, was convinced that anything which Aristotle could prove to be true by reason must be compatible with Christian belief. He set himself the great task of harmonizing the revealed truth of scripture with natural reason. He distinguished faith from reason yet insisted that they supported each other. In *Summa contra Gentiles*, a theological manual written for the use of Christian missionaries seeking the conversion of Jews and Muslims, Aquinas explained his method:

> Muslims and pagans do not agree with us in accepting the authority of any Scripture we might use in refuting them, in the way which we can dispute against Jews by appeal to the Old Testament and against heretics by appeal to the New. These people accept neither. Hence we must have recourse to natural reason, to which all men are forced to assent.[3]

The compatibility of faith and reason was not all that Aquinas borrowed from Aristotle. Augustine had a static view of human nature as fallen, corrupted by an irresistible tendency towards evil. Aquinas adopted Aristotle's dynamic theory of human nature in which the person, like all living things, is dynamically oriented towards the good for that type of living thing. Indeed, said Aristotle, a human being will always choose the good (they may be mistaken as to where the good lies but the rational person always chooses what they see as the good). Aquinas's attitude to the human condition is thus far more optimistic than Augustine's (and it fitted in with the general optimism in thirteenth-century Christianity about human nature and the achievement of earthly good). Living things fulfil their part of God's plan for the world through following their natural instincts and orientations; as rational creatures, human beings must also use their reason in determining how to act. The rationally discernible principles for human fulfilment are called 'natural law'.

This optimism about people yields an optimism about politics. With his bleak view of human beings, the state for Augustine was a damage-limitation exercise; it sought to limit the harm humans do to each other. For Aquinas, the state became something positive. There were natural and earthly goods which could be achieved in society and which were worthwhile (though not as worthwhile as the all-important supernatural ends of human beings). The primary function of the state was no longer the repression of sin but the promotion of the common good (that is, the social preconditions for the achievement of the individual good by all members of society).

Aquinas's major work is the *Summa Theologiae* (Summary of Theology), intended as a textbook for students of theology. Unfinished, at over 2 million words long, it is divided into three parts of which the second is the most cited. This *Secunda Pars*, itself divided into two parts, the *Prima Secundae* (cited I.II) and *Secunda Secundae* (II.II), is over a million words long (it has been calculated that to write it in three years would have required a daily output of 1000 words; Aquinas is said to have dictated to three or four secretaries simultaneously, and to have continued dictating in his sleep). The *Summa* uses a philosophical style known as the 'scholastic' method because it was used by thinkers based in the new universities. The *Summa* is divided into questions and articles and each topic begins with the three strongest arguments against the position to be defended. There then follows a single argument for the other side beginning with the words 'But on the other hand ...' and usually involving the citation of an authoritative text (more often Augustine than any other authority). Finally, Aquinas sets out his own position and its supporting reasons, and the article concludes with a solution of the questions, objections and difficulties. One commentator decries this scholastic method as no more than a ventriloquist's performance: the objections give the appearance of an open debate but are, in reality, carefully chosen easy targets.[4]

The *Summa* was unfinished when, on the 6 December 1273, Aquinas had a mysterious experience while celebrating Mass. Whether a mystical vision or a mental breakdown, it brought a complete end to his scholarly work; asked to continue dictating the *Summa*, he replied that all he had written now seemed like straw. He died three months later and was canonized in 1323. For his contribution to what became the

Western Christian orthodoxy, Aquinas stands on a par with Augustine. This is particularly the case in the Catholic tradition where Aquinas became the pre-eminent theologian, with very many of the terms, theories, and rules for argument used by Catholic thinkers (about human nature, morality, and the relationship between morality and theology and politics) adopted from Aquinas. As regards war, the canonists' treatment of the issue was more influential in Aquinas's own time. But in the sixteenth century, as war was entering the modern period, it was to the work of this great theologian that Church writers, both Protestant and Catholic, looked when developing their doctrine of the 'just war'. In the Catholic Church, Aquinas's pre-eminent status among theologians was to last until the years following the Second Vatican Council (1962–65).

Aquinas's justification of war

Aquinas's reputation as a theologian was built on his prodigious powers of synthesis and systemization. The issue of war, however, never benefited from these powers. He did not undertake a thorough examination of this important issue. Instead, in the thoughts on war scattered throughout his works, Aquinas provides two distinct moral justifications for war. The first is no more than a concise restatement of the established Augustinian reasoning. It is in the section of the *Secunda Secundae* of the *Secunda Pars* dealing with sins against charity that Aquinas deals with war at greatest length. In Question 40, he looks at the lawfulness of war, whether clerics are permitted to fight, whether ambushes and deceits are permitted and whether it is lawful to fight on holy days. In his answer to Article 1 of Question 40, on whether it is always sinful to wage war, Aquinas forwards a concise formula for a just war in the Augustinian mode:

> In order for a war to be just, three things are necessary. First, the authority of the ruler, by whose command the war is to be waged. For it is not the business of a private individual to declare war, because he can seek redress of his rights from the tribunal of his superior ... And as the care of the common weal is committed to those who are in authority, it is lawful for them to have recourse to the sword in defending that common weal [...] Secondly, a just cause is required, namely, that those who are attacked, should be attacked because they deserve it on account of some fault [...]

Thirdly, it is necessary that the belligerents should have a rightful intention, so that they intend the advancement of good or the avoidance of evil.[5]

Here, in answering the question of the lawfulness of war, Aquinas restates the three time-honoured conditions for just recourse to war (it must be declared by a properly constituted public authority, it must be provoked by a just cause, and it must be governed by right intention).

Aquinas's explanation of proper authority moves him away from the punitive model. In giving the reason for this first condition, he refers not to the doctrine of the divine right of kings but to the good of the community: 'as the care of the common weal is committed to those who are in authority, it is lawful for them to have recourse to the sword in defending that common weal'.[6] Aquinas justifies political authority, not by reference to the supernatural realm, but by reference to the human.[7] However, in explaining the second requirement of just cause, Aquinas repeats the core tenet of the Augustinian model of war as punishment for wickedness when he writes that 'those who are attacked should be attacked because they deserve it on account of some fault'.[8] Later in the *Summa* he restates another characteristically Augustinian defence of war when he justifies fighting against enemies on the basis of restraining them from further sinning. This remark is found in a section whose concern is whether we ought to pray for our enemies (II.II Q.83); Aquinas writes:

It is lawful to attack one's enemies that they may be restrained from sin: and this is for their own good and the good of others. Consequently it is even lawful in praying to ask that temporal evils be inflicted on our enemies in order that they may mend their ways.[9]

Despite the profound differences in the political theories of Augustine and Aquinas, Aquinas's first justification of war is simply a reiteration of the established Augustinian one. Wars need not be a contradiction either of the virtue of peace or of the command to love one's enemy, for war can be in defence of peace and for the good of one's enemy (though against his wishes). War is a legitimate means for those in public authority to punish and prevent wickedness as long as they give no place to wrath in their inward disposition. Crucially, the just cause of war is some fault or sin committed by an adversary that needs to be punished and that renders him deserving of attack (though Aquinas specifies no particular crimes). Aquinas follows Augustine and makes the key claim that those killed in war merit death (or benefit from it). They deserve it because of their previous actions; they benefit from it in that they are prevented from repeating those actions. This claim yields a justification of war on the basis of the acts and attributes of the individual enemy combatants. It avoids reliance on consequentialist justifications of war and arguments for war in terms of the greater good. Aquinas's second justification, though, *is* in terms of the greater good – the very type of argument which Augustine had sought to avoid.

Aquinas's other justification of war

Aquinas's second formula for a just war, less concisely but more frequently expressed, sees the just war as a defence of the community and the common good. These consequentialist justifications of political violence are Aquinas's significant contribution to 'just war' thought and are founded on the ethical and political theories of Aristotle. It was such Aristotelian ideas as the naturalness of society and politics, the natural goals of communal life, and the priority of the common good over the individual good which allowed Aquinas to construct his new justification of war. There are hints of Aquinas's new justification of war in his answer to Question 40 Article 1 cited above when he wrote of 'the care of the common weal'. In Question 64 Article 3, on whether a private person can kill a criminal, Aquinas expands on this alternative justification of war:

> It is permissible to kill a criminal if this is necessary for the welfare of the whole community. However, this right belongs only to the one entrusted with the care of the whole community – just as a doctor may cut off an infected limb, since he has been entrusted with the care of the health of the whole body.[10]

Elsewhere in Question 64, dealing with the impermissibility of suicide, Aquinas makes clear how his view of the human community was based on Aristotle (the 'Philosopher'):

> [E]very part that exists is part of a whole. Man is part of the community and the fact that he exists affects the community.

Therefore if he kills himself, he does harm to the community as the Philosopher makes clear.[11]

In claiming that it punished the enemy for their sins and prevented further sinning, Augustine had made killing in war analogous to execution and euthanasia. Aquinas here adds, in relation to political killing within the community, the metaphor of amputation. Princes entrusted with public authority to care for the community could legitimately use lethal force for the sake of the whole community, just as a physician could amputate a limb for the sake of the body. This metaphor illustrates the very different view of the person's relationship to their community taken by Aquinas. To Augustine, individuals were the units of war, and it was to them that a justification of war had to be addressed. To Aquinas, war was between societies and could be justified by reference to the good of societies.

In Aquinas's terms, the common good for which the ruler wages war is merely the good of a city or province and not the good of the world as a whole. It is the common good of separate societies rather than the common good of humankind which Aquinas upholds and for which he thinks wars may be waged. Augustine could claim that a just war benefits all, that even those warred against benefit from the loving punishment inflicted by an adversary in the role of God's scourge. In contrast, Aquinas's new justification could claim only that war is for the good of a society, in the judgment of its prince. He no longer claimed that a divine or universal good is served.[12] The justification of killing in defence of the common good, though more easily applicable to the reality of war than that of Augustine, is problematic for the Christian tradition. For Augustine's justification of killing, despite its many inconsistencies, was founded on a respect for the individual human being. Its implication that only the guilty may be killed (that a person may be killed only if they are legally guilty, if they have done some act that merits punishment) was an expression of this respect for the individual. In practice, of course, it was turned around by Augustine into an inference that the enemy population was legally guilty (or, if not, at least morally wicked). Nevertheless, at its heart, it was a justification of killing in war which refused to accept that people are to be killed because it is useful, because it serves a greater good. Aquinas's second justification of war, as necessary to the common good of society, did not meet this standard. To kill innocent people, simply so that a better situation could result, is at odds with the individualism of the Christian religion. Thus, though Aquinas's second justification of war looked forward to the modern era's justification of war, he himself hastily retreated to the established Augustinian position. Only the established justification could reach the standard set by Augustine, that killing be a just and fitting treatment of the person killed.

To Aquinas, then, war had a twofold purpose: to punish sin and to right a wrong that detracted from the common good. The characterization of a just war as punishment was borrowed from Augustine; the characterization of it as promotion of the common good was borrowed from Aristotle. The two are not complementary and Aquinas's treatment of each is lacking. His novel justification of war on the basis of the good of society was not as explicit and detailed as it could be but even the Augustinian model of war as punishment is not fully analysed by Aquinas. War remained a kind of punishment for sin but the relationship between sin and war was not made fully explicit.[13] Not only is his treatment of each justification rather thin, but there is no successful attempt to bring the two together coherently. They appear at different places in Aquinas's writings on war and never benefit from his famous powers of systematization.

Simultaneous just cause

In relying on the Augustinian model of war, Aquinas follows Augustine in denying the possibility of both sides to a conflict having a just cause. For, according to the Augustinian model, the justification of killing enemy combatants is that they are intentionally participating in an injustice. It is this which generates their legal guilt and makes them deserving of punishment. To allow that both parties to a conflict have justice on their side would be to deny to both sides the right to kill the other. For if there is just cause on both sides, then neither side would merit death as punishment. All killing in such a war would be murder. Therefore Aquinas must follow Augustine and Gratian and reject the possibility of simultaneous just cause. This he does and he denies that war could be just on both sides.[14] However, this rejection of simultaneous just cause is contradicted by other elements of Aquinas's writing on killing. Augustine's opinion that private Christians must allow themselves to be killed rather than kill in self-defence was not shared by later medieval theologians. Aquinas accepts, on an Aristotelian and naturalistic basis, the right of individual self-defence. The human organism seeks to continue living. This is a natural orientation and therefore an orientation towards the good (to Aquinas, no natural orientation of a living thing can be an orientation towards the bad). Human beings, like all living things, have a natural right to defend themselves against attack. This acceptance of the right of self-defence could mean that, once the just had started to fight and kill the unjust, then the latter could, as individuals, justly defend themselves. This implication of Aquinas's teleological approach seriously undermines the Augustinian characterization of war, and the justification of war as punishment.[15]

The combatant

If Aquinas had relied on his second justification of war, he could have justified the killing of all persons in war consequentially, by reference to the peace and well-being of the community. Such a justification of war would permit the killing of any person whose death is required for the well-being of the community. The person targeted need have done nothing to merit punishment or death and there would be no need to establish their guilt or wickedness in order to kill them. All that need be said is that their death would serve the welfare of the community. Yet Aquinas did not take this route; he was reluctant to rely solely on his consequentialist justification of war. The continued presence and primacy of the Augustinian justification of war in Aquinas's work points to a powerful unease at killing people who have done nothing to merit death.

Though the unease at killing the innocent in war continued, there was in Aquinas's time a move away from seeing combatants as incurring guilt through fighting. Though the practice of penance for killing in war continued into the eleventh and twelfth centuries, a change was taking place in the Christian perception of the soldier. An early indication of the new attitude of the Church towards soldiering can be found in the *Vita* of St Gerald of Aurillac, written about 930 by Odo, Abbot of Cluny. Advanced there for the first time was the idea that a fighter could achieve sanctity without laying down his arms. Around 1082, Anselm of Lucca declared that 'soldiers can be just men'.[16] The chivalric ideal was being created and military activity was acquiring a spiritual and redemptive value. Soon weapons, pennants and standards bore pious inscriptions and the cult of martial saints grew with St Maurice and St George as patrons of chivalry.[17] It was not until much later that the new view of the fighter was given a forthright expression by the French count Jean de Bueil, who declared, 'if God be willing, we soldiers will win our salvation by the exercise of arms just as well as we could living a life of contemplation on a diet of roots'.[18] Even by the middle of the twelfth century, though, this ideal of the Christian fighter, the *miles Christi*, was well established.

A sense of honour governed the behaviour of the knight in battle. Cowardice and flight before the enemy were the greatest shames. But there were also standards for the treatment of the enemy during and after battle. The knightly code of honour urged that the beaten enemy should be spared since he was a knight and therefore a brother-in-arms. This principle was supported by self-interest too since captured knights could be ransomed. Perhaps the enemy was also less likely to resist when he knew that he would be taken prisoner rather than killed during pursuit by the victor.[19] In addition to bravery, the ideal Christian knight would also display the Christian qualities of courtesy, truthfulness, loyalty and mercy toward the weak and oppressed. One result of this code of honour known as chivalry was better treatment for other members of the knightly class during and after battle. The code of chivalry is thus seen by some as a source of modern *jus in bello*, secular and separate from the moral concerns of Christianity.[20] Yet the role of the Church in the development of the code should not be overlooked.

Conscientious objection

A reliance on guilt as the justification of war leads one to expect a consequent concern for selective conscientious objection. For, if killing in war is justified as punishment, then ought not potential participants in war to assess the justice of the cause before they fight for it (thereby furthering an unjust cause and committing a sin so serious as to warrant death as a punishment)? It was one of the inconsistencies of Augustine's stance that he was largely opposed to selective conscientious objection and to soldiers' consideration of the justice of their ruler's cause. Aquinas echoes Augustine's grudging acceptance of the right of conscientious objection to war. His acceptance of conscientious objection is every bit as reluctant as

Augustine's though for a different reason. The Doctor of Grace had been fearful of disobedience and wilfulness on the part of the individual and counselled loyalty and obedience. With Aquinas, however, it is the focus on natural law that diminishes the importance of subjectivity, feeling, emotion and conscience. Conscience is of a lower order than natural law in that it can make mistakes and come to wrong conclusions. Subjective definitions of what is good are neither reliable nor adequate. An act which is repulsive to the person doing it, and which seemed to lead to an inadequately good end, may when judged by higher authorities be found to be a rational and justifiable one. Nevertheless, allows Aquinas, it is a sin for man to act against his conscience, however misguided or wrong its judgment. He writes: 'Every conscience, whether it is right or wrong, whether it concerns things evil in themselves or things morally indifferent, obliges us to act in such a way that he who acts against his conscience sins'.[21] An act may be good and right measured by objective standards and yet wrong in that it is not in obedience with a person's conscience; it is the latter judgment which a person must follow.

The issue of whether obedience to princes was to be withheld when their commands contradicted Christian morality or divine truth was a live one for both canonists and theologians of the time. That subjects had the right to debate the justice of a war started by their lord, and on that basis to refuse to participate, was a possibility examined by the scholastic theologian Robert of Courçon (c.1159–1219). Robert's conclusion was that soldiers were not bound to obey their lords in wars they themselves considered unjust. Knights too should not obey orders in a war they knew to be unjust or only partially just. Orders to perform misdeeds such as the burning of churches should be refused even though it would result in loss of the knight's possessions.[22] A century later, Thomas of Cobham (c.1255–1327) was of the same opinion and held that, when princely commands contradict divine ones, knights should refuse the wicked orders of princes.[23] In an unjust war, he said, knights ought to refrain from killing. If they did kill, they were then guilty of homicide and must submit to the penances for homicide on their return from war. Roland of Cremona, a Dominican friar writing about 1230, agreed. A solitary doubter, he thought, should swallow his doubts and obey orders when others think the war to be just. But when all think the war unjust, then they must disobey their ruler. The authority of the ruler, he held, was not sufficient to render a war just.

However, this assertion of the right (indeed obligation) of the individual to assess the justice of their ruler's cause and to refuse to fight for a cause they consider unjust was upheld by few of the theological or canonical successors to Robert, Thomas and Roland. Such supremacy of the individual conscience over political authority would have created practical difficulties. Knights (and also bishops with temporal powers and responsibilities) would have lost their power and possessions by refusing. The view that became dominant was not that of Robert but of his contemporary, Alexander of Hales, the 'Doctor Irrefragabilis'. Alexander followed the stricter stance of Augustine and held that, in nearly all cases, a king must be obeyed in an unjust war. Only if the unjust war was directed ultimately against divine truth could subjects disobey their rulers.[24] Theologians after 1250 followed Alexander and placed obedience to political authority above individual conscience. Full culpability for an unjust cause was restricted to the lord and his knights; non-knightly combatants meeting their feudal military obligations should not concern themselves with the justice of their cause.

The clerical ban

As regards the ban on clerical participation in war, Aquinas concurs with the established opinion. His reasoning, however, is worth noting as he makes changes that are subtle yet significant. It is in Question 40 that he looks at the issue of clerical participation and he again makes reference to Aristotle:

> Several things are requisite for the good of a human society: and a number of things are done better and quicker by a number of persons than by one, as the Philosopher observes while certain occupations are so inconsistent with one another that they cannot be fittingly exercised at the same time; wherefore those who are deputed to important duties are forbidden to occupy themselves with things of small importance. Thus according to human laws, soldiers who are deputed to warlike pursuits are forbidden to engage in commerce.
>
> Now warlike pursuits are altogether incompatible with the duties of a bishop and a cleric, for two reasons. The first reason is a general

one because, to wit, warlike pursuits are full of unrest so that they hinder the mind very much from the contemplation of Divine things, the praise of God, and prayers for the people which belong to the duties of a cleric [...] The second reason is a special one because, to wit, all the clerical Orders are directed to ministry of the altar on which the passion of Christ is represented sacramentally according to I Cor. xi.26: *As often as you shall eat this bread, and drink this chalice, you shall show the death of the Lord, until He come.* Wherefore it is unbecoming for them to slay or shed blood, and it is more fitting that they should be ready to shed their own blood for Christ so as to imitate in deed what they portray in their ministry. For this reason it has been decreed that those who shed blood, even without sin, become irregular. Now no man who has a certain duty to perform can lawfully do that which renders him unfit for that duty. Wherefore it is altogether unlawful for clerics to fight because war is directed to the shedding of blood.[25]

Aquinas here argues for clerical non-participation in war on the basis of social efficiency rather than morality. He upholds the prohibition on clerical participation, but substitutes a new reason for it. Clerics were barred from killing because it clashes, not only with the Christian ideal but also with the practical task of ministry at the altar. Aquinas downplays the moral qualms about the act of killing which were implicit in the clerical ban and says instead that different ways of supporting the war effort are appropriate to the different orders in society. Clerics have a particular vocation, a uniquely spiritual one. Their proper duty in war is to pray for victory and to fight for the divine spiritual good that is the end of all just war. But they fight in their own way, with spiritual weapons and not physical ones.[26] They further the war effort in a way even better than physical fighting. Instead of being something which the most perfect Christians should never do, war becomes something the most perfect Christians can do better – but in their own way.

The move to recast the distinction between clergy and laity in war as a merely functional distinction between social roles deprived this distinction of its moral implications. The Church's prohibition on clerical participation, along with its reluctance to involve itself directly in bloodshed and its hesitation to give crusaders full benediction, were an admission that war fell far short of the Christian ideal. They were an acknowledgment that the most perfect Christian approach is that of non-resistance and love of enemy. In Aquinas's new reasoning, however, the prohibition on clerical participation in war would no longer be a manifestation of the Church's long-standing reservations about the act of killing in war. Such killing would be no longer morally ambiguous; instead, under certain circumstances, it would be a straightforward moral good.[27] The Aristotelian approach transforms war from a bad but necessary phenomenon into an intermediate good. Once considered an evil and a consequence of sin, war became a positive if limited good rooted in the nature of human communities.

To deprive the clerical ban of its theological and moral foundations in this way is to weaken the ban. To kill someone when it was not appropriate to their business or function seems a lesser crime than to kill a person who is innocent and has done nothing to merit death. Yet to acknowledge the *in bello* implications of Augustine's guilt-based justification of war would have been to prohibit war as it was fought. Instead Aquinas changed the reasoning underlying the clerical ban. An Aristotelian focus on social roles became the new basis for clerical immunity in war. This new reason for immunity in war looks forward to the modern age when the PNCI was established in the emerging secular law of nations. For his own times, however, the theological basis of Aquinas's clerical immunity seems peculiar. For Aquinas, war was straightforwardly justifiable and even morally obligatory for Christians. If so, then it ought to be even more so for clerics. It seems odd, given that war is to be seen as a positive though limited good, that clerics are not permitted to join in it. Aquinas's response is simply that it is not part of their job to do so. One commentator suggests that, in refusing to participate in a just war, clerics act as though their jobs were more important than their Christianity.[28]

The non-combatant

Augustine had placed no restrictions on who could be killed in war. As pointed out in Chapter 2, the corollary of the Augustinian defence of killing as punishment (if there are people who do not merit punishment or death then they may not be targeted in war) went unacknowledged by the Doctor of Grace himself. The tenth and eleventh centuries, though, had seen the Peace of God movement and had felt the popular pressures for limitations on war and restrictions on its targets. Aquinas's new justification on war, on the basis of Aristotle's political theories, was able to offer a reason for some degree of discrimination. There are hints in Aquinas's writings of a wish to discriminate between the innocent and the guilty. There are statements that it is never lawful to kill the innocent but they do not lead to any idea of non-combatant immunity nor a moral basis for one. Aquinas does not address the issue of the killing of innocents in the context of war but rather in relation to the judicial process. This occurs in Question 64, Article 6, when he examines 'Whether it is ever lawful to kill the innocent?' Aquinas states that

> he who kills a just man sins more grievously than he who slays a sinful man: first, because he injures one whom he should love more, and so acts more in opposition to charity; secondly because he inflicts an injury on a man who is less deserving of one, and so acts more in opposition to justice ...

Thus, writes Aquinas, it is wrong to kill the innocent. A judge, knowing that a person has been falsely accused, should attempt to find a way to acquit the innocent. If, however, he cannot find one, he can sentence the innocent person to death. The sin is not his but was committed by those who bore false witness. Likewise the executioner should not carry out the sentence on the innocent person if the judgment contains an inexcusable error. On the other hand,

> if, however, [the sentence of death on an innocent person] contain no manifest injustice, he does not sin by carrying out the sentence because he has no right to discuss the judgment of his superior; nor is it he who slays the innocent man but the judge whose minister he be.[29]

Aquinas's opinion that the executioner does not kill the innocent man is an echo of Augustine's description of the soldier and executioner as but the sword in the hand of him who wields it. So, while Aquinas clearly did not approve the killing of innocent people, neither did he absolutely prohibit it.

Even this qualified prohibition on killing the innocent in judicial proceedings is not applied by Aquinas to warfare (this is not surprising as a firm requirement that the innocent should not be killed would negate any justification of war). Aquinas simply follows the Augustinian model which points to the guilt of all on the enemy side (if not for crimes in connection with the war, then for other sins). To this Aquinas adds the defence that a just man unjustly killed would be led to glory by God ('an innocent person ... by death, passes forthwith from the unhappiness of this life to the glory of heaven').[30] Neither provides a satisfactory solution to the problem raised by the killing of innocent people.

The principle of double effect

Aquinas's writing on killing contains in inchoate form one innovation that was to be important for the idea of non-combatant immunity in Western thought. This is the 'principle of double effect' and it appears in his discussion of self-defence.[31] As already mentioned, Augustine had held killing in individual self-defence to be wrong: the individual Christian ought not to resist an attacker with lethal force as such a defence of one's life would probably be motivated by an excessive attachment to life, liberty and other things of this world. Aquinas, in contrast, wished to legitimate the measured use of force in self-defence which he saw as the natural reaction of a living organism (and which therefore could not be bad). In discussing this issue of 'whether it is lawful to kill a man in self-defence?', he utilized what has come to be known as the principle of double effect:

> Nothing hinders one act from having two effects, only one of which is intended, while the other is beside the intention. Now moral acts take their species according to what is intended and not according to what is beside the intention ... Accordingly the act of self-defence may have two effects, one is the saving of one's life, the other is the slaying of the aggressor. Therefore this act, since one's intention is to save one's own life, is not unlawful, since it is natural to everything to keep itself in being, as far as possible ... But as it is unlawful to take a man's life, except for the public authority acting for the common good, as stated above, it is not lawful for a man to *intend* killing a man in self-defence, except for such as have public authority ... [32]

As elaborated by later theologians, this principle of double effect came to mean that one is not to blame for the indirect consequences (or side-effects) of one's actions as long as certain conditions are met.

The first is that the action is in itself either good or indifferent. The second concerns intentionality: one must intend only the good effect of one's action and not the bad one. The third condition is that the two effects be causally independent. The bad effect (in Aquinas's example, the killing of an attacker) must not be the cause of the good effect (the saving of one's life); it must be only a by-product of the good effect. The fourth condition is proportionality: the human good done must be proportionate to the human bad done. The principle of double effect, then, permits killing where it is the foreseen but unintended side-effect of doing good, where the bad does not lead to the good, and where the good outweighs the bad.

Clearly, the principle of double effect can be applied to the killing of civilians in war when civilians are killed as part of the attempted achievement of some military goal. The idea of double effect can be detected in the statement by the US Catholic bishops that

> even justifiable defense against aggression may result in the indirect or unintended loss of innocent human lives. This is tragic but may conceivably be proportionate to the values defended. Nothing, however, can justify direct attack on innocent human life in or out of warfare.[33]

The point being made by the bishops is that, though civilian deaths may be foreseen, as long as they are neither intended nor a direct contribution to one's victory, then they are permissible. The chapter on Augustine looked at his convenient fiction that all in the population whose leadership had done wrong shared in the guilt. Aquinas has here introduced an idea equally strange but every bit as injurious to the health of non-combatants. For, in later hands, it was to make their deaths, though a foreseen consequence of a military act, morally permissible as long as they are not intended, not directly productive of the military goal, and proportionate to the good sought. It is an idea that is still used (and abused) to justify the deaths of civilians in war, and it will be looked at again in Chapter 8.

The end of feudal war

Gratian applied Augustine's guilt-based model of a just war to the feudal combat of his time and found some degree of fit as, in the feudal wars of the seventh to twelfth centuries, a knight could be said to share in the guilt of the cause for which he fought. There was some degree of coherence to the justification of killing in war on the basis of guilt when wars were fought by knights who shared in the political responsibility of their prince or king. However, from the mid-1200s onwards, changes in the technology and personnel of war led to an emerging mismatch between the guilt-based justification and the military and political realities of European warfare. New weapons were introduced to the battlefield and new combatants to use them. With the re-emergence of non-knightly warriors and the standing army, war had new combatants and new targets and it was in need of a new justification. It was no longer fought by combatants who could be said to share in the guilt of the cause for which they fought. A new justification was needed, one which did not rely on guilt. Such a new justification was Aquinas's hesitant innovation.

At the time Aquinas was writing, cavalry was in decline and infantry was making a reappearance in European war. As mentioned in the previous chapter, knights declined in number in the second half of the twelfth century and thirteenth century. The rising cost of defensive equipment was one reason. In the later twelfth century, the hauberk or mail shirt gave way to the great hauberk or long mail shirt. From the middle of the thirteenth century, this was reinforced with metal plates (it was not until the fifteenth century that knights were enclosed in complete plate armour).[34] But in the thirteenth century (the one in which Aquinas was writing), armour was already becoming so expensive that fewer and fewer knights could afford it. From the end of the thirteenth century, horses too had armour. The cost was further increased by the need for armed attendants to maintain the armour and the horse and to help the knight into the former and onto the latter.

Yet all these advances in armour could not keep pace with the innovations in infantry weaponry, principally, the longbow, the crossbow and the pike. The improvements in armour were a reaction to these weapons but the knight had lost his invulnerability. Indeed, attempts by knightly warriors to keep up with the advances in infantry weaponry by strengthening their defensive equipment only hastened their decline. So heavy and unwieldy became the armour of both horse and knight that their mobility and effectiveness were greatly reduced.

The crossbow ban

Of these three innovations in weaponry, the most notorious was the crossbow or arbalest. Known in ancient times, the crossbow returned to use in Western Christendom in the last decades of the eleventh century.[35] Though heavy and slow to operate, it could pierce armour with its bolts. It could also be used by men less skilled than archers and not strong enough to draw the longbow.[36] Upon its reappearance in Europe, it was seen as something novel but also something immoral and diabolical because of its great power. A contemporary description of the new weapon ends with a condemnation of it as devilish:

> This cross-bow is a bow of the barbarians, quite unknown to the Greeks; and it is not stretched by the right hand pulling the string whilst the left pulls the bow in a contrary direction, but he who stretches this war-like and very far-shooting weapon must lie, one might say, almost on his back and apply both feet strongly against the semi-circle of the bow and with his two hands pull the string with all his might in the contrary direction. In the middle of the string is a socket, a cylindrical kind of cup fitted to the string itself, and about as long as an arrow of considerable size which reaches from the string to the very middle of the bow; and through this arrows of many sorts are shot out. The arrows used with this kind of bow are very short in length, but very thick, fitted in front with a very heavy iron tip. And in discharging them the string shoots them out with enormous violence and force, and whatever these darts chance to hit, they do not fall back, but they pierce through a shield, then cut through a heavy iron corselet and wing their way through and out at the other side ... Such then is this monster of a cross-bow, and verily a devilish invention.[37]

The device was effective against knights as it could pierce their armour and their shields. The efficiency and number of crossbows meant greater slaughter on the battlefield.

But it was also the case that enemies could be killed from beyond their range of hearing, vision and retaliation. This aspect of the mechanical device may have made killing in war too remote and inhuman for contemporary opinion. Certainly many theologians were horrified by the effectiveness of the crossbow but also by its indiscriminate slaughter. Relevant too may be that the crossbow was a weapon used by a certain class of combatant. Philippe Contamine suggests that much opposition to the crossbow was aimed not at the weapon but at the type of soldier who used it: a paid one. Mercenarism, or payment for fighting, raised difficulties for the established model of a 'just war'. The difficulties concerned motivation: combatants who receive payment may be motivated, not by the 'right intention', but by money. The cause of the war may be just, it may be waged on proper authority, and yet the intention of the just warriors be wrong. The office of mercenary was held to be dangerous to the soul of the individual concerned. Russell reports too the opinion of the theologian Peter the Chanter that crossbowmen were unworthy of salvation because they made their living by killing innocent victims.[38] The use of the term 'innocent' here is striking. Russell sees Peter's forthright condemnation of crossbowmen as out of step with his more tolerant view of other aspects of warfare. But the reason for stigmatizing bows, crossbows and siege engines may have been based on their inability to discriminate (and the implications of their inability to discriminate for the justification of war). Such missile weapons 'which know not where they strike' were thought to run the risk of killing people who ought not to be killed. A distinction was drawn, however, between the payment of mercenaries and the practice of rewarding knights from the spoils of war though Peter the Chanter warned that such payments, though needed to enable knights to fight, must never be their reason for fighting.

Whatever the reason underlying the objections, they were shared by the papacy. At the end of the eleventh century, Pope Urban II condemned the use of bows and crossbows against Christians. Four decades later, in 1139, the second Lateran Council issued a canon anathematizing all those who used the crossbow or longbow in wars between Christians. The third Lateran Council of 1179 was to confirm the moral stigma on mercenaries as well as the threat of excommunication that applied to them.[39] A few theologians were of the opinion that the prohibition on crossbows applied to all wars; Raymond of Peñafort believed that the prohibition must be upheld even in a just war against Christians (though he thought that these weapons could be used against pagans and persecutors of the faith).[40] Peter the Chanter sought to restrict their use to wars against pagans and heretics while Robert of Courçon believed their employment permissible only in exceptional circumstances such as defence of the

Holy Land. Most canon lawyers, however, held that any weapons could be used in a just war. The theologians came to agree with the canonistic opinion that any weapon was licit in a just war.[41] Gratian makes no allusion to the prohibition in his *Decretum* though it was repeated in the *Decretals* of Gregory IX. Thus, the crossbow ban had only a limited and temporary effect and, by the thirteenth century, most armies had a group of Genoese or other expert crossbowmen.[42]

The longbow and the pike

The longbow also played a significant role in ending knightly dominance in battle and in changing the nature of war in Western Christendom. An invention of the Welsh, the longbow was used by the English in their wars against the Scots at Falkirk (1298), Bannockburn (1314), Dupplin Moor (1332) and Halidon Hill (1333). With greater range and power than the short bow, its arrows could penetrate the knight's mail shirt or shoot his horse from under him. The English had had half a century of experience with the weapon when Edward III invaded France in 1345. The battle of Crecy in 1346, the first of the three great battles of the Hundred Years War, opened with an exchange between English longbowmen and Genoese mercenary crossbowmen.[43] At the second, Poitiers in 1356, the English archers shifted to a position that allowed them to fire at the unprotected hindquarters of the French horses.[44] The French knights had to proceed on foot in unwieldy armour, eliminating the shock effect of the mounted knight and increasing their vulnerability. Knightly warfare was in decline as cavalry suffered defeat by infantry. Less than 30 years after Aquinas's death came the first defeat of a knightly army by foot soldiers since Roman times when the Flemish foot soldiers achieved victory in the battle of Courtrai in 1302. This was followed by the battle of Bannockburn in 1314 when Scottish foot soldiers triumphed over the Anglo-Norman knights of Edward II of England. A year later the Swiss foot soldiers had their first great victory over the Austrian knights at Morgarten.[45] Facing a cavalry overburdened with plate armour and heavy lances, the Swiss pikemen showed Europe the attacking potential of infantry. They showed too the potential of a permanent, disciplined and trained army. Foot soldiers, secondary to cavalry since the ninth century, were suddenly to the fore and their victories in the fourteenth century brought an end to the dominance of knights in European warfare. With the Swiss pikemen, a true infantry had re-emerged, capable of taking the leading role in offence. They were to go on to become the leading mercenary troops of Europe in the fifteenth century. A comparison of the casualty figures from the twelfth and fourteenth centuries highlights the great transformation that was taking place in European warfare in the century in which Aquinas was writing. The previous chapter mentioned battles of the twelfth century in which few knights died or even none. From 1230 on, however, came radical changes as the feudal warfare of mounted knight and fortified castle yielded to mass armies of infantrymen, archers and crossbowmen. At Courtrai in 1302, 40 per cent of the French knights were killed; at Halidon Hill 31 years later, over half of the Scottish cavalry were wiped out; while the last of the three great battles of the Hundred Years War, Agincourt in 1415, saw again 40 per cent of the French cavalry destroyed.[46]

Together these innovations of mercenary archers and crossbowmen, salaried knights, resurgent infantry and indiscriminate weaponry transformed the nature of war in the thirteenth century and rendered the established punitive justification even less applicable. No longer could those killed in war be held to be guilty of a crime and also of the sin of fighting for an unjust cause. Those fighting were no longer principally knights with a share of political power and responsibility; many were now paid fighters with no responsibility for the *ad bellum* aims of their employer. The new weapons also meant that the harm done by war was spread more widely and more indiscriminately. There remained, incidentally, only one type of war to which the idea of war as punishment could be applied with any coherence: the crusades. Pope Urban II called for first Crusade at the Council of Clermont in 1095 and the ensuing wars against Saracens and infidels could possibly be justified as punishment of heresy. This was a rare circumstance in which the claim could plausibly still be made that, not only a ruler, but also his agents and soldiers, merited death because of their own actions and wickedness (in holding to heresy or to a false religion). For the most part, the reality of warfare had moved further than ever away from Augustine's punitive model of a 'just war'.

Conclusion: feudal war and non-combatant immunity

Whereas Augustine had sought to justify war on the individual level, Aquinas constructed a justification of war on the social level. Augustine had attempted to justify killing in war on the basis of the guilt of every person killed; Aquinas, in contrast, developed a justification of war in terms of its consequences for society. One could say that Augustine was concerned with whether war can be justified whereas Aquinas and his contemporaries asked only how war was to be justified. Augustine lived at a time when a woman might be a believer but not her husband, a man might be Christian but not his parents. For Christians to whom Augustine was seeking to justify war, pacifism was still a real option. To Aquinas and other theologians of the later medieval period, the rejection of war was not an option. They lived in a civilization in which all were Christian and in which war was established and accepted.

Though hugely influential, Augustine's justification of war as punishment for guilt never quite fitted reality. In the era when war was waged to defend Roman civilization against barbarism, Augustine's justification of war as a defence, not only of the legal order but also of the moral order was accepted by the Church as it intertwined itself with the civil order. As the feudal system flourished in Western Christendom, Augustine's defence of war as the punishment of wrong maintained some degree of fit with military and political reality. Some guilt and responsibility could be ascribed to combatants on the basis of their feudal rights and duties. Those who fought wars could be said to share in political responsibility for the war; more importantly, those who were targeted in war also shared political responsibility in the feudal society.

But by the time Aquinas was writing, the nature of war in Western Christendom was changing. Developments in the weaponry and personnel of warfare brought great cumulative effects. In the thirteenth century, warfare and its socio-political context was being radically transformed. The monopoly of licit violence held by the knightly class eroded, and the principal role in war was no longer held by knights with social, political and military responsibilities and powers. The long-established Augustinian defence of war was a poor fit with the new political and military realities. There was a need for a new justification. It was at this juncture in the history of European war that Aquinas developed a new justification of war with the resources offered to him by Aristotle's political theories. This teleological justification of war, on the basis of the good of society, justified killing in war without reference to the guilt of those killed. War was fought for the good of society. This new justification brought with it a new reason for immunity in war of certain categories of people: it was their occupation of certain social roles which gave them immunity from harm in war.

Aquinas developed a doctrine neither of the limitation of the means of war nor of the prohibition of the killing of certain categories of people. He did maintain the established immunity for clerics in war though he provided a new rationale for it. The traditional reasoning, with its condemnation of all killing as incompatible with the highest Christianity, was replaced by a new reasoning that presented war straightforwardly as a good means. Clerics were to be immune in war because of their role in society. It was not their business to fight wars and therefore they should not be targeted in war. With its roots in Aristotle's view of the human community, this principle of immunity on the basis of social function had the potential to be expanded into the comprehensive principle of non-combatant immunity which had been sought by the peace movements of the tenth and eleventh centuries. But what the Angelic Doctor gave to non-combatants with one hand, he took away with the other. On the one hand, in defending clerical immunity on the basis of their social role, he provided a moral basis for non-combatant immunity which was to be expanded in later centuries to encompass all civilians. On the other hand, however, the immunity he outlined was to be far from absolute. For Aquinas had also provided, with his moral idea of double effect, a justification for killing supposedly immune non-combatants in war. This principle of double effect asserted that, as long as one does not intend their deaths and certain other conditions are met, then the non-accidental killing of civilians in war can be excused. As regards the fate of non-combatants in war, this principle of double effect was to be every bit as relevant as Aquinas's new functional basis for clerical non-participation in fighting.

Although Aquinas developed a new justification of war, he did not dispense with the old one and the two sit uneasily together in the *Summa* with no synthesis offered. The old Augustinian defence of war was still needed to answer important and persistent questions to which the new Aristotelian justification of war could give no answers. There were two principal ways in which the new justification fell short of what was required. First, Augustine had attempted, not simply to justify war, but to justify it in one particular moral manner: on the basis of the 'right' and not the 'good'. To Augustine, war had to be a just treatment of the individual and not merely a good thing socially. His writings on *bellum justum* are characterized by an unwillingness to rely solely on consequentialist justifications of the use of lethal force in war. He was uneasy with the notion of killing a person simply because some greater good is served by his or her death. Instead he sought a justification of war which focuses on the individual as the locus of value and which justifies the state and its acts by reference to the individual. To establish that war had to be justified in this manner was the important legacy of Augustine. All subsequent Christian writings on war were to be characterized by an unwillingness, to a greater or lesser degree, to rely solely on justifications of the use of lethal force by reference to good ends alone. On both the *ad bellum* and *in bello* levels, the key element of Augustine's attempt to justify war non-consequentially was the notion of 'just cause' interpreted as the guilt of the enemy. The fault required as a condition of a just war must be a subjective one: it is not sufficient that the party without just cause has done wrong; rather they must have knowingly done wrong and it is because of this wilful wrongdoing that they may be killed. It was on this score that Aquinas's new justification of war on the basis of the defence of the common good fell short. It failed to justify the killing of each individual in war by reference to his personal acts and attributes. Secondly, Aquinas's reluctance to let go of the established Augustinian characterization of war in terms of guilt and punishment also allowed his doctrine of war to maintain a clearly biblical foundation. Without it, the Christian character of Aquinas's naturalistic justification of war is much less obvious. With the desuetude of Augustine's two claims (that wars could be divinely ordained as in the Old Testament, and that the king could wage war as God's agent inflicting his punishment on the wicked), the just war approach would lose its distinctively Christian foundation. When that occurred, as John Yoder writes, 'just war' thought would become

> not specifically Christian, and would fit into any honest system of social morality. If Christ had never become incarnate, died, risen, ascended into heaven, and sent His Spirit, this view would be just as possible.[47]

Augustine's guilt-based justification of killing, biblically based but failing to fit the reality of war, was to be replaced by a justification of killing which, though it matched the reality of war, had little distinctively Christian character. Non-Christians earnestly seeking a better world would limit the ends and means of war in a manner similar to modern 'just war' thought, claims Yoder.

To justify war by reference to the good alone, to justify it on some basis other than the acts and attributes of the individual human beings killed, and to justify war in a manner no longer distinctively Christian were steps of such magnitude that even the next great names in Christian just war writing, Francisco de Vitoria and Francisco Suárez, were very hesitant to take them. Writing three centuries after Aquinas, these two theologians were reluctant to relinquish the Christian and non-consequentialist character of *bellum justum* and to move unequivocally to a modern justification of war on the basis of objective justice. These Spanish theologians are the subjects of the next chapter.

5
Innocence and Modern War

How often misused words generate misleading thoughts.
Herbert Spencer[1]

The first important steps towards the modern era's characterization of the combatant were taken by two Spanish theologians who lived in the time of the Renaissance but who continued to write in the manner of Scholasticism. It was they who took the significant (though faltering) step along the route the Angelic Doctor feared to tread, by breaking the connection between objective legal guilt and subjective moral guilt. It was this innovation which began the journey of 'just war' thought from its Christian origins in Augustine's guilt-based model towards the basis in natural law that was to underpin modern international law. This step also had profound implications for the characterization of the combatant and for the justification for his killing in war.

Francisco do Vitoria (*c*.1486–1546) was one of the most influential political theorists of sixteenth-century Catholic Europe.[2] A Basque (taking his name from the town of his birth, Vitoria in Álava) he entered the Dominican order and studied at the University of Paris when the *Summa Theologiae* of Thomas Aquinas was being revived as a Dominican textbook alongside, or instead of, the *Sentences* of Peter Lombard. Paris at this time was the centre for modern ideas and Vitoria was there influenced by Renaissance humanism. In 1526 he was elected to the *prima* Chair of Theology at the University of Salamanca by an enthusiastic majority of students and he devoted his life to teaching theology, incorporating Renaissance scholarship into a scholastic framework (in contrast to the followers of Erasmus who sought to abolish the scholastic method). He applied scholastic methods and Thomistic theology to the issues of his day; in *De indis* and *De jure belli*, he applies them to politics and to war. His writings on war, argued in the traditional scholastic manner, were a genuine attempt to examine the possibility of limiting the harm of warfare and he was the first theologian after Aquinas to make an influential contribution to the doctrine of the 'just war'. Vitoria's innovative contribution to the doctrine of the 'just war' had two elements to it. These two elements formed the two sides to his hesitant rejection of Augustine's punishment model of war. First, he moved towards accepting that a situation which is only objectively unjust could be a sufficient cause of war: there need be no subjective guilt on the part of the enemy against whom a 'just war' is waged. Secondly, and closely linked to this, Vitoria wished to limit war to combatants; he tried to suggest why non-combatants must, on the grounds of justice, be spared. In so doing, Vitoria foreshadowed the modern characterization of the combatant as depersonalized.

A second Spanish theologian of the same era, whose work is worth examining in conjunction with that of Vitoria, is Francisco Suárez (1548–1617), born in Granada of an ancient family which had played a part in the final battles of the wars of the Reconquest of Granada.[3] Initially rejected (twice) by the Jesuits as mentally and physically below the required standard, Suárez entered the Society of Jesus in 1564. He studied theology at Salamanca and rose to the Chair of Theology at the Jesuit College in Rome, one of the highest posts in the Society. Never as brilliant or popular a lecturer as Vitoria had been in his day, Suárez nonetheless achieved a reputation for his clear and thorough scholarship. As the last of the Scholastics, his written work represents a final statement of Renaissance-scholastic philosophy and theology. His 'just war' thought, however, represents a strange transitional stage in the move from the medieval to the modern.

The sixteenth century was one of transition and spiritual crisis, the period in which the disintegration of the medieval world reached its climax. Sovereign states replaced medieval political universalism and the centralization of political power ended feudalism. With the coming of the Reformation, new forms of thought emerged in the West and the end of Scholastic philosophy was in sight. The Spain of

Vitoria and Suárez, however, was largely untouched by the Protestant Reformation or the industrial revolution. The Renaissance revival of literature and scholarship concentrated in Spain on biblical and patristic texts rather than on pagan classics. Thomistic thought was widely attacked in the universities of northern Europe in the fourteenth and fifteenth centuries even before it was largely abandoned by the Protestant countries in the sixteenth. Nonetheless, it continued to dominate in Spain and indeed underwent a revival in the sixteenth century to which Vitoria and Suárez were leading contributors. But the changes in religion, thought and society, along with sudden widening of the horizons brought about by the discovery of the Americas, had rendered the medieval concept of Christendom insufficient.

Although Machiavelli's *Prince* was as widely read and discussed in Spain as elsewhere, political thought there continued to be expounded within a framework of natural law. Vitoria and Suárez operated within the Thomistic system, seeing natural law as a natural system of ethics, independent of Christianity but never contradictory of it. A standard of good and evil, natural law was to be used as a basis for judging human laws (and, as a last resort, for refusing to obey them). Both Vitoria and Suárez were more politically minded and more practical in their advice than Aquinas had been. The last influential thinkers on war to argue in the scholastic manner, they sought to reaffirm the intellectual legacy of the old world and apply it to the problems of the new.

Great changes had taken place not only in European society and thought but also in the wars Europe waged. The century of Vitoria and Suárez was one particularly conscious of the horrors of war: as Europeans, they had seen the divisions in Catholic Christendom faced by a Turkish threat; as Spaniards they were aware of the bloody conquest of the Americas. Feudal war had passed away and the principal combatants of modern war no longer bore any political responsibility for the war being waged. War was now fought by and against people who bore no guilt for the unjust cause of their side. By the fourteenth century, mercenaries and professional soldiers had come to play the central role in the fighting and, as a consequence, there soon came an acknowledgment that enemy combatants could no longer be held politically and morally responsible for the injustice that gave rise to a war.

The Hundred Years War of 1337–1453 has been called the first modern war because of the French creation of a professional standing army as well as the part played by nationalist spirit in the ultimate French victory. In 1439, Charles VII had proposed at Orléans the creation of the first regular army since Roman times in order to end the scourge of mercenary free companies pillaging French cities and provinces. Mercenary companies were taken into royal service on a permanent basis and a French standing army of 6000 men came into being (as did the first permanent system of taxation, introduced to pay for their maintenance).[4] At the same time, the right of feudal lords to keep their own troops was prohibited by the assembly of the estates.[5] The result was the modern standing army, a political, military and fiscal innovation. Greater discipline was possible as the permanent force trained together and captains, themselves now responsible directly to the king, were made fully responsible for the conduct of their men.

As well as the introduction of the first professional standing army, the fifteenth century saw also the development of the other fighting force characteristic of the modern era: the national army of conscripts. The first of these had come into being in fourteenth-century Switzerland. The army was composed of all peasants and burghers who were free, male and physically fit. Such general conscription in a country relying on subsistence agriculture posed problems. The burden of keeping men under arms when the soil had to be tilled and animals tended led to a change in strategy away from the prolonged wars of mercenaries towards the strategy of quick annihilation. An army defeated might fight again; to prevent it from doing so, the Swiss forbade the taking of prisoners. All who fell into their hands were butchered in cold blood (when, in the Burgundian War, a town offered resistance to the Swiss, its population – men, women and children – were killed without mercy. The garrison of one castle were thrown to their deaths from the castle tower and those soldiers who had tried to hide were tied up and thrown into a nearby lake).[6]

With the innovation of standing armies and conscript forces, feudal war was finished. The nature of both war and the combatant had changed. No longer were wars fought by knights who held a share in social and political power and who could be considered politically and morally responsible for the war. War had changed, most importantly, as regards who fought it. The response of Vitoria and Suárez was to attempt to restrict killing in war to combatants only and to exclude many categories of non-combatants from being targeted in war. They tried to do this while maintaining the established justification of killing in war by reference to the guilt of those killed. For this combination of the old and the new, their contribution to 'just war' thought merits Johnson's description of it as 'a transitional stage in the development of a secular theory of just war'.[7] In it, they looked forward to the modern era in its restriction of killing to combatants but they also looked backwards to medieval Christianity for its justification of killing in war. As a result, their approach was incoherent and unsatisfactory.

Isidore of Seville

In breaking away from the Augustinian notion of subjective guilt, Vitoria and Suárez looked back, not only to Aquinas, but also to a much earlier figure. This was St Isidore of Seville (*c*.560–636), a Hispano-Roman bishop who lived two and a half centuries after Augustine. At the time the political turmoil in Spain was ended by the unification of the country under the Visigothic kings of Toledo.[8] The religious conflict between the Catholic Hispano-Romans and the Arian Visigoths was ended in 578 by King Reccared's embrace of the Catholic faith. Spain entered a period of peace and cultural growth, and Isidore, on succeeding his brother to the episcopal see of Seville, set about compiling his *Origines*. Intended as a definitive encyclopaedia of knowledge, it was innovative in its inclusion of pagan knowledge whenever Isidore considered it to be of use to the Christian. A dutiful recorder of the views of others rather than a critical or original thinker, Isidore was, however, tolerant of pagan culture and well read in pagan as well as Christian works. Augustine had been engaged in a struggle to the death with paganism but by Isidore's time this struggle had ended in a decisive Christian victory. Paganism was no longer a threat to Christianity and thus when Isidore came to record the origins of 'just war' thought, he paid attention to Cicero, Roman law and Roman ideas of the community as natural and of the ruler as having natural-law rights to use force.

In setting out the definition of a 'just war', Isidore emphasized, not the Augustinian just cause of punishment but one drawn from Roman law: the recovery of stolen goods. It was just to resort to war in order to recover property illegally taken. This was important as it emphasized a juridical notion phrased in terms of objective material rights. It shifted the focus from a consideration of the enemy's subjective intent and moral guilt to a consideration of the objective injustice of his act.[9] By overlooking the link between objective legal guilt and subjective moral guilt, and justifying war solely on the basis of the former, Isidore took a significant step away from the Augustinian model. It was this step which Vitoria and Suárez were reluctant to take centuries later as to do so would invalidate the claim that the breach of objective legal rights implied the subjective moral guilt of the enemy. It would thenceforth be sufficient justification for a state to wage war if its rights had been violated but it would also mean that people who had done no wrong were having their lives taken as means to political and military ends.

Isidore's inclusion of Roman law in his record of 'just war' thought laid the foundations for the later secularization of 'just war' doctrine. Isidore's definition of a just war, avoided by Aquinas, was adopted in the late Middle Ages and early modern period by those who sought to move from a divine authority to wage war towards one deriving from the natural order.[10] The writings of the Bishop of Seville were important to those in the later Middle Ages who sought to make judgments about the justice of wars on a rational and natural-law basis rather than a supernatural or theological one. However, the shift of 'just war' doctrine to a natural-law basis and into the sphere of secular international law yielded some troubling moral implications. It was to overcome these implications that Vitoria and Suárez struggled without success.

Vitoria's and Suárez's justification of war

Aquinas had not accepted the claim, implicit in Isidore's definition, that an action that is only objectively unjust can be a legitimate cause of war. Instead, he had required also a subjective injustice, giving a clear punitive element to his characterization of war. Yet, as we saw in the last chapter, Aquinas was not consistent on this point. Elsewhere, he raised the possibility that war could be justified, not as punishment, but merely as something necessary for the maintenance of justice and order and the safeguarding of the common good. Any violation of such order could bring about an aggressive war – even if no subjective injustice existed (and therefore no cause for punishment). He did not, however, put this justification of war to the fore but continued to give prime place to the Augustinian punitive model of a just war as a justified punishment of a sinful enemy who merits punishment on account of their wickedness. However, in the three centuries after Aquinas, the justification of war as punitive justice faded from European thought, and the characterization of war as defence of the social order took its place. The emphasis on natural law had fundamentally altered the 'just war' approach making it, not primarily an assertion of God's judgment against evildoers, but a description of the right of princes to use force to defend their rights and the good of the society they governed.[11] The *jus ad bellum* of Vitoria and Suárez is built on the natural law idea that everything instituted by God has within itself the powers necessary for its maintenance, fulfilment and proper functioning. So a community must have the power to protect itself, avenge itself and recover its property because otherwise it could never maintain itself or achieve its fulfilment. For Vitoria and Suárez, in common with others of their time, the justice of war was grounded in nature rather than religion and war could be justified only for causes provided for in natural law. Both reject paganism, idolatry, unnatural sins and difference of religion as just causes for war as well as extension of empire and the private gain or glory of the prince.[12]

As regards the cause for a 'just war', Vitoria wrote:

> There is a single and only just cause for commencing a war, namely, a wrong received ...
>
> Not every kind and degree of wrong can suffice for commencing a war. The proof of this is that not even upon one's fellow-countrymen is it lawful for every offence to exact atrocious punishments, such as death or banishment or confiscation of property. As, then, the evils inflicted in war are all of a severe and atrocious character, such as slaughter and fire and devastation, it is not lawful for slight wrongs to pursue the authors of the wrongs with war, seeing that the degree of the punishment ought to correspond to the measure of the offence.
>
> ... war is waged: Firstly, in defence of ourselves and what belongs to us; secondly, to recover things taken from us; thirdly, to avenge a wrong suffered by us; fourthly, to secure peace and security.[13]

According to Vitoria, then, both defensive and offensive wars could be just. The former could be in defence of life, property or honour while an offensive war must be to right a wrong. The 'just cause' for an offensive war must be an injury suffered and war must be the last resort to remedy that injury. In addition, there must be proportionality between the evils brought about by war and the good that is its aim. An offensive war must also be declared by a competent authority and it must be carried out in the right manner. Suárez repeated the standardized formula of a 'just war':

> First, the war must be waged by a legitimate power; secondly, the cause and reason must themselves be just; thirdly, it must be properly conducted and a sense of proportion kept at the beginning, during hostilities and after victory ...[14]

Suárez reiterates here the requirement that war be waged by a 'legitimate power'. In the time of Vitoria and Suárez, the perception of the authority vested in the ruler was very different to that of previous centuries. In Gratian's time, the doctrine of the 'divine right of kings' had still meant that the ruler waged war as God's scourge and inflicted God's punishment on the wicked (a crucial element of the punitive model of war). By the sixteenth and seventeenth centuries, the authority to wage war was secularized, based in natural law and directed towards serving the social good. Natural law had become separated from divine law and from God; it may still have been seen as enclosed with divine law, but the latter was seen as no longer relevant to war. Thus, by the time of Vitoria and Suárez, the divine right of kings meant no more than that the ruler could act as he pleased. The requirement of 'legitimate authority' lost its central role in making war just and became no more than a pragmatic bar on private war making.[15] This new *jus ad bellum* had positive practical implications for *jus in bello* in that the shift of focus from subjective guilt to objective unjust act permitted a less severe treatment of war's victims. In contrast, the new *jus ad bellum* raised profound moral problems as to why human beings may have their lives taken as a means to the end of securing the social order.

Simultaneous just cause

In the established Augustinian *jus ad bellum* as reiterated by Aquinas, only one party to a conflict could have justice on its side. Both sides could be at fault (in which case the war would be unjust on both sides) but both sides could never have just cause. There could not be justice on both sides for if each side is just then for either side to kill any of the other's combatants is to commit murder (it was the injustice on the *ad bellum* level which permitted, on the *in bello* level, a person to be killed in war). Without that injustice on one side, such killing would be murder. By the sixteenth and seventeenth centuries, the changes in European warfare had made untenable this accusation of guilt on the part of one side's combatants. The wars of the 100 years following the Reformation cast doubt on the possibility that a just cause could be known to exist, while the rise of mercenaries and professional soldiers meant that combatants could not be held responsible for an unjust cause even if one could be shown to exist. Given this, the acknowledgment of simultaneous just cause seems no more than a commonsense acceptance of political and military reality, but its implications for the moral justification of killing in war are huge. For acceptance of the possibility of simultaneous just cause would seem to mean the rejection of the punishment model of war: the 'just war' could maintain its role as an instrument of justice only if justice happened to be the outcome of a military struggle. However, Vitoria and Suárez strove to maintain the moral characterization of war and did so by relying on the notion of 'invincible ignorance'. In a very important development for the characterization of war and of the combatant, they accepted that a war can be (subjectively) just on both sides but only because of invincible ignorance. In response to the question 'whether a war can be just on both sides?', Vitoria writes:

The following is my answer: First proposition: Apart from ignorance the case clearly cannot occur, for if the right and justice of each side be certain, it is unlawful to fight against it, either in offence or in defence.

Second proposition: Assuming a demonstrable ignorance either of fact or of law, it may be that on the side where true justice is, the war is just of itself, while on the other side the war is just in the sense of being excused from sin by reason of good faith, because invincible ignorance is a complete excuse.

Also, on the side of the subjects at any rate, this may often occur; for even if we assume that a prince who is carrying on an unjust war knows about its injustice, still (as had been said) subjects may in good faith follow their prince, and in this way the subjects on both sides may be doing what is lawful when they fight.[16]

Vitoria here maintains the Augustinian position that, from an objective point of view, a war can be just only for one of the parties to it. Subjectively, however, he allows that a war can be just for both sides if both are acting in good faith. When he discusses the issue in *De indis*, he maintains this position that there could not be justice on both sides. It could be, though, that one side has justice and the other mistakenly believes that it does. Because of this possibility, Vitoria writes, there 'is no inconsistency, indeed, in holding the war to be a just war on both sides, seeing that on one side there is right and on the other side there is invincible ignorance'.[17]

The presumption of guilt and innocence

Vitoria's acknowledgment that both parties to a war may believe that they have justice on their side also raised grave problems for the justification of killing in war. The Augustinian model, which used guilt as the justification of killing in war, saw that guilt as derived from the unjust cause of one party to the conflict. Such guilt was assigned to one side's combatants and non-combatants. Both combatants and non-combatants on the side at fault were held to be guilty of participation in the wrongdoing of their ruler and, for that reason, they could be killed. As regards the combatants and non-combatants on the side with just cause, there was no justification for their killing in war: their deaths were murder. It was in this way that Augustine's model met the standard required of a justification of war, justifying the killing of each person in war by reference to the acts and attributes of that individual. However, the Augustinan model had major problems, the most serious being the connection between the ruler's legal fault and his subjects' moral guilt. This connection is crucial to the whole Augustinian justification of killing in war and yet it is unproven and improbable. It seems unfair in the extreme to blame soldiers and subjects for their participation in their ruler's unjust causes. Indeed, to lay the blame on them for things that were not their concern may seem insulting to otherwise honourable fighters and powerless subjects. A practical drawback with the Augustinian model is that it did not have the effect of limiting the scale or harshness of wars. In theory, charity was to be a motive of one's actions in war as well as justice and punishment, but the punishment motive could make wars merciless and vicious as one's enemies were considered at fault and deserving of punishment.

Vitoria tried to remedy this practical problem by loosening (though not severing) the connection between the ruler's legal fault and his subjects' moral guilt which was the weakest link in Augustine's model. Vitoria's model brings a fundamental change in the basis on which people are classified as targets. The division of people into two categories, legitimate and illegitimate targets, is no longer on the basis of the just or unjust cause of their ruler; rather it is on the basis of combatancy and non-combatancy. Crucially – and extraordinarily – combatancy is held to carry with it a presumption of guilt. In Augustine's model of a just war, soldiers fighting for a just cause did nothing wrong when they killed soldiers fighting for an unjust cause. But for soldiers on the side without just cause to kill their adversaries was to commit murder. In Vitoria's model, soldiers on both sides may be presumed to be 'guilty' and may be killed without murder being done. While a war is in progress, the issue of just cause is set aside and all combatants are accorded the same status. Belligerent equality is gained and those engaged in injustice have the same status as those engaged in furthering a just cause. Vitoria accomplishes this major change by linking guilt to combatancy by presumption. While war is being waged, combatants on both sides may be presumed to be guilty of participation in an unjust cause (unless proven otherwise) and killed. It is not the bearing arms and engaging in fighting which is wrong, a wrong of such magnitude that one may be killed for it (this would be to reject all fighting in war as wrong which is not Vitoria's intention). Rather, combatants may be presumed to be guilty of participation in an unjust cause. That Vitoria links combatancy/non-combatancy to guilt/innocence so closely that they become virtually synonymous is clear from his discussion of whether the innocent may ever be killed:

> I discussed this with a member of the Royal Council who thought it expedient for the proper waging of a war that everyone should be killed. My opinion is, firstly, that everyone able to bear arms should be considered dangerous and must be assumed to be defending the enemy king; they may therefore be killed unless the opposite is clearly true, i.e. unless it is obvious that they are

harmless. I believe, secondly, that when it is essential for victory it is lawful to kill the innocent. For example, a town is besieged and must be bombarded: the death of the innocent results from the bombardment, but the result is incidental: let them perish! (There can be no doubt about this; it is the same as besieging a fortress.) But thirdly I say that if a town were captured, and innocent persons came near the scene of victory because they no longer felt in danger, it would not be lawful for the king to kill such people as, for example, children, religious and clerics who were not taking part. The reason for this limitation is evident: they are innocent, and their death is not necessary for victory. It would be heretical to say that they might be killed at such a time. Hence, one must not kill the innocent on purpose when it is possible to separate them from the guilty.[18]

Vitoria writes that the bearing of arms is only an indicator of guilt while a war is in progress and as long as the issue of wilful participation in an unjust cause is still unsettled. It may be found that both rulers and ruled on the side without just cause believed, in good faith, that they had justice on their side. If this is so, then they were wrong only because of invincible ignorance:

Note, however, that sometimes, nay, frequently, not only subjects, but princes, too, who in reality have no just case of war, may nevertheless be waging war in good faith, with such good faith, I say, as to free them from fault; as, for instance, if the war is made after a careful examination and in accordance with the opinion of learned and upright men. And since no one who has not committed a fault should be punished, in that case, although the victor may recoup himself for things that have been taken from him and for any expenses of the war, yet ... it is unlawful to go on killing after the victory ... [19]

Indeed, soldiers too may well be innocent (in the sense that they did not knowingly and wilfully participate in injustice and wickedness) and, if this is so known, they must not be harmed unless military victory requires it: 'if there should even be a soldier who is clearly innocent, and our soldiers are able to let him go free, they must do so, whether during the war or after victory has been won...'[20] Suárez built on Vitoria's work and sought to maintain the strange marriage of moral innocence and legal innocence. Like his predecessor, Suárez held that natural law forbids the killing of the innocent. Or, to be more precise, it forbids the killing of any one who is actually *known* to be free from guilt. Like Vitoria, he sought proof of innocence in order to spare life rather than proof of guilt in order to take it. Suárez then asserts that it is involvement in the perpetration of a crime that makes one a legitimate target of attack and he holds that immunity from attack is to be granted to those who are to be considered innocent in an objective legal sense (they may or may not be innocent in a subjective moral sense of intending to do wrong). So, on this basis, immunity is to be granted to women and children and also to ambassadors and clergy because of objective material fact.[21]

The non-combatant

With Vitoria and Suárez the immunity of non-combatants in war took a great step forward. The justice or injustice of one's cause was downplayed and an attempt was made to grant immunity to non-combatants on both sides. This feat was accomplished by assuming the guilt of combatants on both sides (unless it is known to the contrary) and assuming the innocence of non-combatants on both sides (unless it is known to the contrary). The flaws of this approach are profound and obvious but it had a practical benefit as the shift of focus from subjective guilt to objective unjust act permitted a less severe treatment of war's victims. No longer was war a punishment of their wickedness. This weakening of the link between *ad bellum* legal fault and *in bello* moral guilt opened the way for firm *in bello* restrictions. It did so in two ways. First, it did so by narrowing down the enemy from the entire population of one's adversary to just its combatants. By weakening the connection between the ruler's legal fault and his subjects' moral guilt, Vitoria's innovation allowed a distinction to be drawn between combatant and non-combatant members of the enemy population. Only those who bear arms or engage in fighting were to be presumed guilty in the absence of evidence to the contrary. Non-combatants on both sides (regardless of the justice of causes) are to be presumed innocent unless it can be shown that they knowingly and wilfully promoted injustice and wickedness. As such, non-combatants should not be killed as the 'deliberate slaughter of the innocent is never lawful in itself'.[22] This is a very powerful moral basis for non-combatants' immunity from targeting. To kill the innocent would be a breach of natural law.[23] Classes of people who must be presumed innocent until proven guilty are women, children, clerics, religious, foreign travellers, guests of the country, 'harmless agricultural folk, and also ... the rest of the peaceable civilian population'.[24] Secondly, if guilt could be linked to combatancy, then innocence could be made into, in Hartigan's words, 'a concrete reality'.[25] Guilt and innocence would be easy to identify in war, assigned on the basis of the bearing and non-bearing of arms respectively. In the Augustinian model, subjective moral guilt was assigned on the basis of objective facts alone: Augustine (unjustifiably) ascribed guilt to individuals whose ruler had an unjust cause. Vitoria continued to ascribe subjective moral guilt on the basis of objective facts but he ascribed it to both sides of the conflict. Those who fight for either side may be assumed, while the war is in progress and in the absence of evidence to the contrary, to be guilty. With Augustine's approach, one did not have to ascertain the subjective moral status of each individual; one only had to decide where justice lay on the *ad bellum* level before one could say which side's combatants could kill without doing murder. Vitoria avoids even this question. Guilt can be presumed on the basis of combatancy alone.

With Vitoria's model of war, the connection between legal fault (on the *ad bellum* level) and moral fault (on the *in bello*) is weakened. The possibility of invincible ignorance means that ruler and combatants on both sides may be subjectively innocent. Divorcing *in bello* conduct from *ad bellum* fault permitted humanitarian restrictions to be placed on both sides in a war; regardless of the justice of their cause, both parties to a conflict could be required to abide by restrictions on their means and methods of fighting. Fighters on both sides could be offered the privileged status of lawful combatant, and non-combatants on both sides could be granted some protection. On this issue of the collateral killing of the innocent, Vitoria relies on Aquinas's principle of double effect though he applies it more strictly than the Angelic Doctor in some instances:

> Sometimes it is right, in virtue of collateral circumstances, to slay the innocent even knowingly, as when a fortress or city is stormed in a just war, although it is known that there are a number of innocent people in it and although cannon and other engines of war can not be discharged or fire applied to buildings without destroying innocent together with guilty.

The proof is that war could not otherwise be waged against even the guilty and the justice of belligerents would be baulked ... In sum, it is never right to slay the guiltless, even as an indirect and unintended result, *except when there is no other means of carrying on the operation of a just war.*[26]

As Palmer-Fernández points out, Vitoria's restriction on killing civilians is stricter than Aquinas's in two ways.[27] First, Vitoria requires there to be no other way of 'carrying on the operations' and, second, civilians may be killed only in a war known to be just. If there is doubt about the justice of a war, then the war must be fought without killing civilians, even as an indirect and unintended side effect of a military action. Where there is other than certainty about the *ad bellum* justice of a war, the PNCI functions as an exceptionless rule.

That the PNCI functions as a moral absolute in wars of doubtful justice is unsurprising given that Vitoria and Suárez justify non-combatant immunity on the basis of 'the right' rather than 'the good'. To Vitoria and Suárez, it is justice that requires that non-combatants should not be targeted and not merely the good end of reducing the casualties of war whoever they may be. Non-combatants are not to be killed because they are to be presumed to be innocent and to kill them would breach the fundamental principle of natural justice that the innocent may not be so treated. What is surprising is that in cases where the justice of one's cause is not in doubt, they permit the immunity of non-combatants to be ignored whenever the chances of victory would thereby be improved. Instead, the focus is on the principle of proportionality:

> Great attention, however, must be paid to the point already taken, namely, the obligation to see that greater evils do not arise out of the war than the war would avert. For if little effect upon the ultimate issue of the war is to be expected from the storming of a fortress or fortified town wherein are many innocent folk, it would not be right, for the purpose of assailing a few guilty, to slay the many innocent by use of fire or other means likely to overwhelm indifferently both innocent and guilty.[28]

In wars of certain justice, Vitoria writes, an act of war that would kill non-combatants but add little to the achievement of victory must not be done. But if military victory requires an act that will kill non-combatants, then they may be killed. In these cases Vitoria is not as far as he might think from the member of the Royal Council who thinks (in the Augustinian manner) that all in the enemy population may be killed. For he allows all – combatant and non-combatant, guilty and innocent – to be killed should killing be necessary for military victory or even should such killing improve the likelihood of military victory.[29]

The combatant

The characterization of the combatant in Vitoria and Suárez is closer to that of the Augustinian model than the modern one. The distinction between combatants and non-combatants is not one of guilt and innocence nor even one of participation and non-participation in a possibly unjust war. Rather, Vitoria and Suárez permit combatants on both sides to be killed while a war is in progress because we cannot discern, while the war is still in progress, whether they are fighting, knowingly or unknowingly, for a just cause or an unjust one. As there is no chance of settling these two questions while war is being waged, combatants may be assumed (in the absence of evidence to the contrary) to be guilty of knowing participation in an unjust cause. For this reason, they may be killed. In the case of non-combatants, a presumption of innocence applies instead; they may be killed only if their guilt may be established. For Vitoria and Suárez, combatancy and non-combatancy do not imply guilt and innocence. Rather the combatancy and non-combatancy may in war be taken as temporary indicators of the guilt and innocence (until the issue can be settled more definitively). Combatants on both sides may be killed in war (without murder being done) because it is permissible to assume while a war is in progress (unless one actually knows to the contrary) that the enemy is guilty of injustice and that enemy combatants are guilty of wilful participation in that injustice.

By this means, Vitoria and Suárez attempted to align the combatancy/non-combatancy distinction with the guilt/innocence one. Their starting point was the demand of natural law that the innocent should not be killed. Their innovation was the claim that in war non-combatancy may be taken as prima facie evidence of innocence (a fuller investigation may reveal individual women or foreigners to be guilty of engaging 'in actual fighting' in which case they are legitimate targets). The bearing or non-bearing of arms becomes an indicator of guilt or innocence with the result that the only legitimate target in the enemy population is the person who is armed and therefore dangerous.[30] But the bearing of arms is not the reason why a person may be killed. The reason why an armed person may legitimately be killed is not because they are armed but because their bearing of arms may, in the particular circumstances of war, be taken as an indicator of their possible involvement in the commission of a crime. For the Spanish theologians, then, guilt remained the justification of killing in war. This presumption of combatant guilt permits the killing of combatants only while a war is still in progress. Once war has ended then combatancy and non-combatancy may no longer be used as indicators of guilt and innocence; guilt and innocence must instead be investigated and determined. As Vitoria writes, 'there is nothing to prevent the killing of those who have surrendered or been captured in a just war'; however, their involvement in injustice must be established before such captured and surrendered combatants may be killed.[31]

Conscientious objection

Vitoria and Suárez made a significant contribution to the modern law of war with their assertion that non-combatants on both sides have an equal and just claim to immunity in war. Their characterization of the combatant, however, was more Augustinian than modern. This is evident too in their treatment of the issue of selective conscientious objection. They both place heaviest responsibility on the ruler to discern just cause. Vitoria writes: 'It is essential for a just war that an exceedingly careful examination be made of the justice and causes of the war and that the reasons of those who on the grounds of equity oppose it be listened to'.[32] Likewise Suárez requires a ruler considering a resort to war to make an examination of his cause and to satisfy himself that he has justice on his side: 'I hold, first, that the sovereign ruler is bound to make a diligent examination of the cause and its justice and that, after making this examination, he ought to act in accordance with the knowledge thus obtained'.[33] However, both Suárez and Vitoria also place some responsibility on the subject in this matter. They hold that, when the prince's cause is manifestly unjust, then the subject may not serve in the war. If a subject is convinced of the injustice of his prince's cause, he ought not to fight in the war even if commanded to do so. Soldiers are not excused when

they fight in bad faith. Vitoria starts with the straightforward demand
that those who, in conscience, believe a war to be unjust must play
no part in it but he asks subjects to give a wide margin of trust to
their political rulers. In the serious and complex matter of war, they
ought to give their government the benefit of the doubt:

> Subjects whose conscience is against the justice of a war may not
> engage in it whether they be right or wrong.
>
> Senators and petty rulers and in general all who are admitted on
> summons or voluntarily to the public council or the prince's
> council ought, and are bound, to examine into the cause of an
> unjust war.
>
> Other lesser folk who have no place or audience in the prince's
> council or in the public council are under no obligation to exam-
> ine the causes of a war, but may serve in it on reliance on their
> betters.
>
> Nevertheless the proofs and tokens of the injustice of the war
> may be such that ignorance would be no excuse even to subjects
> of this sort who serve in it.[34]

The Spanish theologians offered a clear justification for selective
conscientious objection to particular wars by the individual subject.
They did not require that the Church declare a war unjust before an
individual could refuse to serve in it but saw it as the individual's
responsibility to dispel doubts and satisfy his own conscience. If his
inquiries result in a confident belief in his ruler's injustice, then he
must in conscience refuse to serve. In less clear-cut cases, though, both
Vitoria and Suárez held that the subject is not required to consider the
justice of his ruler's cause too deeply but may in good conscience rely
on the judgment of the ruler (not that the ruler is under any obligation to give his subjects his reasons for making war). In cases of doubt,
says Suárez, the prince is better placed to decide on justice. In any
case, Vitoria had pointed out, should the subject find the war to be
unjust he has no ability to affect the prince's decision. For these reasons, the common subject has no obligation to inquire into a war's
justice. In fact, Vitoria and Suárez discouraged such attempts at
enlightenment by soldiers: they suggested that while soldiers have a
right to assess the justice of their ruler's cause, they have no obligation
to do so. It is only if the war is manifestly unjust that they must refuse

to serve. They hold, in contrast to Augustine, that to fight in an unjust cause endangers a soldier's soul more than a refusal to obey his sovereign. Thus, holds Suárez, subjects 'may go to war when summoned to do so, provided it is not clear to them that the war is unjust'.[35]

Vitoria and Suárez, then, allowed for the possibility of selective conscientious objection, albeit in limited circumstances. However, conscientious objection was very soon to be eroded. For selective conscientious objection is most obviously an implication of the Augustinian model of war, and not of the modern characterization of the combatant as an instrument. Their recommendation to soldiers not to fight for an unjust cause ties in with the old punitive model of war rather than with the modern one. Vitoria and Suárez had not moved to the modern era's view of the combatant as an unthinking tool of his military and political masters but still saw participation in war as dependent upon individual conviction of its just cause. From the sixteenth century, as Western thought moved towards the modern era's depersonalization of the combatant (both as killer and as victim), there was an increasing lack of concern, even among theologians, about the personal moral aspects of warfare. In its place came a greater concentration on external issues such as the defence of territory and the protection of the social order.[36]

Conclusion: innocence and non-combatant immunity

Vitoria and Suárez took only a small step in the direction to which Aquinas's work had pointed three centuries before: the elimination of the subjective factors of intention and motive and a reliance on objective justice alone to make a war just. Building on Isidore as well as Aquinas, the two Spaniards forwarded a new justification of war in terms of secular politics, natural justice and the good of society. On the *ad bellum* level, they went beyond Aquinas's position as regards the possibility of both sides to a war having just cause but they did not go all the way. They allowed, not that both sides may have justice on their side in a war, but that both sides may believe they do. By this means, they kept to the traditional Augustinian position that one side only could have just cause while nonetheless acknowledging that the other side might wrongly (though in good faith) believe it had justice on its side. With this deft manoeuvre, they created a half-way position between the medieval and modern views of the combatant and the non-combatant. Their reliance on 'invincible ignorance' to allow for the possibility of simultaneous just cause had very significant benefits for the treatment of the enemy during war, and also after it. The principle of belligerent equality, so crucial for the *in bello* limiting of warfare, was built by Vitoria and Suárez on the possibility of ignorance and uncertainty. The impossibility of seeing into people's souls to discern their subjective moral state (which had led Augustine to permit the killing of all in war) now led Vitoria and Suárez to limit the killing to as few as is necessary for military victory. The uncertainty about subjective fault and sin (and the possibility of invincible ignorance) led the Spaniards to seek the restriction of targeting to combatants alone. Their acknowledgment that enemy combatants may not be wicked but only mistaken led them to eliminate the punitive element of war. There ought to be no punishment of the enemy who may be innocent. The acknowledgment that enemy combatants are most probably innocent was the starting point for a more humane treatment of the enemy in war. It fitted in with the post-Reformation age of greater cultural and political diversity in which both sides to a war were likely to believe in the rightness of their cause. The most that could be done in such an age was to urge humane limitation on the conduct of war and the removal of punitive measures. Vitoria and Suárez can be seen as providing the theoretical basis for this. War was no longer to be seen as punishment of the guilty and, as both sides may sincerely believe that they are in the right, so war should be conducted and concluded in as limited and humane a manner as possible.

Yet there are profound problems with the Spaniards' attempt to move away from the Augustinian model and to find some basis for restrictions on the savagery of war. Their strange half-way position is based on linking the powerful moral concepts of guilt and innocence to the material facts of combatancy and non-combatancy. Yet they can link them only by presumption. Guilt remains the justification of killing in war, and combatancy and non-combatancy are held to be satisfactory indicators of guilt and innocence. This guilt is the guilt that derives from participation (by at least one side to a war, possibly both) in an unjust cause. In Vitoria and Suárez's model of war, it is still the likely case that one state is guilty, with its combatants participating in a wrong, while the other side has just cause. The killing of the just side's soldiers is still wrongful killing (though no longer murder if it is done by combatants acting in good faith). To kill on the presumption of guilt is hardly defensible: later investigation may reveal innocent people to have been killed. Indeed, later investigation would nearly always reveal innocent people to have been killed. This is so for two reasons. First, all the combatants and non-combatants on the side with just cause will have been innocent. Secondly, many of those on the side without just cause may have been acting in good faith too. It is therefore likely that the guilty killed in war will amount to very few indeed. War may, in fact, kill none but the innocent. If combatants are likely to be innocent (objectively innocent on one side, subjectively innocent on the other), and if it is improbable that combatants on either side will bear a guilt derived from their wilful participation in an unjust cause, then why may we presume them to be guilty while a war is in progress? Why may we kill them on the presumption of their guilt when such guilt is unlikely and when their innocence is far more likely? The Spaniards' defence is that, though combatants are probably innocent, they cannot be clearly identified as such and, because of this, they may be deemed guilty on the basis of combatancy and they may be killed. This is the only basis to Vitoria and Suárez's vain hope that they can still claim that innocent people have not been targeted and killed in war. It is not enough. To kill on the presumption of guilt is hardly defensible when it is actually known that, in fact, the vast majority or even all of the combatants will be innocent.

Why do Vitoria and Suárez put forward this incoherent position? Why do they place at the heart of their justification of killing combatants in war the presumption of guilt? Because, without it, they would be accepting the killing of innocent people as a means to political and military ends. This was something they were not prepared to accept; indeed, they held it to be contrary to natural law. Vitoria and Suárez attempted a convenient but highly questionable union of moral intention and material fact when they held that guilt and innocence may be deduced from participation or non-participation in a possibly unjust activity. This link was vital if they were to maintain guilt as the justification of killing in war and if they were to avoid the admission that innocent human beings have their lives taken as a means to the end of securing the social order. The result was a truly transitional model of war. On the one hand, they looked back to the Augustinian model of war in which killing is justified as punishment for guilt. On the other hand, they looked forward to the modern justification of killing in war on the basis of the depersonalization of the combatant. They tried to acknowledge that the innocent made up the majority, or even all, of those killed in war and yet still allow them to be targeted in war should military success require it. They tried to have both a justification of killing which accords to human life the status it should have and also humanitarian restrictions on warfare founded on belligerent equality. But their attempt was built on no more than a claim that those targeted in war may have been innocent but that this was neither known nor knowable at the time they were killed. They hoped that the presumption of guilt on the part of combatants (while war is still being waged) would allow them to avoid sanctioning the intentional killing of the innocent as a means towards political ends.

Vitoria, ever sensitive to the status of the individual in Christian morality, seems to have looked ahead to the modern characterization of war and of the combatant and become reluctant to adopt it. To eliminate issues of *ad bellum* fault and wickedness and to adopt the characterization of the combatant as a depersonalized instrument whose life may be taken in war for any reason or none would allow war to be limited to combatants only but only by also erasing war's moral characterization.[37] In other words, Vitoria could objectify the justice of war (and eliminate subjective moral guilt on the part of the enemy as a necessary condition of a just war) only by also objectifying the humans who fight and die in war. The objectification of the justice of war requires the objectification of the humans who fight war. For if the enemy state is not guilty, then individual enemy combatants cannot be said to merit death as punishment. To take this step would be to permit the maiming and killing of people without any claim that they were guilty or deserved it on account of some fault. Killing in war would no longer be linked to individual guilt. People who serve as soldiers would become expendable, things, impersonal means to just ends. One can detect the apprehension that Vitoria felt, though writing long after Aquinas, about taking the step towards killing non-guilty combatants in order to further the ends of a secure and just social order. It is this apprehension which explains his unsatisfactory attempt to connect combatancy to guilt (or the presumption of it) in order to avoid killing the innocent. Vitoria, and Suárez after him, sought instead to maintain the only justification of killing that accords to human life the status it should have. They tried both to maintain the standards of justice in the treatment of human beings and yet to justify war as it really is.

There can be no other conclusion than that, in the modern model of war foreshadowed by Vitoria, innocent human beings have their lives taken as a means to the end of securing social and political goals. In this model, war was no longer the scourge of God and those killed in war need no longer be those who merited death as punishment for their wickedness. Now innocent lives could be sacrificed to secure the social order. Such a trading in innocent human life, whether or not it dressed in the language of Christianity, is repellant. As Joan Tooke puts it:

> The idea that war can be justified as a purely impersonal means so that ... blameless human lives can be used casually as mere ... things or weapons to put right a situation which is only objectively unjust is clumsy, inhuman and more cold-bloodedly cruel than any savage natural instinct.[38]

Yet such is the view of war and its combatants towards which Vitoria and Suárez moved Western thought. Guilt and innocence, combatancy and non-combatancy, the bearing and non-bearing of arms, danger and defencelessness, harmfulness and harmlessless, the military value of killing someone and the military pointlessness of killing them: the confusion of these concepts is all too evident in the 'just war' writings of Vitoria and Suárez. This confusion arises from their attempt to avoid the admission that innocent people have their lives taken as a means to military and political ends. However, their work serves only to show how the concepts of guilt and innocence cannot be used both to justify and to limit modern war. No attempt to grant immunity to non-combatants on the basis of their innocence can be coherent if, as the other side of the coin, it permits the killing of combatants by reference to their guilt. For it is not the guilt of combatants which is the reason they may be targeted in war but their combatancy. An acknowledgment that combatants are innocent must lead to a complete rejection of the Augustinian justification of war as punishment. A new justification for killing combatants would have to be found. It would be a moral justification for killing combatants which is much weaker than one based on guilt. Indeed, as we will see in the next chapter, the modern era's justification for killing combatants in war has been based more in custom than in morality.

6
Non-combatancy and Formal War

It's good in practice but will it work in theory?

Garret FitzGerald[1]

The modern characterization of the combatant came to the fore in the age of nation states and formal war that emerged at the end of the Thirty Years' War (1618–48). The Reformation, and the religious wars that followed it, had changed the political and intellectual context of war. Papal authority, long weakened, was repudiated utterly by the Protestant states. The centralization of political authority culminated in the development of the large nation states of England, France, Spain, Sweden and the Netherlands. The Thirty Years' War had begun as a religious conflict between Protestants and Catholics in Germany but developed into a bloody struggle for the balance of power in Europe when, as a Catholic victory seemed imminent, the Danes, Swedes and French intervened to stop the Habsburgs gaining control of Germany. The war ended in 1648 with the Treaty of Westphalia which ended the supremacy of the Holy Roman Empire (leaving the Emperor with only nominal control) and recognized the sovereignty of Switzerland, the Netherlands and the German states. By upholding the doctrine of state sovereignty, the Treaty marks the start of the modern system of fully independent, sovereign nation states. The state became the sovereign unit as remaining imperial powers were ceded to it from above and the last local feudal powers to it from below.

Each of these sovereign states was to be served by its own unified, professional standing army. In France under Louis XIV, the *roi soleil* and the very model of royal absolutism ('L'état, c'est moi'), mercenary elements were eliminated from the army. Every French soldier became the soldier of the king, swearing a personal oath of loyalty to him. The feudal duties to serve militarily faded away and soldiers became professional fighters in a unified force. Training was better, cohesion greater, and discipline more severe than had been possible with collections of mercenary forces. With Louis's reforms, the French army became a state army, unified and subject to the king. Recruitment was voluntary and as many foreigners as possible were recruited so as not to deplete the number of French peasants and workers (Swiss, Italian, German, Hungarian, Scots and Irish soldiers formed their own regiments).[2] As a result of these changes, the French army became the most formidable fighting force in Europe.

After the Thirty Years War came changes in the weaponry of infantry. The old musket and harquebusier were replaced by flintlock muskets (still muzzle-loaders, they were quicker to reload using a combination of paper cartridge, gunpowder and bullet though they were still vulnerable to wet weather).[3] The new weaponry increased the firepower of infantry but their high cost put them beyond the resources of the mercenary captains. The one power with sufficient funds for modern equipment was the monarchy. The introduction of firearms thus played a role in the assumption of overall control of the armed forces by the central political authority. It contributed to the ongoing concentration of political power in centralized hands, added to the power of monarchs, and helped to make war into a political instrument.[4]

These developments in military organization and equipment made war more destructive and brought demands for the limitation of war. The savagery and atrocities of the Thirty Years War had provoked revulsion and a realization that, unless curbed, war would cease to be a means to any worthwhile ends.[5] Religion ceased to mould political and legal thought. The intellectual climate of the time favoured a limitation of war, particularly the rationalist abhorrence of extremism, its emphasis on moderation, and the belief that all humans were entitled to natural rights. With the Treaty of Westphalia, Europe entered a phase of formal war that was to last until the French Revolution. Wars were fought between states by their standing armies for limited aims, and the civilian population was largely excluded. For ideological, political, social and technological reasons, war had become limited in its scope, duration and impact on the civilian population.

It was in this political, military and intellectual context that the PNCI came to be established in law. It can be seen in the works of two of the founding figures of international law. One is the famous Dutch jurist, moralist, theologian, politician and diplomat Hugo Grotius (1583–1645), whose *De Jure Belli ac Pacis* (On the Law of War and Peace) was an early and great work of international law. The second is the Swiss jurist Emmerich de Vattel whose *Le Droit de gens* (The Law of Nations) was published 133 years after Grotius's work.[6] In Grotius's work can be seen the modern view of war and of the combatant in an early and formative stage while, in Vattel's, this modern view is recorded in a precise manner. Their works will be examined together in this chapter.

Grotius (or Huig de Groot) was the more brilliant and original of these two jurists. A composer of Latin verse from the age of 8, he enrolled as a student at the University of Leiden aged 11 (less remarkable then than it would be today). He was 15 when he received his doctorate in law from the University of Orléans (while accompanying the Prime Minister of the United Netherlands, Johan van Oldenbarnevelt, on a diplomatic mission to France) and he was 16 when he was called to the bar and began to practise law in The Hague. His first published work on international law, *The Free Sea* (1609), challenged the right of any nation to claim part of the open sea as exclusively its own (such a claim, he argued, was contrary to natural law). As Pensionary of Rotterdam (secretary and legal adviser to the city's Council), Grotius became embroiled in religious as well as political debates, arguing against the Calvinist doctrine of predestination. His activities led, in the wake of the Calvinist coup d'etat of 1618, to his arrest and trial for treason. Sentenced to life imprisonment and incarcerated in the castle of Loevestein, he escaped in 1621 (at his wife's suggestion, he hid in the large chest used to carry legal texts to and from his prison), and fled the United Provinces. It was while in exile in Paris that he wrote *De Jure Belli ac Pacis*, and a second work, *De Veritate Religionis Christianae* (On the Truth of the Christian Religion), which was published in 1627. Though as much a treatise on religion and ethics as on law, the former work won legal fame for its author and exerted an immediate influence on the development of international law in the modern period. In it, Grotius drew heavily on Aquinas and Vitoria. He nonetheless moved the law of war and peace onto a new basis for the new age of nations when he based it unequivocally on custom and natural law rather than on the gospel. In 1634, while still in exile in Paris, he was appointed Ambassador of Sweden to France, a position he held for 11 years during which time he helped negotiate a treaty to end the Thirty Years War. He died (of exhaustion and exposure following a shipwreck) in 1645 with the final words 'By understanding many things, I have accomplished nothing.'

Like Grotius, Vattel had practical experience of politics and diplomacy as well as an interest in philosophy and theology. He was born almost 70 years after Grotius's death, in the principality of Neuchâtel, Switzerland. The son of a Reformed clergyman and the younger brother of professional soldiers, Vattel first thought of life as a theologian. His interests turned later to law and philosophy and he published a philosophic work on Leibnitz. The Elector of Saxony appointed him Minister to Berne, and Vattel worked as a diplomat and minister and was made Privy Councillor, in which position he served in Dresden until his death. Like Grotius, Vattel was witness to war though, by Vattel's time, war in Europe had become less severe and less cruel as a result of the practice of discriminating between civilians and combatants. As Vattel wrote in 1740:

> It is with good reason that this practice has grown into a custom with the nations of Europe, at least with those that keep up standing armies or bodies of militia. The troops alone carry on war, while the rest of the nation remain at peace.[7]

The fate of civilians in war has always been a product, not only of the predominant military technology and the prevailing socio-political structure of combatancy, but also of ideas, morals and law. That the Seven Years War of 1756–63 was conducted on a very different basis to the Thirty Years War of 1618–48 was a result of all three of these factors. Certainly the more humane customs of the time are reflected in Vattel's work on the law of war.

Grotius's concern to prevent and limit war was intimately related to his faith. He was appalled by war yet saw no possibility of its eradication in a Europe divided by the Reformation. As he wrote in the Preface to *De Jure Belli ac Pacis*:

> Throughout the Christian world I have seen a lawlessness in warfare that even barbarian races would think shameful. On trifling

pretexts, or none at all, men rush to arms, and when once arms are taken up, all respect for law, whether human or divine, is lost as though by some edict a fury has been let loose to commit every crime.

Confronted by this hideous spectacle, many of our best men have concluded that all armed conflicts must be forbidden to Christians, whose chief duty it is to love everyone ... But their very effort to force a thing back too far toward the other extreme frequently does more harm than good, because the exaggeration in it is easily detected and detracts from the influence of what else they say that is actually true. A remedy must therefore be found for both sets of extremists, that men may neither suppose that nothing in the way of war is lawful, nor that everything is.[8]

Grotius's aim, then, was not to abolish war but to establish a body of principles which could lessen its frequency and mitigate its cruelty. In seeking to persuade his audience of the merit of generosity and mercy, he quotes extensively from Greek and Roman philosophers, historians, poets and orators, as well as the Old and New Testaments and the fathers of the Church (only rarely are the writers he cites more recent than these). His approach to the law of war was not to be one that relied on Christian revelation. Rather, he sought to promote that law as something independent of religious opinions, as a set of rules, founded in custom and natural justice, which all states could accept and follow thereby preventing anarchy and restraining the ferocity of war.

At the heart of Grotius's approach to the law of war is a threefold distinction between what is legal, what is just, and what a Christian ought to do. Grotius distinguished between what is permitted by nature and what is permitted to Christians; he was clear too that natural justice is inferior to Christian morality and he criticized those who claimed that what the gospel forbids is forbidden also by the law of nature. It is the teachings of Jesus and not justice, he pointed out, which require us to give up our life for others.[9] He acknowledged the rule of law as it existed between nations and promoted obedience to it by states. But he also urged political and military leaders to go beyond that law; their aim should be justice, not simply in the sense of what is legal, but also in the sense of what is 'right and godly'.[10] His acceptance of war as, in some circumstances, just and right was to be based on natural law and in particular on the natural right of

self-defence (a move with far-reaching implications for the status of
the combatant in war). He argued that it is natural justice that gives
us a right to wage war in certain circumstances and not the Christian
gospel. With his reliance on natural law to determine what is just in
war, Grotius was closer to Aquinas than to many of his Protestant contemporaries. However, Grotius was critical of Aquinas's teachings on
war, seeing them as not only incomplete and unsystematic but also
insufficiently Christian. Grotius's own consideration of the relevance
of Christianity to war was to be more detailed and more thorough
than Aquinas's.[11]

Grotius's and Vattel's justification of war

The most important and lasting step taken by Grotius in his justification of war was to sever finally the link between *ad bellum* and *in
bello* justice. In the Augustinian model of war, *ad bellum* just cause
was required for *in bello* just killing. The punitive justification of war
had implied that combatants were (on the side with *ad bellum*
just cause) the executioners of justice or (on the side without *ad bellum* just cause) murderers. Fundamental to this justification of war
as punishment was the notion of collective guilt. By the time of
Aquinas, this assumption seemed untenable; by the seventeenth century, it was undeniably so. Yet Vitoria and Suárez had stopped short
of breaking from the punitive justification of war. They sought only
to lessen the *in bello* implications of the *ad bellum* justification of war
as punishment by allowing that combatants on the side without just
cause may have fought in good faith (they were not guilty of murder
if, through their invincible ignorance, they believed their cause to be
just). It was left to Grotius to make the decisive break and to reject
outright the notion of collective guilt that was central to the established Augustinian justification of war:

> But the law of nature does not allow inflicting reprisals, except on
> the actual persons who committed the offense. Nor is it enough
> that by a kind of fiction the enemy may be regarded as forming a
> single body.[12]

Grotius here asserts that innocent people may not be punished for
the crimes of others and acknowledges that innocents comprise most

of the enemy population in war. In doing so, Grotius discards the justification of war that had served Christendom for over a thousand years.

If war is not punishment, then what is it? To Grotius, war was a method of settling legal disputes when all other methods fail. Legally, the requirements of *jus ad bellum* are met by the formal declaration of war by the ruler of a sovereign state. The reasons for the war may be stated in the declaration but no reference to any substantive understanding of justice is required. Grotius holds the use of force to be justified 'to protect rights and maintain order'. Such a war in defence of rights and order may, he wrote, be justly waged 'for injuries either not yet committed or actually committed'.[13] The injuries may be against persons or property and war may be waged to defend them, to recover property and to punish the offender. At the heart of this argument is the human being's natural right of self-defence. Grotius allows that such self-defence can include offensive war when the opponents' warring intentions are clear and the danger is immediate. However, he rejects the use of lethal force against distant or potential dangers:

> that the bare possibility that violence might some day be turned on us gives us the right to inflict violence on others is a doctrine repugnant to every principle of justice. Human life is something that can never give us absolute security ... the fear of an uncertainty cannot give a right to resort to arms.[14]

By Vattel's time, the justification of war as punishment had long faded and the acceptance of war as a means to states' rights had become established in law. For Vattel, as for Grotius, just cause is interpreted in a wholly legal, rather than moral, manner:

> War is that state of affairs in which we promote our rights by force ... Whatever constitutes an attack upon these rights is an *injury* and a just cause of war.[15]

Again the injury that is the just cause of war may be one already received or one threatened. So, of the three principal requirements of *jus ad bellum* bequeathed by the Middle Ages (proper authority, just cause and right intention), only just cause remained in the period of

Grotius and Vattel. The requirement of 'proper authority', so important in the Middle Ages when it rested on the doctrine of the divine right of kings, had faded in significance by the start of the modern era of nation states. The ruler was no longer the minister of God punishing wrongdoers on his authority but instead the protector of his people, their property and their prosperity. 'Right intention', the most subjective of the three classic criteria, had also diminished in importance as Vitoria's and Suárez's emphasis on purely external factors is taken to its culmination by Grotius and Vattel.

Simultaneous just cause

With this legal approach to war, Grotius and Vattel were less inclined than the medieval theologians to see justice residing wholly and clearly on one side of the conflict. Strictly, Grotius points out,

> a war cannot be just on both sides, any more than a lawsuit can be. For, by the very nature of the case, there can be no moral sanction given us to do opposite things, such as acting and preventing action. Yet it may indeed happen that neither of the warring parties is acting unjustly. For no one is acting unjustly unless he knows that he is doing an unjust thing ... [16]

Vitoria and Suárez had relied on 'invincible ignorance' to make a war just on both sides; Grotius too allows a war to be just on both sides in the moral sense for the same reason. Grotius also allows a war to be just on both sides in the legal sense: 'If we understand the word "just" to apply to certain legal aspects, undoubtedly in this sense a war may be lawful for both sides'.[17] With the *jus ad bellum* reduced to a set of legal formalities, both sides to a conflict can observe the formalities, both sides can make the correct declarations and, in the legal sense, both sides to the war can have just cause. Vattel follows Grotius as regards the possibility of simultaneous just cause. He too holds that, strictly, both parties to a war cannot have just cause. If one party claims a right and the other disputes the justice of the claim, or if one complains of an injury and the other denies having done it, it cannot be that both are right. However, like Grotius, he allows that both sides may believe, in good faith, that they have just cause:

> [I]t can happen that the contending parties are both in good faith; and in a doubtful cause it is, moreover, uncertain which side is in

the right. Since, therefore, Nations are equal and independent, and cannot set themselves up as judges over one another, it follows that in all cases open to doubt the war carried on by both parties must be regarded as equally lawful, at least as regards its exterior effects and until the cause is decided.[18]

Grotius and Vattel completed the move (started by Vitoria and Suárez) from the requirement of subjective fault towards objective fault. No longer was the side with unjust cause said to have knowingly and wilfully done wrong; rather, the injury done could be merely objective and unintended. They believed that the side committing the wrong or injury may honestly and earnestly believe themselves to be in the right. No longer was a legal fault taken to imply moral guilt and desert of punishment. Building on this, they acknowledged the possibility of 'simultaneous just cause'. They accepted (though reluctantly) that both parties to a conflict could have just cause, in a legal sense, and even in a subjective moral sense. Together, these two changes to the principle of 'just cause' de-emphasized the *jus ad bellum* and moved the focus to the *jus in bello*. They also had a great huge impact on the moral status of the combatant and of the non-combatant in war.

The combatant

Having rejected the punitive model, Grotius and Vattel needed a new characterization of the combatant and a new justification for killing by combatants in war. They rejected the notion that one side's combatants are guilty. Why then may combatants be killed in war? If they are not guilty, then why is it not murder to kill them? Grotius's answer was that there is a natural right of all people to fight in self-defence (and defence of property and defence of others) and it is this which permits combatants to fight and kill without incurring guilt in war. He takes the position implicit in Aquinas's claim that self-preservation, an in-built orientation of living things, could not be said to be wrong. Natural law, argued Grotius, gives even combatants on the side without just cause the right to kill:

> when our bodies are violently attacked with danger to our lives, and there is no other way of escape, it is lawful to fight the aggressor, and even to kill him ... We must note that this right of self-defence derives its origin primarily from the instinct of self-preservation,

which nature has given to every creature, and not from the injustice or misconduct of the aggressor. Wherefore, even though my assailant may be guiltless, as for instance a soldier fighting in good faith, or one who mistakes me for someone else, or a man frantic with insanity or sleeplessness, as we read sometimes happens, in none of these cases am I deprived of my right of self-defence ... [19]

With this natural right to defence, the link between *ad bellum* just cause and *in bello* just conduct was severed. No longer did the justice of one's sovereign's cause have any implications for the rights of combatants (or non-combatants) in war. All combatants in war had equal status and the same right to kill. Even when the ruler was in the wrong, combatants could fight in his war without blame.

Grotius's reliance on a natural right to self-defence was a significant innovation in 'just war' thinking. Augustine had placed war in an overarching moral framework when he claimed that all those fighting in an unjust cause were guilty of a wrong, so guilty that they could be killed. He had linked the *in bello* morality of killing directly to the *ad bellum* morality of the war when he allowed only those whose ruler's cause was just to kill without committing murder. Augustine had urged combatants to fight even when they doubted the justice of their ruler's cause, on the grounds that a treasonous refusal to obey was worse than furthering a possibly unjust cause. Vitoria and Suárez absolved from blame those combatants who fight for unjust causes in good faith on the grounds of their invincible ignorance. Grotius took this further and permitted combatants to fight even for causes they knew to be unjust, on the grounds of their natural right to self-defence. According to Grotius, subjects may fight against enemies, even enemies furthering a just cause, if they are about to harm them or their property, or indeed are about to harm others or their property. This, says the Dutch jurist, is because all human beings have a natural right to self-defence, even combatants fighting for an unjust cause. Grotius thus dissolves the link between the justice of war and the justice of fighting in war.

Subjects may justly fight even when the cause motivating their sovereign is an unjust one. Unlike Augustine, Grotius does not argue from the greater picture to the smaller, from the justice of the war to the justice of killing in war. No longer was all killing in an unjust cause to be considered murder. No longer did the morality of the combatant's acts depend on the morality of the war. Grotius arrived at a situation in which a party to a conflict could have a cause that is unquestionably unjust and yet that party's combatants could not be blamed for killing. Regardless of the justice of the cause of one's country, all combatants could fight in defence of themselves and of their property, and in defence of the lives and property of others. *Ad bellum* guilt, the very basis of Augustine's model of war, had no implications for the *in bello* level of Grotius's model of war. Guilt was no longer the reason why some people may be killed in war.

Vattel followed Grotius and upheld the principle of belligerent equality and the divorce of *in bello* just conduct from *ad bellum* just cause. However, in place of Grotius's natural right to self-defence Vattel gave the notion of combatants' instrumentality as the reason why combatants may kill in war without being guilty of murder. Grotius had described combatants as instruments when he distinguished principal actors from their assistants and their instruments. In war, he wrote, the principal is the sovereign authority and the instruments are his subjects who willingly fight ('When we say "instruments", we do not mean by it arms and things of that kind, but men who in action voluntarily make their wills dependent on another's will').[20] Vattel adopted the metaphor and made it central to the modern era's characterization of the combatant:

> The sovereign is the real author of war, which is made in his name and at his command. The troops, both officers and soldiers, and in general all the persons by whom the sovereign carries on war, are only instruments in his hands. They execute his will and not their own.[21]

For Vattel, as for Grotius, combatants on both sides could kill without being guilty of murder. Vattel's reasoning, though, is different. He does not argue from the right of self-defence, as Grotius had done, but instead holds combatants to be mere instruments of their states with no responsibility for the justice or injustice they further. Even when they kill in an unjust cause, combatants are not guilty of murder: the ruler alone bears responsibility for the injustice of war. When the cause of war is unjust, 'the sovereign alone is guilty' for the 'bloodshed, the desolation of families, the pillaging, the acts of violence'; his 'subjects, and especially the military, are innocent' for they killed and destroyed 'not of their own will but as instruments in the hands of their sovereign'.[22] In Vattel's characterization of combatants as instruments, combatants are no longer responsible for the lethal acts they perform. They do not have to enquire into the justice of their cause and be satisfied that they serve a good cause. Indeed they should not consider those war aims and have no right to selective conscientious objection should they believe them to be unjust.

Selective conscientious objection

Grotius and Vattel differ greatly in their attitudes to conscientious objection and selective conscientious objection. Grotius's stance looks back towards the punitive model while Vattel's fits the modern view of war with its characterization of combatants as instruments. In the previous chapter it was seen that Vitoria was more insistent than Aquinas or Augustine on the right (though not the duty) of Christians to refuse to participate in a particular war they believed unjust or indeed in war at all. Aquinas had reluctantly admitted that one ought to follow one's conscience in the matter of war even though conscience was a fallible guide to conduct and could be misled. Vitoria was more in favour of the right of conscientious objection but he required the injustice to be manifest before conscience forbids one to fight. Also, for Vitoria, a subject was under no compulsion to inquire into the causes of a war in order to ascertain their justice; he could simply trust his superiors and accept their judgment. It was only if a subject came to believe that a war was manifestly unjust that he should refuse to fight. A further point of relevance is that, for Vitoria, the ruler was under no obligation to divulge his just cause for war to his people. The idea of a right to selective conscientious objection, then, developed gradually through the centuries from Augustine to Grotius. It was a right that Augustine was very reluctant to acknowledge. Aquinas was less grudging in his acceptance that a subject must follow the dictates of his conscience and refuse to fight in a war he considers unjust. Vitoria and Suárez accepted the right to selective conscientious objection but did not require subjects to enquire into the justice of a war nor did they require the ruler to explain his cause. Finally, with Grotius, came the idea that combatants have a duty to question the justice of the cause and that the ruler has a duty to explain it. The acceptance of a right to selective conscientious objection was very slow in coming. In one way, this was strange since it could be argued that the punitive model of war, upheld by Augustine, Aquinas, Vitoria and Suárez, implied a right to selective conscientious objection: when war was justified as God's punishment on the wicked, then the combatant ought to satisfy himself that the enemy was indeed wicked; for if the enemy was not wicked, then the combatant was committing murder in killing the enemy. Despite this, it was not until Grotius that a right to selective conscientious objection was unequivocally accepted.

Grotius moved the issue of selective conscientious objection a step further on all fronts. He upheld conscientious objection to warfare, not simply as a right, but as a duty on the grounds that every individual has the obligation to obey God and not man:

> if they are commanded to do military service, as usually happens, and if it is clear to them that the reason for the war is unlawful, they should absolutely refuse to serve. God is to be obeyed rather than men ... [23]

As well as asserting the right and duty of selective conscientious objection (i.e. a refusal to fight in a particular war that one thinks unjust), Grotius also upheld a right to general conscientious objection (a refusal to fight in any war):

> And, even if there be no doubt as to the grounds for war, still it does not seem right that Christians should be compelled to fight against their will, since to take no part in warfare, even when it is legitimate to do so, is a mark of a higher holiness, which has long been demanded of clergy and penitents and recommended constantly to everyone else ... [24]

What if the subject is not certain that the war is unlawful, but only doubtful? Grotius's answer is that the subject should still refuse to obey the order to fight. Augustine had thought treasonous disobedience worse than the possible killing of the innocent; Grotius disagrees. There is, he declares, a duty of conscientious objection:

> if a subject not merely hesitates but is led by reasonable arguments to incline to the belief that the war is unlawful ... It seems reasonable too that even the executioner who is to put a condemned man

to death should understand the merits of the case, either by being present at the examination and the trial, or by hearing the criminal's confession, so that he may be sure that the man deserves to die.[25]

As the reference to the executioner shows, Grotius departed from the approach of Vitoria and Suárez in asserting a duty of rulers to make public their cause for war so that it may be examined by subjects and citizens. Only when this is done, he argued, can subjects assess its justice and decide whether or not to fight. Any soldier who had doubts about the justice of his cause should refuse to fight. Grotius preferred that those in doubt should choose disobedience rather than the moral danger of fighting unjustly.

The traditional exemption of clergy, religious and penitents from military service was upheld by Grotius as a holy tradition and something to be recommended to all. Christians unwilling to fight in any war should be excused. Aquinas's attempt to relocate the traditional clerical exemption onto a new basis of social roles was rejected by Grotius. He argued that clergy were, and should be, exempted from military service because of the wrongness, the unholiness, of killing. Anyone else objecting to killing on the same grounds should be granted exemption from military service too. In his *De Jure Belli ac Pacis*, Grotius is firm that, though natural law and justice gives us the right to wage war, Christian revelation urges us to give up that right, to sacrifice our interests and even our lives in order to further the lives and salvation of others. The Dutch jurist approves of the pacifism of the pre-Constantinian Christians, praising their refusal to participate in war. He makes the point too that, if Jesus wanted his followers to give up small things in order to avoid strife, then how much more must he want us to give up greater things in order to avoid war:

> Sometimes the circumstances are such that to relinquish a right is not merely a praiseworthy act but one obligatory on us, by reason of the love we should feel for mankind, even for our enemies, whether considered in itself or as a command of the most holy law of the Gospel.[26]

Oddly, though Grotius praises Christian pacifism, he does not see pacifism as an essential element of Christianity.[27] He sees the refusal to fight as something counselled, but not commanded, of Christians:

> Christ commanded us to relinquish the object of dispute rather than engage in lawsuits. But this saying, taken in so general a sense, was rather by way of counsel, to indicate a sublimer mode of life, than a positive command ... All these counsels are praiseworthy, excellent, highly acceptable to God, yet they are not imposed on us by any binding law.[28]

Even though he stops short of advocating pacifism to all Christians, Grotius advances the cause of conscientious objection to a new point. He upholds the right to general conscientious objection. As regards selective conscientious objection, he asserts a duty on the part of the subject to enquire into the justice of his ruler's cause before fighting for it.

The idea of conscientious objection to military service had developed slowly over many centuries. It culminated, in the work of Grotius, in a right to general and selective conscientious objection. But, only one and a half centuries later, the right to selective conscientious objection was rejected by Vattel. It was Vattel's characterization of the combatant as an instrument which led him to deny any right to selective conscientious objection. With his view of war as equally legitimate for both parties, and his characterization of the combatant as an instrument, the issue of selective conscientious objection lost its importance. Since, according to Vattel, combatants do not incur guilt by killing in war, there is then no longer any need for combatants to consider the issue of the justice of causes. Hence, says Vattel:

> Every citizen is bound to serve and defend the State as far as he is able ... Whoever is able to bear arms must take them up as soon as he is commanded to do so.[29]

Vattel's rejection of conscientious objection was backed up with an attack upon the traditional exemption of religious from military service. His rejection of the clerical ban shows both his hostility to the Catholic Church and his belief in the primacy of the state over the individual. Vattel tolerated an exemption from fighting for ministers of religion only on the basis that they could serve the state better by teaching religion, governing the church and celebrating public worship. He pays no attention to the established basis for the traditional ban on clerical fighting: that the shedding of blood is something that those Christians who aim highest ought never do. Vattel reserved a special contempt for contemplatives:

> No one is naturally exempt from bearing arms in the service of the State, for the obligation of every citizen is the same ... The clergy cannot naturally, and as a matter of right, claim any special exemption. To defend one's country is a duty not unworthy of the most sacred hands. The law of the church which forbids ecclesiastics to shed blood is a convenient device for dispensing from the duty of fighting persons who are most often ready to fan the flame of discord and to provoke bloody wars.
>
> ... as for that huge crowd of useless persons who, under the pretext of consecrating themselves to God by the vows of religion, in fact give themselves up to a life of idleness and ease, on what ground do they claim an exemption that is ruinous to the State? ... I do not mean by this to advise a sovereign to fill his armies with monks but merely that he should gradually lessen the number of a useless class of men by taking away from them harmful and ill-founded privileges.[30]

Vattel's dismissal of the right to selective conscientious objection was in line with his espousal of the formal model of war in place of the punitive model. In the punitive model, killing for an unjust cause was murder, and so the right of selective conscientious objection was firmly grounded. In Vattel's model, combatants were merely instruments who bore no guilt for their actions, and so the right of selective conscientious objection no longer fitted. That selective conscientious objection does not fit with the modern era's model of war and its characterization of the combatant as instrument is evident from the treatment of war-resisters in the twentieth century. In the First and Second World Wars, many countries acknowledged a right of general conscientious objection but not of selective conscientious objection: conscientious objector status was accorded only to those who opposed all wars, usually on religious grounds. Those who opposed only the particular war in question, often for reasons of socialist internationalism, were refused exemption from military service.[31]

Mercenaries

Another implication of Vattel's new characterization of the combatant was his acceptance of mercenarism. The medieval opposition to mercenarism had its roots in the 'just war' requirement of 'right intention'. When war was justified as punishment, there was a concern that combatants be motivated by loving punishment of the wrongdoer. If the combatant was not so motivated (if his primary motivation was hatred, malice or money) then his killing was not justified. But with Vattel's view of the combatant as a guiltless instrument of the sovereign with no obligation or right to inquire into the justice of the cause for which he fought, the concern with motivation faded away. Vattel was unappreciative of the moral concerns of the medievals about mercenarism and saw no problem with payment for fighting. He discussed the issue solely in terms of state authority and made no mention of morality:

> The question has been much discussed whether the profession of a mercenary soldier be legitimate or not, whether individuals may, for money or other rewards, engage as soldiers in the service of a foreign prince? The question does not seem to me very difficult of solution. Those who enter into such contracts without the express or implied consent of their sovereign are wanting in their duty as citizens. But when the sovereign leaves them at liberty to follow their inclination for the profession of arms, they become free in that respect.[32]

Vattel's favourable attitude to mercenaries, perhaps unsurprising for a Swiss given his nation's service to Europe as paid fighters, is also an implication of his new view of combatants as instruments.

The non-combatant

Grotius's assertions, that natural law does not sanction punishment except of those who have done wrong and that the enemy cannot be conceived as a single body, are rightly famous. For with them, Grotius dismissed the punitive model of war. In its place, he sought to establish the principle of non-combatant immunity with a firm foundation in law and justice. This immunity was to be given to all non-combatants; not only women and children but also all 'men whose way of life is opposed to warmaking' were to be immune from targeting in war (in the latter category he placed clergy, religious, agricultural workers, merchants and 'other workmen and artisans, whose callings demand peace, not war').[33] For Grotius, civilians were not to be killed in war except when that killing was necessary to defence or when that killing was collateral:

> an enemy, though he may be fighting a lawful war, does not have a true and inherent right to kill innocent persons, clear of any blame for the war, except as a necessary measure of defence or *as a result of something not a part of his purpose*.[34]

Grotius lays great emphasis on civilian immunity in war. However, the rule against attack on civilians is not absolute. The words 'as a result of something not a part of his purpose' is Grotius's phrase for the principle of double effect: innocent civilians may be killed when it is an unintended though foreseen side effect of an act necessary to achieve the aims of the war. He thus allows indirect attack on civilians:

> A ship filled with pirates, or a house with brigands, may be bombarded even though in that same ship or house there are a few children, or women, or other innocent persons, who are endangered by the attack.[35]

In such cases, the principle of tactical proportionality still holds as Grotius makes clear when he cautions that:

> We should beware of things which happen and which we foresee may happen beyond what we intended, unless the good which is the aim of our act is much greater than the harm we fear, or unless, when the good and the harm are equal, the expectation of good is much stronger than the fear of harm, which is a question to be left for prudence to reflect on. But, as always, in case of doubt we should favour, as safer, the course that protects the other person's interest more than our own.[36]

Grotius strengthens his plea for the immunity of civilians in war by claiming that it is very often not necessary to kill them or that there are advantages to not killing them which outweigh any military disadvantages. First of all, he argues, it is to one's own military advantage to fight in a just and honourable way. One's own soldiers fight best when they are fighting justly and in a just cause. Furthermore, he says, a lack of moderation and mercy in fighting may make the enemy more difficult to defeat: 'we should fear the recklessness of men driven to desperation'.[37] Moderation in war is to be advised as such moderation

> deprives the enemy of one powerful weapon – despair ... Furthermore, moderation in the midst of a war gives an appearance of great confidence of victory. Clemency also is apt of itself to break down determination and win over the enemy's heart.[38]

When it is not militarily necessary to kill non-combatants, then it is not honourable to kill them; indeed, as such, non-combatants are not guilty, the motive for such militarily pointless killing of them can only be malice. Justice, charity, clemency, humanity and military honour and professionalism all support a general principle of non-combatant immunity. Sparing non-combatants will usually not reduce military efficiency. It may do so some times but even then it will be a minimal reduction; in any case, there are advantages to abiding by this principle (as well as precedents in the codes of chivalry for taking risks in an honourable cause).

For his part, when Vattel outlines the laws of war, he writes that these rules forbid both acts which are 'essentially unlawful and obnoxious' and also acts which 'contribute nothing to the success of our arms and neither increases our strength nor weakens the enemy'. The use of poison and assassination he puts in the first category and the destruction of temples, tombs and public buildings of remarkable beauty he forbids on the second basis ('What is gained by destroying them?', he asks).[39] The killing of civilians is outlawed, not because it is unnecessary but because it is obnoxious and essentially unlawful. The killing of civilians may (like poisoning or assassinating) weaken the enemy and add to the chances of victory over them but it is still wrong. Vattel follows Grotius in establishing as immune all those who are not in the business of fighting, regardless of age or gender. 'Women, children, feeble old men and the sick' and also 'ministers of public worship and men of letters and others persons whose manner of life is wholly apart from the profession of arms' are categorized by Vattel as 'enemies who offer no resistance, and consequently the belligerent has no right to maltreat or otherwise offer violence to them, much less to put them to death'. He continues that 'as they do not resist the enemy by force or violence, they give the enemy no right to use it towards them'.[40] Thus, the immunity of these non-combatants is based on justice as well as humanity and charity. Justice, says Vattel, does not permit us to use violence against those who do not use force against us. It is wrong to kill civilians, not because harming them is unnecessary, but because they are not themselves engaged in harming others.

For both Grotius and Vattel, then, the foundation of the PNCI was justice. Justice requires that non-combatants be spared. Justice permits us to kill those who are guilty and those engaged in harming us; non-combatants are neither. Given this, justice requires that those not directly involved in trying to harm us be spared. Vattel's emphasis on justice is significant. He could have argued for non-combatant immunity on the basis of its lack of military benefit since, in the formal wars of his time, the targeting of non-combatants may have added no more to the chances of military victory than the chopping down of fruit trees. Had he done so, his reasoning would have been of limited interest to us now as, for almost a century, technology has offered the possibility of destroying an enemy's war effort by demoralizing the civilian population. A PNCI resting on the claim that killing non-combatants is of no military benefit would crumble to nothing in an age when military technology allowed the destruction of enemy morale and civilian support for the war effort.

For both Grotius and Vattel, the PNCI was a principle that could yield to the requirements of military success: civilians were to be immune only as military circumstances permit. Grotius and Vattel did much to expand the categories of immune people and to establish the PNCI as a principle of justice and law but, in this regard, they made no departure from the established position. Like Aquinas, Vitoria and Suárez, *in bello* just conduct was subordinated to *ad bellum* just cause. The prohibition on killing civilians in war could be overruled by the end for which the war is fought. If the defence of lives or property required it, then the prohibition on killing civilians might be ignored. Ultimately, both Grotius and Vattel allowed all necessary means in pursuit of a just cause though they sought to qualify this right of necessity on the grounds of humanity, charity, military honour and even military expediency. As Vattel put it:

> When the end is lawful, he who has a right to pursue that end has, naturally, a right to make use of all the means necessary to attain

it ... a sovereign has the right to do to his enemy whatever is necessary to weaken him and disable him from maintaining his
unjust position; and the sovereign may choose the most effica-
cious and appropriate means to accomplish that object, provided
those means be not essentially evil and unlawful, and consequently forbidden by the law of Nature.[41]

The PNCI was not, for Grotius and Vattel, an exceptionless rule of
conduct in war (one which can never be breached in any circumstances, even if the goal of war is thereby lost). This implies that the
immunity of the innocent, though a high-ranking moral value for
them, was not the highest one. It might be overridden by the ends
for which war was fought (and by the natural right to self-defence).

Conclusion: formal war and non-combatant immunity

Many factors in the seventeenth and eighteenth centuries eased the
acceptance within the European society of states of the right of non-
combatants to immunity in war. Political, social, military and technological factors generated the era of formal war in Europe in which war
was waged between states by their professional and disciplined standing armies. Aims were limited and so were the extent and the ferocity
of warfare. Combatants could be clearly distinguished from non-combatants and the latter could be granted immunity with little impact
on the conduct of war. Emerging ideas about humanitarianism reinforced the existing practice of limited war. It was in this age that the
PNCI was established in international law on the firm foundation of
justice. Hartigan sees the status achieved by the civilian by the end of
the nineteenth century as 'a gratuitous achievement, a structure built
upon an artificial foundation, which required only a slight maladjust-
ment of its composite elements to bring about its collapse.[42] This is
not so. At the heart of the PNCI there is a timeless principle of justice
which demands that innocent civilians should not be killed in war
because, as innocents and as civilians, neither the justification of
punitive killing nor that of preventative killing can be applied to
them. They are innocent of *ad bellum* injustice and may not be killed
punitively; they are non-combatant and may not be killed preventatively. It is this which gives enduring force and appeal to the PNCI.

The establishment of the PNCI on the basis of justice was one side
to the new view of war promoted by Grotius and Vattel. The other

side concerned the characterization of the combatant and the justification of the killing of combatants in war. The important innovation
in this regard (suggested by Grotius and adopted by Vattel) was
the view of combatants as instruments of the state. This is the view
of combatants that persist to this day. It is based on a forthright
acknowledgment that the justification of punitive killing does not
apply to combatants (they are as innocent as civilians of *ad bellum*
injustice). Yet it permits combatants to be killed at any time in war
even when the justification of preventative killing does not apply.
This is because of the customary acceptance in the Western world
that members of armed forces may in war be treated as instruments,
both by their own commanders and by their enemy's. The members
of armed forces have volunteered (or, if pressed to join, they have at
least acquiesced) in being treated, not like individual human beings,
but as instruments. In hostilities their lives may be taken as the
means to a military or political objective. They have given up their
right to be treated as persons (their right not to have their lives taken
as a means to some end) and they have simultaneously been absolved
of culpability for the killing they commit. So combatants are doubly
depersonalized: they need not be guilty in order to be killed, and they
do not incur guilt by killing. They are depersonalized when they are
killed for reasons not to do with them as persons and also when they
are not held responsible for the killing they commit. The justice of
this convention – that in war those in uniform may be treated as
other than human beings – depends on the degree of consent to it by
combatants (an issue we will return to in Chapter 8). But the moral
reason why civilians may not be killed remains a powerful one. Non-
combatants may not be killed because they are human beings and
their lives may never be taken as a means to an end. The prohibition
on killing non-combatants is not simply customary. It is based on the
most fundamental principles of justice. Non-combatants have not
agreed or acquiesced to have their lives taken as means to an end.

Grotius and Vattel produced both a characterization of the combatant and a basis for non-combatant immunity that have endured
up to the present. The PNCI's foundation in justice was obscured in
the nineteenth century as positivism came to dominate international
law. After Vattel, legal writers promoted the positivist view that the
customs and positive agreements of states were the only source of
international law. They rejected Grotius's natural law-based approach

and denied that international law could be constructed on universal principles. Their aim in doing so was to make the restrictions on warfare less contestable. They sought to establish the laws of war without reliance on such unprovable ideas as natural justice or a set of values common to all peoples. The outcome, however, was the establishment of the PNCI in law without a clear moral reasoning to support it. Thus the moral force of the principle was obscured. The criterion used to distinguish those with immunity from those without was function: those whose function was to fight could be targeted in war; all others were to be immune. But function cannot be the moral basis of the PNCI as the question must still be asked: *why* are those whose function is not combatant to be granted immunity? To answer simply that international law as it exists requires non-combatants to be granted immunity in war deprives the PNCI of potentially crucial moral support.

The PNCI was established in law in an age of professional armies, limited aims and formal war. The normative grounding of the principle was expressed famously by a francophone Swiss philosopher and theorist, far more eminent and eloquent than Vattel. Jean-Jacques Rousseau's *Contrat Social* was published four years after *The Law of Nations*. There is in it a much-quoted passage about people in war:

> War, then, is not a relation between men, but between states; in war individuals are enemies wholly by chance, not as men, not even as citizens, but only as soldiers; not as members of their country, but only as its defenders. In a word, a state can have as an enemy only another state, not men, because there can be no real relation between things possessing different intrinsic natures.[43]

Rousseau urges us to recognize our membership of a particular state as something accidental and our membership of universal humankind as fundamental. Even when enlisted to fight, we should acknowledge the common humanity we share with our enemies. In his distinction between people-as-subjects and people-as-humans, Rousseau expresses the view of the combatant-as-instrument held established by Grotius and Vattel. As non-combatants do not occupy the role of instrument, they ought to be spared the horrors of war. This characterization of the combatant was a product of the age of formal war but, 11 years after Rousseau's death, this age came to an end. The French Revolution of 1789 (inspired in part by Rousseau's writings) changed the context and nature of war in Europe. Politically and militarily, the Revolutionary and Napoleonic wars of 1792–1815 brought huge changes to Europe as revolutionary politics struggled with enlightened absolutism, as national armies of conscripts fought professional armies, and as a new military rationalism contested with the traditional military aristocracy. With these changes, the age of formal war gave way to the age of total war and Europe entered a new military era. To say that we are enemies only accidentally, not as persons but as soldiers, was the antithesis of the idea of national and total wars that Napoleon was very soon to launch. The new mode of war making, and its accompanying patriotic fervour and nationalist hatreds, threatened the immunity of non-combatants in war. Yet the PNCI survived. Neither the characterization of the combatant nor the basis of non-combatant immunity changed as Europe entered the era of total war though they were put under strain. The PNCI was sufficiently firmly based in Western civilization's most fundamental rules of human justice to persist in a very different set of political, social, technological and military circumstances. This new era is the subject of the next chapter.

7
Involvement and Total War

> And if you don't care who you kill, why should you care who you
> save?
>
> John Le Carre[1]

With the Revolutionary and Napoleonic Wars of 1792–1815, Europe
was plunged into the era of total war. These wars between France
under Napoleon and a series of European coalitions were a marked
break from the limited wars between small armies of professional soldiers that had been characteristic of the eighteenth century. There
was a broadening of war in all its elements: the combatants, the targets, the victims, the weapons, the aims and the battle plans. Small
armies of volunteers gave way to mass armies of conscripts; technological advances yielded more efficient weapons which the industrial
revolution supplied in vast quantities; and nationalism produced an
ideological fervour not seen in Europe since the wars of religion.

It was a shortage of troops to fight the Revolution's enemies that
led Robespierre, on 20 February 1793, to introduce mass compulsory
conscription. The *levée en masse* was born as all able-bodied males
between 18 and 40 years old were declared eligible for military service.
That war was to be total in national effort and popular participation
was clear from the law passed by the French National Convention on
23 August 1793:

The young shall fight; married men shall forge weapons and trans-
port supplies; women will make tents and clothes and will serve
in the hospitals; the children will make up old linen into lint; the

old men will have themselves carried into the public square to rouse the courage of the fighting men, to preach hatred of kings and the unity of the Republic.[2]

Using the mass army made available to him by Robespierre's innovation, Napoleon became the master of the strategy of annihilation, exploiting to the full the superior numbers, mobility and patriotic fervour of his forces.[3] The aim of Napoleonic warfare became the total annihilation of the enemy. All available forces were concentrated to break the enemy's will to resist, to eliminate his sources of supply and to render him defenceless. Inevitably, larger armies meant larger losses on the battlefield and, in all, Napoleon's campaigns cost 3 500 000 dead and wounded. The Prussians reformed their army during the wars against Napoleon and made military service permanent in 1814. Conscription alarmed the conservatives in Prussia for political as well as financial reasons ('Arming the nation means the organisation of revolution' warned Prince Wittgenstein).[4] The Franco-Prussian War of 1870–71 showed the Prussian army to be the most modern and efficient in Europe. France and Russia saw no option but to follow suit and introduced permanent peace-time conscription in 1872 and 1874 respectively. By 1914 all European powers (with the exception of Britain) had conscript armies.

Conscription increased the size of armies and the industrial revolution improved the quantity and quality of their weaponry. The nineteenth century saw rapid developments both in the technology of armaments and in the industrial capacity to mass produce them. Breech-loading weapons, with a rate of fire twice that of muzzle-loading ones, were adopted by the Prussian army in 1843. The Austro-Prussian War of 1866 demonstrated their 'advantages' to all: the Prussian rate of fire was three times that of the Austrians which, combined with their exploitation of geography on the battlefield, gave victory to the Prussians. Machine-guns appeared on the European battlefield shortly afterwards. A forerunner of the modern machine-gun, the *mitrailleuse* was used to deadly effect by the French against German cavalry in the Franco-Prussian war of 1870–71.[5] A true machine-gun, recoil-operated and capable of firing several hundred rounds a minute, was patented in 1884 by the American Hiram Maxim. Nearly 30 years before, at the siege of Sebastopol during the Crimean war, gas was used for the first time in war when the British used sulphur in an attempt to smoke out the Russian defenders from their fortress.[6]

The Great War of 1914–18 showed the Napoleonic Wars to have been, not the exception that many thought and hoped, but the prototype for the total war to which the wars of the twentieth century tended. These wars tended towards totality both in their ends and in their means. By the 1940s, the ends of war had become total victory, unconditional surrender and the reconstruction of the defeated country's social, economic and political system in line with the victor's ideology. The means of war tended towards totality too. Restraints on strategy were loosened and the delineation of legitimate targets was broadened as nearly all sectors of society and the economy made some contribution to the war effort.

In this era of total war, civilians became targets. The targeting of the enemy's civilian population was made possible by the use of aircraft as bombers. More than any other weapon hitherto, the bomber airplane made the civilian population a target of war. The aircraft changed the course of warfare as much as the horse and gunpowder had done in previous eras but in ways which had particular significance for the non-combatant. Strategy could now include destruction of civilian morale as well as the destruction of transportation, communication and industry. The first use of airplanes as bombers came in October 1911 when the Italians bombed Turkish troops and Arab tribesmen in Libya during the Italian-Turkish War (the Austrians had, in the mid-nineteenth century, launched unmanned bomb-carrying balloons at the city of Venice). Aerial bombing began in the first World War on 11 October 1914 when two German planes dropped 22 bombs on Paris, killing 3 people and wounding 19.[7] Propeller-driven Zeppellin airships caused panic by bombing London from May 1915. Though airpower had arrived, it made little difference to the course of the First World War; it was left to the British strategy of naval blockade to take the war to the German people, undermining German industrial production and civilian morale.

In 1921 the Italian strategist Guilio Douhet predicted airpower's ending of civilian immunity: 'now it is actually populations and nations', and not their armies or navies, 'which come to blows and seize each others' throats'.[8] Douhet and other advocates of airpower claimed that bombers could deliver a quick and decisive knock-out blow by spreading misery, terror and massacre among the civilian

population. Though this strategy of aerial bombing was strongly condemned,[9] it was to be crucial to the war of 1939–45: what had been
done by naval blockade in the First World War was to be achieved by
aerial bombing in the Second. Motivated in part by revulsion at the
huge military casualties of the First World War, and a consequent
unwillingness to treat soldiers as cannon fodder, the British and
Americans invested huge resources in creating heavy bomber forces
to attack the German economy. The vulnerability of these bombers
to flak and fighter aircraft led the RAF to adopt a strategy of bombing
at night. The bombers were now safer from attack by German fighters but they could now no longer locate and bomb targets with any
precision (in 1941, only 20 per cent of bombs fell within five miles
of their target). The result of this discovery was a switch of strategy
from bombing military and industrial sites to bombing enemy cities
and society. Instead of bombing factories or rail yards, the RAF
bombed the workforce and their families. The workers, their houses,
their families and morale, became the targets of the night air raids.
By 1943, the British had the quantity of planes and the guidance
technology (radar and radio beams) to pursue city bombing with
devastating effect (in 1943, 60 per cent of bombs fell within three
miles of the target).[10] The first successful attempt at creating a
firestorm came in July and August 1943 when an RAF force of 731
bombers attacked Hamburg. Incendiary bombs were dropped
(though also some high explosive bombs to make the city unsafe for
firefighters) creating a firestorm which generated, and was sustained
by, a rush of air inwards to feed the flames. The air heated to 800
degrees Celsius and civilians in underground air shelters, who would
usually be safe, were killed by the heat or by suffocation. On 13 and
14 February 1945, British and American bombers attacked Dresden,
a city teeming with refugees fleeing westwards ahead of the advanc-
ing Soviet army. A firestorm was successfully kindled and 50 000
civilians killed.

Such strategies of total war, utilizing attacks on cities and civilian
morale in a quest for unconditional surrender, were made easier by
the invention of nuclear weapons in 1945. The atomic bombs
dropped on Hiroshima and Nagasaki in August 1945 had an explosive force, generated by the chain reaction fission of uranium
(Hiroshima) or plutonium (Nagasaki), that was thousands of times
greater than any previous bomb. After the war thermonuclear

weapons were developed, in which the fission explosion was used to start the chain reaction fusion of hydrogen isotopes, giving even greater destructive blasts. Once the rockets used to carry these weapons could achieve escape velocity, their range became unlimited (these Intercontinental Ballistic Missiles – ICBMs – placed the weapons in orbit around the planet where they continued on their journey ballistically, that is, under the effect of gravity). The re-entry speeds of these weapons made attempts at their destruction futile[11] and, with the deployment of the nuclear-powered submarines in the 1950s, nuclear missiles gained an undetectable and invulnerable launching pad.

In the early decades of nuclear weapons, the primitive state of guidance technology did not allow the large liquid-fuelled rockets to strike targets smaller than cities (the same justification of technological limitation had been used for city bombing in World War 2). With rapid advances in technology came greater precision in nuclear targeting although the blast, radiation and fallout from nuclear use (not to mention the possible 'nuclear winter' effect of dust and smoke in the atmosphere) would still devastate the civilian population. Even in a 'limited' nuclear war or one composed solely of 'counterforce' strikes against enemy missiles and command and control facilities, the civilian population would suffer from radiation and radioactive fallout. Such weapons of mass destruction brought the era of total war to its culmination. Nuclear war was never waged between the superpowers but total war resulting in the total destruction of the enemy was an ever-present possibility. In such a total nuclear war, the combatant/non-combatant distinction would have faded away completely. All in society would be its victims and yet, in such a push-button war, very few of the military would be its 'combatants'.

The Cold War was total war in suspended animation. Another form of total war was waged with increasing importance through the second half of the twentieth century. This was informal or guerrilla war. Again, it had its origins in the Napoleonic wars of 1792–1815. In those wars, one momentous innovation of modern warfare, the mass national army of conscripts, met another: the irregular or partisan. In 1797 the French forces were initially defeated by a mass popular uprising of Tyrolean peasants (the Tyroleans had previous experience of irregular warfare having expelled the Elector of Bavaria and his forces in 1703). In Spain too, Napoleon's conscripted army met resistance from partisans. These Spanish 'guerrillas' were volunteers with no uniforms, motivated by religion or patriotism or loyalty to the monarchy. They operated independently, interrupting the army's lines of communication, ambushing its supply columns, and capturing its couriers. Though not decisive in the war, their harassment of the 300 000-strong occupying army helped the Duke of Wellington's forces to establish themselves in Spain. While Wellington, as commander of the Anglo-Portuguese forces, obeyed the established rules of war, the guerrilla units did not. They hanged French prisoners, killed French wounded and, in return, were given no pardon when captured. The French themselves were to use irregulars (the *franc tireurs* from private rifle clubs) to little effect against the Prussian army in 1870–71. Again, they were not recognized as lawful combatants and were summarily executed when captured by the Prussians. In the South African War of 1899–1902 a European army had to fight a numerous, well-armed and effective partisan force. By the end of that war, both the British and the Boers had resorted to using terror against the civilian population. The guerrilla fighter, fitting the formal category of neither regular combatant nor civilian, was to become a major issue for the twentieth-century law of war. In blurring the distinction between combatants and non-combatants, guerrillas placed great strain on the established basis of the PNCI.

The extreme form of guerrilla war is terrorism. Often it is the most informal of all informal wars with the combatant posing as a civilian and becoming, in effect, a 'stealth soldier'. But terrorism is also practised by states (the first use of the term was in connection with the Jacobins' use of force in the wake of the French Revolution). Regardless of its perpetrators or its goals, terrorism is a form of total war. The essence of terrorism is the totality of its targeting. Terrorism targets civilians and civilian property. It uses the same target list as total war, and the same justifications. Its perpetrators might claim that, in a modern society, all are involved in the maintenance of the disliked regime or of the military effort of their opponents. They can point to the significant precedent of World War 2 and the victorious allies' strategy of terrorizing the civilian population, 'de-housing' them and breaking their morale. Terrorists can claim too that they have no alternative: they are limited by the quantity and quality of weaponry available to them and cannot target their violence more precisely.

The justification of total war

How may total war be justified? Two claims may be made to justify the targeting of civilians in war. The first is the claim that the supposed 'innocent civilians' are not in fact innocent. The second is the claim that they were not civilian. Those making such claims can point to the changes in the social, economic and political context of war in the nineteenth and twentieth centuries. Democratization, nationalism and industrialism in this period certainly altered the citizen's relation to his state and its wars. Industry, technology and culture became important elements of state power. The industrialization of war in the nineteenth century made a country's engineering industry and raw materials trade part of its war machine. The broadening of the franchise also appeared to put political power in the hands of more and more of a country's population. As a result, the support of the civilian population became crucial and morale was built and maintained through propaganda. That public support for war also became a target of the adversary and attempts were made to break civilian morale.

The first approach to justifying total war denies that civilians are innocent.[12] It claims that they may be held responsible for their country's wrongdoing. Such guilt may be ascribed to the enemy population collectively or individually. Neither, however, seems tenable. To ascribe guilt to a society as a whole is to take a holistic view of societies and nations in which the people are held to constitute a unified entity. Such a view was famously rejected by Hugo Grotius (when he condemned the 'fiction' that people in the enemy state form a single body) and by Edmund Burke in the eighteenth century (when he declared that he knew no means of bringing an indictment against a whole nation). Indeed it is to its foundations in Greek and biblical thought that Western culture can trace the principles of justice which do not permit the execution or punishment of individuals except for their own crimes. It is also true that collective guilt cannot be ascribed to the enemy population as individuals. Enemy civilians cannot be said to be guilty on the basis of either their acts or omissions for the wrong committed by their government or armed forces. All in the civilian population can only be guilty by virtue of their acts if all agreed to the evil act, if the decision was reached by consensus. They can only be guilty by virtue of their omissions if some duty of rebellion against evil political leaders is claimed.[13] Such a duty may exist but, even so, not all in the civilian population can be guilty on the grounds of omission. The civilian casualties of war include babies, infants, toddlers and small children. Their guilt, by act or omission, cannot be claimed.

The killing of enemy civilians cannot be justified on the basis of their guilt. In any case, as the previous chapter claimed, the killing of combatants in war is not justified on the basis of their guilt. Combatants too were acknowledged to be equally innocent of *ad bellum* guilt. The immunity of non-combatants in war has been based neither on their innocence of *ad bellum* guilt nor on their non-contribution to the war effort. Augustine's punitive justification of war gave way to the formal model of war precisely because the justification of punitive killing could not be applied coherently. The justification of preventative killing could be applied neither to non-combatants nor to combatants. The basis of the immunity of non-combatants in war was not their innocence. Rather non-combatants were to be immune in war because they did not occupy the formal role of combatant; they were not instruments of their sovereign and they could not have their lives taken as a means to an end in war. Given this, the attempt to justify total war on the basis of the non-innocence of the civilian population is unconvincing.

The second attempt to justify total war denies that innocent civilians are actually civilians by claiming that, in a modern industrial state, all people contribute to the war effort (however indirectly) and thus may be considered combatant. Why should those who contribute to the war effort through the manufacture and supply of weaponry and ammunition be treated so differently to those who contribute through fighting? Such suggestions are made, for example, by Jenny Teichman when she writes that a scientist involved in making nuclear weapons 'cannot be regarded as anything but a legitimate target'[14] and by Maurice Pearton when he asks: 'At what point did a workman, en route from his home to his job in a factory cease to be a non-combatant, particularly if he had been exempted from conscription into the armed forces on the grounds of his skills?'[15] Again, it is relevant to point out that the civilian casualties of war include individuals for whom no involvement in the war effort, direct or indirect, can be claimed. These include, but are not limited to, children.

In any case, the broadening of contribution to the war effort in a modern industrial society does not undermine the civilian's right to non-combatant immunity in war. It is a requirement of justice that only combatants be targeted in war and this is not negated by the changes in technological, military, social and political factors that made total war. The PNCI was established in international law in an age of formal war but the force and justice of the principle does not depend on any particular set of social, political and military circumstances. The notions of the civilian population's involvement in, or contribution to, the maintenance of a political structure or process are as irrelevant to the legitimacy of killing as notions of guilt and responsibility. Guilt, responsibility, involvement, contribution are not the reason why combatants may be killed in war and they are not a reason why civilians may be targeted in war. The value of one's product to warriors has never been the determinant of one's legitimacy as a target. Food has always been necessary to fighting; armies have long marched, and fought, on their stomachs yet agricultural producers were an early inclusion on medieval Christians' list of illegitimate targets. The PNCI was based on a customary acceptance that those in uniform could in war be treated as instruments rather than as human beings. No implication of guilt or responsibility was laid against combatants nor did combatants have to be engaged in a combatant act to be targeted in war. The attempt to justify total war on the basis of civilians' contribution to the war effort fails.

The civilian

In the twentieth century, technology developed so as to allow attacks upon the whole population of an enemy country even though the principles of justice did not permit this. The Hague Conventions of 1899 and 1907 had clarified the protection of non-combatants under international law. The Hague Conference of 1899 was the first meeting of the world's major powers to agree upon norms of international warfare and it had both an ambitious purpose and a lasting effect on international law. At this conference, and its successor in 1907, many aspects of the law of war were dealt with, including the declaration of war, the rights of neutrals, and the status and rights of non-combatants. The resulting Hague Regulations on Land Warfare committed states to the protection of non-combatants in war, recognized in four categories: prisoners, civilian inhabitants of occupied territory, citizens of neutrals and medical personnel. They required that the persons and property of civilians should not be violated, that civilians should not be taken hostage, and that the right of civilians to freedom of transit, of correspondence and of religious practice should be respected.[16] Despite the clear protection of non-combatants under the Hague Conventions, civilians were the main victims of the aerial bombings of the second World War and of the use of nuclear weapons that brought the war to a close.

The years after 1945 gave the opportunity for a reconstruction of the law of war and advances were made on the protection of the civilian in war. This was accomplished in two ways: first, by lengthening the list of acts that may not be done to civilians and, secondly, by including more people in the category of civilian. The charter of the International Military Tribunal which sat at Nuremburg set out a long list of forbidden acts. Most of the 'war crimes' prescribed there are offences against the PNCI expansively defined (murder; ill-treatment or deportation of civil population; plunder of public or private property; wanton destruction of cities, towns or villages; devastation not justified by military necessity). So too with the Tribunal's new category of 'crimes against humanity', all of which were breaches of the PNCI: murder; extermination; enslavement; deportation; other inhumane acts committed against a civilian population; and persecutions on political, racial or religious grounds. The 1949 revision of the three Geneva Conventions of 1929 (dealing with prisoners of war, and the wounded, sick and ship-wrecked) added to the list of acts which may not be done in war. In addition, a new fourth convention was created, dealing with civilians.

The Civilians Convention of 1949 outlawed forced civilian labour (A51) and the forcible transfer of civilians, except temporarily (A49). The destruction of property was forbidden, except where 'absolutely militarily necessary' (A53), and adequate food was required to be provided for civilians even if this necessitated the occupier bringing it from outside (A55).[17] Articles 33 and 34 declared it illegal to use collective punishment, intimidation, or terror against civilians or to take them hostage. Articles 27, 31 and 32 prohibited the physical or moral maltreatment of civilians and the death penalty was restricted to the offence of attacking occupying forces or its property (A68). Article 5, however, did permit states, in their own territory or in occupied territory, to hold incommunicado civilians suspected of spying, sabotage or other activities 'hostile to its security'. These revisions to the three 1929 conventions and the creation of the new convention were done at Geneva, orchestrated by the International Committee of the Red Cross. The resulting four Geneva Conventions of 1949 delineated the roles of combatant and non-combatant and set out formally how a person could exchange the role of combatant for that of non-combatant through capture, wounds or shipwreck.

The Civilians Convention, although it advanced the protection of civilians in war, dealt mainly with the issue of civilians under enemy occupation. The most important issue as regards the protection of civilians, their suffering in consequence of enemy attack, was omitted. The reasons for this omission related not just to the past (the victims of much aerial bombing, Germany and Japan, were not present in Geneva but the victorious allies were) but to the future. At the same time as diplomats and jurists were meeting in Geneva to draft the Convention on civilians, military strategists were developing 'counter-value' strategies based on the use of nuclear and thermonuclear weapons against enemy cities. Clearly much work remained to be done as regards the protection of civilians during military engagements. In the post-war years, the International Committee of the Red Cross continued to seek improvements in the protection of civilians in war. Its ICRC's 1956 'Draft Rules for the Limitation of the Dangers Incurred by the Civilian Population in Time of War', though not accepted by governments, did lead to the two Additional Protocols of 1977 (known as AP1 and AP2) which were accepted. These two Additional Protocols were appended to the Geneva Conventions of 1949 and it is in their delineation of non-combatant immunity that we find the current legal requirements. The first Additional Protocol (dealing with international armed conflicts) lays down the basic rule about civilian immunity in Article 48 and expands on the protection of the civilian population in war in Article 51. The provisions of these articles are regarded as customary international law, binding on all states:

Article 48 – Basic Rule
In order to ensure respect for and protection of the civilian population and civilian objects, the Parties to the conflict shall at all times distinguish between the civilian population and combatants and between civilian objects and military objectives and accordingly shall direct their operations only against military objectives.

Article 51 – Protection of the Civilian Population

1. The civilian population and individual civilians shall enjoy general protection against dangers arising from military operations. To give effect to this protection, the following rules, which are additional to other applicable rules of international law, shall be observed in all circumstances.
2. The civilian population as such, as well as individual civilians, shall not be the object of attack. Acts or threats of violence the primary purpose of which is to spread terror among the civilian population are prohibited.
3. Civilians shall enjoy the protection afforded by this Section, unless and for such time as they take a direct part in hostilities.
4. Indiscriminate attacks are prohibited. Indiscriminate attacks are:

    (a) those which are not directed at a specific military objective;
    (b) those which employ a method or means of combat which cannot be directed at a specific military objective; or
    (c) those which employ a method or means of combat the effects of which cannot be limited as required by this Protocol;

    and consequently, in each such case, are of a nature to strike military objectives and civilians or civilian objects without distinction.
5. Among others, the following types of attacks are to be considered as indiscriminate

    an attack by bombardment by any methods or means which treats as a single military objective a number of clearly separated and distinct military objectives located in a city, town, village or other area containing a similar concentration of civilians or civilian objects; and
    an attack which may be expected to cause incidental loss of civilian life, injury to civilians, damage to civilian objects, or a combination thereof, which would be excessive in relation to the concrete and direct military advantage anticipated.[18]

These articles are very explicit. Civilians must not be targeted in war. The threat or use of force must at all times be directed only against military personnel and military assets. Military actions whose primary purpose is to assault the civilian population are forbidden as are acts which indiscriminately assault civilians. Every person who is not a combatant (not taking a direct part in hostilities) is declared to be a civilian. In cases of doubt, the status of civilian is to be assumed.[19] Even with the uncompromising language of AP1, however, the immunity of civilians in war is still not absolute. Acts which are certain to cause civilian deaths are permitted as long as the loss of civilian life is still not excessive in relation to the military advantages sought.

The combatant

The era of total war brought greater variety in the types of European combatant. In the war that was never waged, strategic nuclear war between the superpowers, the combatant was so remote from his target and the effects of his action as hardly to be engaged in 'combat' at all. But where the characterization of the combatant as instrument became problematic was in its application to other forms of total war: guerrilla war and terrorism. Combatants participating in these informal wars present a fundamental problem to the established characterization of the combatant as instrument. The developments in the social, economic and political context of war which allowed nearly all members of a belligerent's population to be construed as contributors to the war effort did not undermine the PNCI: the principle's basis in justice remained firm through the twentieth century. The most serious problem for the PNCI in the twentieth century has instead been informal combatants. Informal combatants create a problem for the PNCI precisely because combatant status has been, since the time of Vattel, ascribed on the basis of the formal occupation of the role of combatant. By not formally occupying this role, informal combatants (partisans, guerrillas and terrorists) instead appear to be, and claim at times to be, civilians who must be granted immunity.

The 1907 Hague Regulations set out the attitude to informal combatants which persisted for 70 years. Articles 1 and 2 of the Regulations, concerning 'The Qualifications of Belligerents', read:

Article 1
The laws, rights, and duties of war apply not only to armies, but also to militia and volunteer corps fulfilling the following

conditions:

1. To be commanded by a person responsible for his subordinates;
2. To have a fixed distinctive emblem recognisable at a distance;
3. To carry arms openly; and
4. To conduct their operations in accordance with the laws and customs of war.

In countries where militia or volunteer corps constitute the army, or form part of it, they are included under the denomination 'army'.

Article 2
The inhabitants of a territory which has not been occupied, who, on the approach of the enemy, spontaneously take up arms to resist the invading troops without having had time to organise themselves in accordance with Article 1, shall be regarded as belligerents if they carry arms openly and if they respect the laws and customs of war.[20]

The Hague Regulations, then, recognized two formal and distinct categories of person in war: combatant and non-combatant. Each was granted its own privileges and responsibilities and, provided people remained in these roles, they were to be protected to some extent from the violence of war. The Regulations accepted armed resistance as lawful only when it tended towards regular combatancy, for if combatants are to be targeted even when they are not engaged in a combatant act, then they must be recognizable as combatants at all times. Article 1 of the Regulations thus set out four conditions to be met by a partisan, guerrilla or informal fighter if he was to qualify for privileged status of a combatant. To carry arms openly and an emblem recognizable at a distance would be to abandon the stealth, surprise and subterfuge which are the guerrilla's main hope of victory. Yet only if these conditions were met was the combatant considered to a lawful combatant and his killing considered to be other than murder. Only lawful combatants were required to be treated, on capture, as prisoners of war.

The Hague Regulations were founded on the approach to non-combatant immunity that developed in the period from Grotius to

Vattel. According to this approach, what matters is not whether a person forms part of an enemy country's armed strength, or makes a contribution toward it, but simply whether that person occupies the formal role of combatant (in practice whether they are dressed in a markedly military way and enlisted in a military organization). Those in the role of combatant in war may be attacked; civilians may not. A person no longer able to perform the function of a combatant (through wounds, sickness, shipwreck or capture) reverts to the status of a noncombatant and re-acquires the immunity from wanton attack that such status implies. They may no longer be killed, and the civilian population are encouraged to come to their aid. Civilians are protected when treating and tending those rendered *hors de combat*, as is the Red Cross.

The formal approach to combatancy of the Hague Regulations yielded a clear delineation of the categories of combatant and civilian. However, this clear delineation also meant that there was a gap between the two lawful categories of combatant and civilian. There was a third category of person in war: the unlawful combatant. Those who did not abide by the rules set out in the articles quoted above were unlawful combatants and were accorded no protection. These people had the status and privileges of neither combatant nor civilian: on capture, they could be executed for their deeds. As we will see, the rise of the irregular (and unlawful) combatant in the twentieth century was to call into question the justification of the killing of combatants in war on the basis of their formal occupation of the role of combatant.

The formal approach to combatancy taken by the 1907 Hague Regulations was still in place when the Second World War broke out in 1939. During that war, the activities of unlawful combatants emphasized the need for change in the law of war. Many partisans, guerrillas and informal combatants fought for the USSR, Greece, Yugoslavia, Poland and France. Attitudes to their activities were sharply divided. The Germans reacted to them with ruthlessness and indignation, considering their activities to be illegal and unethical.[21] The war's eventual victors, however, were proud of their partisan activities, and wanted the stigma of illegitimacy removed. Despite pressure from countries that treasured their resistance to German occupation, the post-war Geneva Conventions did not change the definition of the lawful combatant but persisted with the definition of the combatant set out in the Hague Regulations. The 1949

Conventions did not directly address the issue of informal war. Article 4 of the Prisoner of War Convention declared that armed resistance in occupied territory was legitimate. However, the Prisoner of War Convention, with 143 articles and 5 annexes, did not apply to informal war and its informal combatants; the status of prisoner of war remained totally dependent upon the prisoner having had the status of lawful combatant. The Conventions maintained the same restrictive conditions of the Hague Regulations, requiring partisans to have a commander, to wear a fixed distinctive sign recognizable at a distance, to carry arms openly and to conduct their operations in accordance with the laws and customs of war. The status of lawful combatant still depended on the formal occupation of the role. So too the justification for killing such combatants continued to be based on their formal occupation of the role of combatant.

The Geneva Conventions, in leaving intact the formal delineation of combatancy, left unresolved the issue of the informal combatant. The gap between the civilian and the regular combatant remained and those irregular combatants who fell into this gap were accorded no status in war. Yet the wars of the second half of the twentieth century were to be characterized by their informal nature: in most wars of this period, the formal army of a state fought the informal fighters of a non-state group. The guerrilla, revolutionary and nationalist wars of decolonization in the post-1945 period greatly increased the pressure on the formality of combatancy and on the characterization of the combatant as an instrument of a sovereign authority. Informal combatants could not be brought under the protection of the laws of war without discarding the established characterization of the combatant based on his formal occupation of the role of combatant. Yet to do this would be to discard also the established justification for the killing of combatants in war.

It was left to the two Additional Protocols of 1977 and the Convention on Conventional Weapons (CCW) of 1980 to close the gap between the formal combatant and the civilian, that is, to eradicate the no man's land of the informal combatant and to eliminate the space between the roles of civilian and lawful combatant. AP1 did so by ending the formality of the categories of combatant and non-combatant. It allowed the role of combatant to be no longer formally occupied. It allowed a person to move from combatant status to civil status depending on what he or she is doing at any time. Sections 3, 4 and 5 of Article 44, which deals with combatants and prisoner of war status, read:

3. In order to promote the protection of the civilian population from the effects of hostilities, combatants are obliged to distinguish themselves from the civilian population while they are engaged in an attack or in a military operation preparatory to an attack. Recognising, however, that there are situations in armed conflicts where, owing to the nature of the hostilities an armed combatant cannot so distinguish himself, he shall retain his status as a combatant, provided that, in such situations, he carries his arms openly:

    (a) during each military engagement, and
    (b) during such time as he is visible to the adversary while he is engaged in a military deployment preceding the launching of an attack in which he is to participate.

   Acts which comply with the requirements of this paragraph shall not be considered as perfidious within the meaning of Article 37, paragraph 1(c).

4. A combatant who falls into the power of an adverse Party while failing to meet the requirements set forth in the second sentence of paragraph 3 shall forfeit his right to be a prisoner of war, but he shall, nevertheless, be given protections equivalent in all respects to those accorded to prisoners of war by the Third Convention and by this Protocol ...

5. Any combatant who falls into the power of an adverse Party while not engaged in an attack or in a military operation preparatory to an attack shall not forfeit his rights to be a combatant and a prisoner of war by virtue of his prior activities.[22]

Civilians enjoy their protected status 'unless and for such time as they take a direct part in hostilities'.[23] In Best's reading of Article 44, civilians become combatants upon engaging in, or preparing for, guerrilla activities but revert to the privileged status of civilian on stopping such guerrilla activity. AP1 took a realistic approach to irregular warfare when it required guerrilla fighters to distinguish themselves from the civilian population only 'while engaged in an attack or in a military operation preparatory to an attack', thus allowing them to look and live like civilians during non-operative periods and to gain the protection of civilians status. Guerrillas may not pretend

to be civilians during combatant operations (those doing so, if captured, forfeit the benefits of PoW status)[24] but they may move from
the status of lawful combatant to that of protected civilian, subject
only to the minor requirements that they be members of 'the armed
forces of a party to the conflict' possessing 'an internal disciplinary
system which, *interalia*, shall enforce compliance with the rules of
international law applicable in armed conflict'. AP1 removed the gap
that had existed since the Hague Regulations between the categories
of combatant and civilian. No longer were irregular combatants
declared to be unlawful and criminals. Rather, they could move from
the category of combatant to the category of civilian (and back again)
depending on their activity at any given time. In attempting to reconcile civilian immunity with civilian participation by permitting the
same persons to be both combatant and non-combatant in the course
of a day, AP1 eliminated the formality of the categories of combatant
and non-combatant. It is no longer the role of combatant, but the act
of combatancy, which matters. The role of combatant need no longer
be formally occupied and the activity of combatancy becomes the
indicator of combatant status. A person moves from combatancy to
civil status depending on what he or she is doing at any time.

With AP1 the categorization of all in war as either combatant or
civilian has been completed. The no man's land of unlawful combatancy has been eliminated. But in doing so, AP1 also brought a
huge shift in the characterization of the combatant and in the justification of the killing of the combatant in war. For, unlike regular
combatants who may be killed at almost any time in war, those who
engage in irregular combatancy cannot. They can only be killed when
actually engaged in an act of combatancy. The reason for killing
them is no longer that they formally occupy the role of combatant
and may be treated as an instrument of their political and military
authority. The reason for killing them is that they are engaged in
harming or killing others. This is a very significant alteration to the
justification of killing combatants in war. Indeed it is the first step in
ending the justification of the killing of combatants in war based
only on their occupation of the role of combatant.

Conclusion: total war and non-combatant immunity

In the age of total war, the primary victim has come to be the civilian. The numbers of civilians killed in war have risen to overtake the

numbers of combatants killed. In World War 1, only 14 per cent of casualties were civilian. In World War 2, the proportion was 67 per cent.[25] In Korea, it was 84 per cent and in Vietnam 90 per cent.[26] In the 1990s, and the wars in Somalia, Bosnia, Rwanda and Chechnya, the percentage of civilian casualties remained at these very high rates. In the post-1945 period, weapons of mass destruction were developed that could not be used discriminately. Throughout the Cold War, NATO threatened escalation to nuclear war in Europe, as complete a breach of the PNCI as is imaginable. In the wars of the 1990s, the genocide, systematic rape, 'ethnic cleansing' and forced flight of civilian populations came to be the principal means, and indeed the ends, of war.

Yet the century that saw unprecedented slaughter of both civilians and combatants ended with concerns to lessen the violence of war and to target it more precisely. Calls to reduce unjust killing in war have not focused solely on civilians; combatants (one's own and the enemy's) have also been the subject of concern. In the final decades of the twentieth century, great efforts were made to respect the status of the non-combatant in war. Technological innovations brought about by the application of electronics to warfare (the so-called 'revolution in military affairs') permitted more precise targeting. Developments in information technology, remote sensing and communications yielded pilotless spy planes on the battlefield and spy satellites in space. Advances in the guidance and accuracy of weaponry are enabling forces to take advantage of that intelligence. The result is 'smart' weapons whose greater accuracy permits the use of smaller warheads to do the job. Less collateral damage is done and more precise discrimination between civilian and combatant is possible, especially when the new technologies are combined with (or themselves lead to) military superiority. The closing decades of the twentieth century even saw accelerated research into and development of non-lethal and low-lethality weapons. Such weapons are the very opposite of the 'neutron bomb', a weapon which evoked public protest in the 1970s because it was designed to kill people without harming property. Non-lethal weapons diminish fighting capacity without killing people. Some are already in use, such as radio waves to jam enemy transmissions and the graphite bombs employed by NATO to short out an electricity grid in its war against Serbia in 1999. Non-lethal weapons still under development use a great diversity of approaches. Electronic means may be used to hack into an enemy's computers or microwaves to damage electronic equipment. Sound waves may be employed to cause pain and disorientation to people, or light to blind people or equipment. Chemical weapons may incapacitate people or damage equipment (by degrading materials or rendering surfaces slippery), or they may immobilize people (by spraying them with sticky foam).[27]

The motivation to lessen killing in war, and to discriminate between combatant and civilian, has been strengthened by the electronic mass media and its coverage of war. Public support is crucial for any Western military involvement and that public support is detrimentally affected by TV footage of civilian casualties and damage. If this is to be avoided, then the issue of discrimination between civilian and combatant must remain a priority at the top of the military and political agenda. The concern to maintain public support by respecting civilian status in war was evident in NATO's engagement in Kosovo in the 1990s. A military alliance, which for decades threatened escalation to nuclear war in Europe,[28] waged a war there in which it put great effort into minimizing civilian casualties. Air strikes were cancelled, and the use of cluster bombs suspended, when civilians died as a result of NATO attacks.

The NATO wars against Iraq and Serbia in the 1990s also highlighted the concern of Western countries to avoid casualties among their own combatants. The century which started in Europe with the senseless slaughter of the First World War, when waves of infantry were sent to their deaths, ended with a marked reluctance on the part of Western countries to risk the lives of their combatants in war. In the USA, the impact of the Vietnam War on popular and political culture is frequently cited as a cause of the growing sensitivity to combatant casualties.[29] Again, the 'revolution in military affairs' is being put to use to reduce combatant casualties. Developments in intelligence gathering and processing and remote weapons systems are aimed to reduce the risk of combatant casualties while pilotless planes and crewless ships ('arsenal ships') would eliminate it in some operations.

The unjust killing of enemy combatants also raises concerns. The Vietnam War generated unease with the scale of enemy casualties, and the more recent cases of the *Belgrano* and the 'Highway of Death' show the extent to which the unjust killing of combatants in war stirs consciences. On the 2 May 1982, during the Falklands/Malvinas war, the Argentinian cruiser *General Belgrano*, outside the war zone and sailing away from the islands, was attacked and sunk by the British submarine *HMS Conqueror*. Almost 400 crewmen died. The sinking of the *Belgrano* during the Falklands war caused deep unease in Britain because it seemed to many to be an unjust use of lethal force. The combatants on that vessel were not engaged in, or about to be immediately engaged in, an act of combatancy. The 'highway of death' episode occurred on 26 and 27 February 1991 when Iraqi soldiers were withdrawing from Kuwait at the end of war there. US planes trapped the long convoys by disabling vehicles at the front and rear, and then bombed the halted convoys for hours. Since the killing of withdrawing soldiers violates the Geneva Conventions of 1949 (which outlaws the killing of soldiers who are out of combat), the British and US governments in these cases sought to justify their actions. The Thatcher government in Britain claimed that the *Belgrano* was sailing not away from the islands but towards them. The Bush administration's defence of its action was based on the claim that the Iraqi troops were retreating to regroup and fight again. Such an intention on the part of the Iraqis would make the killings legal under international law. The British and American actions may have been legal under the existing law of war but they provoked a profound unease on the part of many of their own peoples, and outrage on the part of some. The days of widespread public acceptance of the mass slaughter of enemy combatants are over.

A concern to use force justly is evident from these episodes as well as from the developments in weaponry, intelligence gathering and intelligence processing which have as their aim greater discrimination and lower lethality. But the means to discriminate accurately can be put to good effect only if we are clear whom we should discriminate between. The issue is not the undeniable practical difficulties in distinguishing combatants from non-combatants in informal wars which are fought by a regular state army on one side and an informal force of a non-state group on the other. Rather the issue is a fundamental theoretical one. Who may justly be killed? Who precisely should count as a legitimate target in future wars? Answers to those questions will be offered in the final chapter.

8
Conclusion

Forgive me if I still prefer people who kill people because they think it's right, not necessary.

Gavin Lyall[1]

This work has examined the evolution of the idea that certain categories of people ought to be granted immunity from violence in war. Of each stage of the Western justification of war over the past 1600 years, the questions have been asked: Who may be killed in war? Why? Who may not? Why not? These questions were asked in order to discover the reasoning and motivations behind the development of the PNCI. Some conclusions can now be reached and some pointers to the future development of the principle given.

The first conclusion that can be reached is that PNCI has long been considered a rule of justice. The introductory chapter of this work drew attention to the two ways in which we commonly think about ethical and moral issues, one on the basis of justice ('the right') and the other on the basis of goals ('the good'). The latter judges some actions to be good or bad by referring to certain goals while the former approach evaluates actions by referring to justice. The history of the evolution of the PNCI shows it to be a principle of justice: the targeting of non-combatants in war is prohibited because it is unjust and not because it leads to better consequences.

Furthermore, the focus of that conception of justice has been the individual. The Western world has sought to justify both the immunity of some in war and the killing of others on the basis of justice. It has sought to justify the killing of a person in war as an appropriate treatment of that person (Western thought has long been reluctant to accept a justification of war in terms of the greater good alone). This standard is required by approaches, Christian or liberal or other, which view human beings in an individualistic manner. The Christian world-view has seen individual human beings, not as mere parts of a greater unit, but as separate (though not as complete in themselves: they are made complete and whole only through a relationship with their creator). This emphasis on the separateness, the uniqueness and the importance of each human being was strengthened by the Protestant Reformation. For modern liberalism, the view of each person as a separate individual, whole and complete, came to be a fundamental tenet.[2]

It is this standard of justice in the treatment of people which has been central to the long history of attempts to justify war as well as to the evolution of the PNCI. As was suggested in Chapter 2, justifying war in this manner was the achievement of the first distinctively Christian justification of war: that of Augustine. His attempt to reconcile Christianity and war yielded a justification of killing in war on the basis of the guilt of soldiers fighting for an unjust cause. By fighting for an unjust cause, soldiers shared in the guilt and their legal guilt in breaching the peace was accompanied by the moral guilt of choosing to do wrong. Because of this moral wrong, Augustine claimed, those fighting for an unjust cause could be said to merit death as a punishment. Augustine's punitive justification of war may not have fitted reality very well but it did set the standard to be met by all subsequent Christian justifications of war: killing in war was to be an appropriate treatment of the person killed.

By the thirteenth century, that poor fit with the reality of warfare was all the more glaring as, with the move from knightly warfare towards mass armies and mercenarism, there were no grounds at all for the ascription of guilt to soldiers on the side without just cause. A new justification was required and it could be found in the *Summa Theologiae*: yet this justification of war on the basis of the good of society was not given priority by Aquinas. Because only the guilt-based justification of killing in war met the standard that those killed must merit death because of their acts, Aquinas gives continued primacy to Augustine's definition of a 'just war'. In that Augustinian model of war, all on the side without just cause (combatant and non-combatant) could be killed in war or after. None on the side with just cause (combatant or non-combatant) could be killed without murder being done. The Augustinian model thus offered little basis (apart from charity) for granting immunity to non-combatants in war. Aquinas did raise the possibility of granting immunity to certain categories of people, not on the basis of justice, but on the basis of their social role. Though role came to be important in the characterization of combatants, justice has remained the primary force in the development of immunity for non-combatants.

In the sixteenth century came an attempt to justify the immunity of non-combatants on the basis of justice while retaining also the justification of the killing of combatants on the basis of justice. Vitoria and Suárez's transitional approach was built on a presumption of guilt on the part of combatants (while war was in progress and unless their innocence could be established) and a presumption of innocence on the part of non-combatants (while war was in progress and unless their guilt could be established). If successful, this would have maintained justice as the reason why combatants may be killed (they merit punishment for furthering a possibly unjust cause) while founding the immunity of non-combatants on justice too (they ought not to be killed in war because their responsibility for, or wilful participation in, an unjust cause has not been satisfactorily established and the issue of their guilt or innocence can, and should, be postponed until the end of the war). But the Spanish theologians' attempt could not be successful: although it gave a grounding in justice to the principle of non-combatant immunity, its claim that combatants could justly be killed on a presumption of guilt was untenable. To kill on the presumption of guilt was unacceptable given that both Vitoria and Suárez acknowledge that the combatants on one side are innocent (their side had just cause) and that the combatants on the other are very possibly innocent too (they fought for an unjust cause in good faith, led astray by their invincible ignorance). The Spaniards established why the killing of non-combatants was unjust but they failed to establish why the killing of combatants was just. For if it was unjust to kill non-combatants because of their likely innocence then it was equally unjust to kill combatants, few or none of whom could be said to be guilty (and half of whom, in any case, were fighting for a just cause).

It took until the seventeenth century for Western thought to develop the justification of non-combatant immunity that is underpinned by

modern international law. This was based on the customary acceptance in Western culture that, in war, those formally occupying the
role of combatant may have their lives taken as means to military
and political ends. They need not actually be engaged in an act of
combatancy to be killed nor is there any claim made that they are
guilty of wrongdoing and that their death is merited as punishment.
Combatants may be killed because of the customary acceptance (in
Christendom and Western culture) that, in war, the occupant of the
role of combatant may be treated as a means and not an end and
may be killed even when not engaged in an act of combatancy. This
is the approach of Grotius and Vattel and the one which came to be
the basis of the Hague Regulations and Geneva Conventions. Under
these laws, combatants need not be engaged in an act of combatancy
to be thought legitimate targets: as long as they are not *hors de combat*, they may be killed in war even when they are not engaged in a
combatant act and when there is nothing about the soldier as a person which makes hostile treatment justified. This is the characterization of the combatant that persists in international law.[3] In its favour
is that it established a sortal distinction between combatants and
non-combatants.[4] Issues of involvement, responsibility and guilt (all
scalar concepts)[5] were avoided by the PNCI's focus on formal role. No
assessment was required of a person's responsibility for the resort to
war or contribution to the war effort. Issues of involvement, responsibility, or guilt were avoided as they would require a judgment by
the attacker of the victim's degree of involvement or responsibility
(the sort of flexible assessment that the laws of war have sought to
avoid).

No sooner had this new justification of killing in war become
established in law and convention in the late nineteenth and early
twentieth centuries than it came under pressure. For the twentieth
century was the century of total war: technology permitted war without restrictions on persons targeted or suffering inflicted. The terror
bombing of the Second World War was an attack, not just on societies, cities and housing but on the distinctions between the guilty
and the innocent, the combatant and the non-combatant. Such terror bombing reached its nadir on 6 August 1945 when the centre of
an undefended city was destroyed by a single bomb. The informal
wars of the second half of the twentieth century further eroded
the distinction between combatant and non-combatant. Terrorism

breached the PNCI to an even greater extent: its targeting of civilians and civilian property is what makes it repellent and wrong.

Just and unjust killing

The search for an explanation of the normative basis of the PNCI has continued in contemporary moral philosophy and political theory. The Introduction briefly outlined many suggestions for the moral foundations of the PNCI, as it exists in law and custom now. The suggested foundations were of a wide variety but none gave a persuasive moral grounding for the current delineation of the 'combatant' category and for the differing treatment of the 'combatant' and the 'non-combatant'. Some failed to justify the precise delineation of legitimate target from illegitimate; some could not account for the very different treatment of combatant and non-combatant; and others failed to account for the perceived moral force of the principle. Clearly, the search for a coherent moral basis for the current demarcation of combatancy and the current position on the proper treatment of combatants and non-combatants is not the most pressing problem. (There may, indeed, be no coherent moral justification for the PNCI as it currently stands in law.) More important is to assess what justice requires of us in our treatment of other human beings in war. In other words, rather than starting from the PNCI as it exists now and working backwards to find a normative basis for it, we should start from fundamental moral values and move forward from them to principles for the proper treatment of people in war.

It is nonetheless worthwhile to look at recent attempts to justify the PNCI. Some of them try to provide a normative grounding in justice; they claim that it is right that civilians should not be killed in war. Others propose a basis in 'the good'; they claim that it is beneficial if states abide by the PNCI. I will look first at explanations in terms of 'the good'. Two will be outlined, the first by George Mavrodes and the other by Gabriel Palmer-Fernández. Both writers turn their attention to such an approach having found no convincing explanation in terms of absolutist morality or justice for the PNCI as it stands. Mavrodes suggests that the PNCI is a convention-dependent obligation, similar in nature to the obligation to pay tax or to drive on one side of the road and not the other.[6] Such obligations are entirely dependent on laws and customs; if no such law exists, then no duty to obey exists (in contrast are those independent moral obligations which can be understood without reference to the laws and customs of any society, e.g., the prohibition on wantonly murdering one's neighbours). For Mavrodes, the PNCI is one of the 'rules of the game' of war, similar in nature to the rules of the road. One is obliged not to kill civilians in war only if a rule exists forbidding the killing of civilians. 'The immunity of non-combatants', he writes, 'is best thought of as a convention-dependent obligation which substitutes for warfare a certain form of limited combat'.[7] That form of limited combat, less costly in human life and human suffering, is warfare in which civilians are spared.

Palmer-Fernández's suggested normative grounding for the PNCI is that 'civilians are illegitimate targets of deliberate attack *because* their immunity is a crucially important feature of the modern understanding of war'.[8] He gives the reason why states should accept this limitation in the conduct of war. This is that every 'nation wants to preserve the institutions necessary for its continued existence and way of life'.[9] Small and weak states, by upholding the PNCI in war, can avoid total devastation at the hands of the strong; a military superpower avoids biological, viral and 'other future weapons of mass destruction' being used against it by the weak. To Palmer-Fernández, the 'fairness requirement' imposes a duty on states to abide by the PNCI if they wish other states to do so.

There are problems with such attempts to justify the PNCI in terms of 'the good'. One is that, if the rule is justified on the grounds that sparing civilians will, in the long run, bring about a better state of affairs than will otherwise result, then there will be occasions when overriding the rule is the better means to such a state of affairs. There will always be cases where targeting civilians in *this particular war* would lead to lower overall death tolls. It is difficult to argue that the rule should not be overridden when it is thought likely that targeting civilians will produce a greater present balance of good over evil than any alternative course of action. It is difficult (even for a rule-consequentialist) to forego the quick and less bloody end to the war in progress. In the heat of combat, such assessments are all too likely to be biased and self-interested. A particular problem with Mavrodes's approach is that the obligation not to attack civilians is dependent on the existence of a convention and contingent on the adversary's adherence to it. If the enemy abandons the convention, then there is no longer anything immoral about attacking civilians.[10] In contrast to Mavrodes (and to the legal positivists who came to dominate international law after Vattel), most writers on the PNCI see the obligation not to target civilians as an independent moral rule; it is wrong to attack civilians regardless of what one's enemy is doing. It is wrong to target civilians in war even if the enemy targets civilians. It is, in short, an obligation similar to the one not to wantonly kill one's neighbours.

Such a status for the PNCI is backed up by the history of the principle. In both justifying the killing of some persons in war, and granting immunity to others, Western thought has been motivated by an individualist conception of justice. This justice requires that human life be treated as an end in itself and never as a means; that no one be punished except for their own crimes; that the life of an innocent human being should not be taken as a means to some end; and that an innocent person should not be killed no matter how advantageous it would be to his fellow human beings. To kill an innocent human being, even to save two or more innocent human lives, is unjust. It is the uniqueness and separateness of individual human lives which require that human lives never be traded off, one against another, or bartered and exchanged. An individualist conception of justice does not rule out the taking of human life. It can be just to kill a person. It is possible to kill a person while still treating them as a person. But, for it to be just to intentionally kill a person, there must be some fact about that person or their action that renders them liable to lethal violence. As Thomas Nagel puts it,

> whatever one does to another person intentionally must be aimed at him as a subject, with the intention that he receive it as a subject. It should manifest an attitude to *him* rather than just to the situation.[11]

It is unjust to kill someone because of their geographic location, organizational affiliation or anticipated future action. Nor is the justice of killing a person established simply by the fact that killing them would avert a mortal threat to someone else. However, to kill them for their past or current actions may be just. There are four types of just killing which have been claimed to be applicable to war. These are punitive killing (an example of which is capital punishment), preventative killing (e.g. in self-defence or other-defence), charitable killing (e.g. involuntary euthanasia or mercy killing) and consensual killing (e.g. voluntary euthanasia and violent sports where the risk of death is accepted by participants). Of these four types of killing, three are used to justify the killing of combatants in war (and combatants only, thus giving a moral basis to the immunity of civilians from violence in war). The principles of punishment, self-defence and consent are used still to argue for the immunity of civilians in war. These claims will be examined now. The claim of charitable killing in war will not be examined. First made by Augustine when he claimed that killing soldiers on the unjust side spared them from sinning further, this justification was repeated for at least 700 years but it has no advocates today. Though mercy killing sometimes occurs in war in the case of severely wounded and incapacitated combatants, it is not a justification applied to the killing of all enemy combatants (or to the sparing of enemy non-combatants) and will thus not be discussed.

Punitive killing

It can be just to kill someone punitively. Capital punishment may meet the standards of justice.[12] A person can be punished and yet still be treated as a person because punishment involves treating them as responsible for their own action. If one kills another person as punishment, then the reason for killing is connected to the person killed as an individual. To kill them as punishment for an act for which they are responsible is to treat them as a person. Procedures for just punitive killing are well established in legal practice. Such killing can be just when it is truly punitive (indeed capital punishment is only 'punishment' if the person executed was responsible for the crime: execution for crimes committed while a child or while severely mentally impaired is not punishment).

Augustine's punitive model of war (with the secular ruler waging war as God's agent and inflicting his punishment on those who choose to do wickedness) was one of only two distinctively Christian approaches to war (the other was pacifism). It is thus no surprise that there persists to this day the attempt to justify war as punishment, and the associated attempt to use the guilt/innocence distinction as the basis of the combatant/non-combatant distinction). Recent neo-Augustinian approaches include those of the Catholic philosophers Elizabeth Anscombe and John C. Ford SJ.[13] They claim that combatants are morally guilty and may therefore be violently treated, while non-combatants are morally innocent and may not.

Anscombe's starting point is the basic principle of justice that no one is to be punished except for their own crime.[14] She writes:

> what is required, for the people attacked to be non-innocent in the relevant sense is that they should themselves be engaged in an *objectively unjust proceeding* which the attacker has the right to make his concern; or – the commonest case – should be *unjustly attacking* him.[15]

Anscombe here puts forward the classic Augustinian punitive model of a just war. She sees (at least) one side to any conflict as necessarily engaged in an 'objectively unjust' campaign. Hence (following Augustine) soldiers on that unjust side are guilty of fighting an unjust war (even when they are under orders and obey all the laws of war); it is for this guilt that they may justly be killed. Non-combatants may not be targeted because thy are not participating in the enemy's wrongdoing. As they are not engaged in the prosecution of the war, they are committing no wrong.

The objections to this stance have already been outlined with regard to Augustine. First, it permits only one side's soldiers to kill; soldiers fighting on the side without just cause may not legitimately kill in war. This is incompatible with the modern era's principle of belligerent equality. Secondly, it may be unclear which side has the unjust cause. Vitoria pointed out, many centuries ago, the difficulties in establishing objectively the causes of a war and the difficulties in assessing their comparative justice. It was for these very reasons that he allowed soldiers to fight 'in good faith' in a war whose injustice was known only to the ruler. Thirdly, even in cases where the injustice of a belligerent is clear, it does not follow that the combatants on that side are knowingly participating in an evil act of such magnitude that death would constitute a just punishment for them. It is simply not plausible that all combatants on the side without just cause have always chosen to do wrong. Some may never have chosen to fight in this particular war and, even if they have chosen, membership of armed forces in wartime is not an evil so great as to merit death as a punishment. It may be claimed that, even if enemy military and war-related personnel are not conscious of the wrong they are committing against the victim nation, they are nonetheless committing the wrong, and the victim nation is accordingly justified in authorizing its military forces to kill them.[16] But to kill soldiers punitively for a wrongdoing of which they are not aware is unjust. Soldiers are not the proper objects of punishment, even when the cause for which they fight is unjust. In all, Anscombe offers no persuasive reason why we should reject now the enduring innovation of Grotius and Vattel: their acknowledgment that combatants are innocent of *ad bellum* guilt.

A variant on the punitive model comes from the Jesuit priest, John Ford. Writing during the Second World War, he claimed that combatants are morally guilty because of their participation in war. War is wicked and evil; to participate in it makes one liable for the punishment due to the participant in wickedness. Likewise, the non-participation of the non-combatant in war implies their moral innocence:

> Catholic teaching has been unanimous for long centuries in declaring that it is never permitted to kill directly noncombatants in war. Why? Because they are innocent. That is, they are innocent of the violent and destructive action of war, or of any close participation in the violent and destructive action of war. It is such participation *alone* that would make them legitimate targets of violent repression themselves.[17]

This variant of the punitive justification for killing in war offers the possibility of reconciling the Augustinian model of war with the modern era's principle of belligerent equality. Combatants on both sides may be justly killed because they are guilty; they are guilty of the wickedness of war. This justification contends that war is wicked, so wicked that those who wage it may be punitively killed for their participation in it. This variation on the punitive model would seem to support an anti-war position (if both side's combatants do wrong by warring, then neither should war). This is not an implication that Ford would wish drawn from it.

The punitive approach offers no convincing reason why combatants may be killed in war. Even if very great blame could justly be laid on individuals in war, their killing may still not be a just punishment. Punitive killing without a fair trial is unjust (vigilante justice and summary execution are illegal because they lack the protections of an impartial judge, legal representation and a right of defence). Even if guilt could be fairly established with regard to combatants, death may not be a punishment proportionate to the crime (the wrong they have committed in fighting may merit a lesser punishment). And even if death were a proportionate and just penalty, the forms of killing found in war are such that many would constitute 'cruel and unusual punishment' and thus would not be meted out even to a convicted criminal guilty of the most heinous crime. Killing in war, even when genuinely punitive, would often still be unjust.[18]

The conclusion must be that punishment can justify the killing in war of very few combatants in war. Punitive killing may occur in some instances but it is not the killing characteristic of war. The means and methods of warfare available are still too undiscriminating to serve as legitimate instruments of punishment. They cannot be used discriminatingly between the innocent and the guilty. Even with perfectly discriminating weapons, of course, the lack of a trial to establish the desert of retribution undermines the ability of warfare to serve as punishment. Standards such as a fair trial, an impartial judge, a right of defence and legal representation cannot be met on the battlefield. For this reason, just punitive killing has been carried out *post bellum*, as in the trials of the International Military Tribunal at Nuremburg, and not *in bello*.[19] Indeed the Geneva Conventions prohibit the summary killing of prisoners without trial. In all, desert of punishment cannot be claimed of the whole enemy population or even of all of the enemy armed forces. Mark Osiel writes of the Balkan war of the 1990s: 'most Serbian officers, and even many Serbian enlisted personnel, had good reason to know that the war their superiors ordered them to wage was aggressive in nature'.[20] Osiel can claim only that 'most' officers and 'many' enlisted personnel should have known. This leaves many officers and most enlisted personnel innocent of knowingly participating in wrong. Their deaths in war cannot be justified punitively. The justification of punishment may apply to those military or political leaders who chose to do wrong, or those of lower ranks who knowingly played a role in the commission of such serious crimes as massacre, systematic rape or genocide. But it does not apply to those combatants fighting lawfully for their country. It therefore cannot provide a basis for the distinction between combatants and non-combatants.

Preventative killing

Preventative killing is the second heading under which some modern explanations of the normative basis of the PNCI can be grouped. It can be just to kill another person preventatively, that is, in self-defence, in defence of others, or to prevent them acting in a certain harmful way. Again the reason for killing is connected to the person killed. They are killed because of the action they are doing or about to do. To stop someone from killing you (or someone else) by killing them is still to treat them as a person.[21] That it can be just to kill a person preventatively has long been accepted. Augustine believed in the justice of using lethal force in other-defence, though not in self-defence (he worried that the latter showed an undue attachment to the things of this world). Aquinas, however, believed that all living things have a natural right to self-defence. It could not be wrong for a human being to follow their instinct for survival, if need be by recourse to lethal violence. Grotius, as we saw, accepted Aquinas's idea of a natural right to self-defence and sought to justify the use of lethal force by combatants on both just and unjust sides by reference to it. Nowadays it is popularly accepted (and axiomatic in ethical theory) that it can be legitimate, at times, deliberately to kill an attacker in defence of oneself or another. The wrongness of killing an innocent bystander in order to save an innocent victim is also widely accepted.[22]

To be a just treatment of a person, preventative killing must be killing in self- or other-defence (that is, the killing of a lethal attacker) and not killing in self- or other-preservation (as an example of an act of self-preservation that was not an act of self-defence, Kemp cites the case of *R. v. Dudley and Stephens* (1884) in which two starving seamen were convicted for killing and eating a boy with whom they were shipwrecked).[23] Self-defence entitles the victim to use lethal force only against the attacker. Acts of self-preservation may have the same end as acts of self-defence but they are directed at a party who is not themselves threatening. The intentional killing of non-combatants in war is never justified by the principle of self-defence (for if the civilians are attackers then they are no longer non-combatants). Soldiers who kill intentionally civilians in war can usually invoke only the excuse of self-preservation, and claim that they killed civilians to save their own lives from a threat that did not emanate from the civilians.[24] Such self-preservative killing of an innocent non-attacker fails to treat the person justly. It is, as Anscombe writes, murder: 'For murder is the deliberate killing of the innocent, whether for its own sake or as a means to some further end'.[25]

Two contemporary writers who seek to justify the killing in war of combatants, and the immunity of civilians, by reference to self-defence are Thomas Nagel and Robert Fullinwider. Nagel looks at what is here termed the justification of preventative killing after rejecting attempts to justify the killing of combatants in war as punishment. He writes: 'we must distinguish combatants from noncombatants on the basis of their immediate threat or harmfulness'.[26] According to this view, justice permits the killing of those who put in mortal jeopardy the lives of others. Those who are not engaged in violent or threatening activity may not be attacked. The justification of preventative killing thus permits the killing of many combatants in war. The problem with it (if it is to explain the PNCI as it exists) is that it does not permit the killing of *all* in military uniform in wartime. There are many non-combatant soldiers who pose no threat. It is not just the cooks, bandsmen and administrators in military uniform who are not putting anyone in mortal jeopardy. There are also soldiers in a combatant role who are not at that moment putting anyone in mortal jeopardy (they may be behind the front line, or away from a scene of combat, or asleep). The justification of preventative killing cannot be used to justify the killing of them. Only in the case of a direct and immediate threat to life may the principle of self-defence be invoked to justify killing. The principle of self-defence does not justify the use of lethal force against those who are causally remote threats or potential threats.

Robert Fullinwider attempts to apply the justification of self-defence on the collective level. He asserts that not only may a person justifiably kill in self-defence but so too may a nation. In the latter case, that killing is inflicted by a nation's armed forces. As civilians do not kill, they may not be killed in self-defence. He writes:

> Our obligation not to kill noncombatants stems from our obligation not to kill without justification; and the principle of Self-Defense justifies killing only combatants.[27]

Does Fullinwider avoid the problem with Nagel's position? Can the fact that enemy soldiers are all engaged in a joint endeavour justify their deaths preventatively? I suggest not. For not all people whose activity or existence plays a role in the causal chain of a threat to another's life may be killed in self-defence (or other-defence). If killing a soldier punitively is just, then it may also be just to kill punitively those who order the soldier to the frontline. However, if a soldier is justly killed preventatively, then it is not just to kill others in the chain of command or responsibility, or others engaged in the joint endeavour with the soldier. Justice permits the preventative killing only of those persons causing an immediate mortal threat. Political leaders, army cooks, munitions workers and weapons research scientists pose no immediate mortal threat. They cannot justly be killed preventatively.

Procedures for just preventative killing are well established in police practice. Such killing can be just when it is truly preventative (when the police use of force is a last resort against a genuine threat). Proper policing treats people justly, even when lethal force is used. In such policing, there is discrimination between the dangerous and the harmless and between the guilty and the innocent. Force is used only as a last resort. If the aim of the operation is achievable only through excessive or unjust force, then the aim is foregone. A set of guidelines for the just use of lethal force preventatively was developed to direct soldiers in their use of force against informal combatants in Northern Ireland. Since 1969 in Northern Ireland, the British Army has provided aid to the civil power: its soldiers have been used in the role of police. To guide military personnel in that role, rules about when to open fire were developed and given to all soldiers on a card. Though these guidelines were drawn up for a situation of informal war and terrorism, they nonetheless set out the requirements of the just use of lethal force preventatively. These rules are guidelines for the just killing of a person on the grounds of prevention and, as such, are worth quoting in full:

INSTRUCTIONS FOR OPENING FIRE IN NORTHERN IRELAND

General Rules
1. In all situations you are to use the minimum force necessary. FIREARMS MUST ONLY BE USED AS A LAST RESORT.
2. Your weapon must always be made safe: that is, NO live round is to be carried in the breech and in the case of automatic weapons the working parts are to be forward, unless you are

ordered to carry a live round in the breech or you are about to fire.

Challenging

3. A challenge MUST be given before opening fire unless:

   a. to do so would increase the risk of death or grave injury to you or to any other person;
   b. you or others in the immediate vicinity are being engaged by terrorists. ˙

4. You are to challenge by shouting 'ARMY: STOP OR I FIRE' or words to that effect.

Opening Fire

5. You may only open fire against a person:

   a. if he* is committing or about to commit an act LIKELY TO ENDANGER LIFE, AND THERE IS NO OTHER WAY TO PREVENT THE DANGER. The following are some examples of acts where life could be endangered, dependent always upon the circumstances.
      (i) firing or being about to fire a weapon
      (ii) planting, detonating or throwing an explosive device (including a petrol bomb)
      (iii) deliberately driving a vehicle at a person and there is no other way of stopping him*;
   b. if you know that he* has just killed or injured any person by such means and he* does not surrender if challenged, and THERE IS NO OTHER WAY TO MAKE AN ARREST.

6. If you have to fire you should:

   a. fire only aimed shots;
   b. fire no more rounds than are necessary;
   c. take all reasonable precautions not to injure anyone other than your target.

* 'She' can be read instead of 'he' if applicable.[28]

Much killing of combatants in war can be justified as preventative killing: persons are killed in circumstances in which they, as individuals, present a threat. The killing of them in such situations is a response to their actions. They are still treated as persons. Though they are killed, they are not treated unjustly. However, the principle of self-defence alone cannot justify all the killing in war that the current law of war allows. Not all killing in war is self-defensive or other-defensive, that is, as a response to a direct and immediate threat to life. The dramatically increased proportion of civilian casualties is a widely noted feature of war in the mid- and late-twentieth-century, but the killing of members of armed forces also changed in its nature. There were long periods of warfare in which nearly all killing of soldiers in wars could be justified as preventative killing. Soldiers were killed when they themselves were attempting to kill others. This era of warfare lasted from prehistory into the twentieth century. Even the First World War had, in trench fighting, much killing that was preventative. It was only as technology changed the nature of warfare in the twentieth century that the killing of combatants could become more and more non-preventative. Longer-range and more destructive weapons allowed the killing of members of armed forces who were not at that moment engaged in combatancy. Such killing in war of soldiers who at that moment pose no threat cannot, however, be justified by the justification of preventative killing. Self-defence cannot justify all the killing of combatants that is held to be legal in war today. Soldiers away from the scene of fighting are only a potential threat. Those who constitute only a potential threat cannot be justly killed preventatively any more than can those who contribute to a present threat (suppliers, munitions workers, tax-payers).

Consensual killing

A third instance in which killing may be just is that of consensual killing. An informed adult, *compos mentis*, can consent to death, or to the risk of death. Examples of consensual killing include duels, voluntary euthanasia, assisted suicide and violent sports. In such cases, certain conditions are required for death or the risk of death to be just; these include that the person be adult, of sound mind and free from duress at the moment that they consent to death, or to the risk of death. The justification of consensual killing fits with the characterization of the soldier as depersonalized, in the role of an instrument of war. This characterization of the combatant was foreshadowed in Aquinas's attempt to base the PNCI on the different social roles occupied by different people. This idea was developed by Grotius and Vattel (and stated famously by Rousseau). The rules of the game are that only those in the role of combatant may be attacked and killed at almost any time in war. The justification of consensual killing provides a normative grounding for this characterization for the combatant. If soldiers had volunteered to occupy that role, knowing the rules of the game, then their deaths in war could be justified on the grounds of their consent.

A volunteer soldier can consent to be treated as an instrument of war, to have his life imperiled by his commanders or the enemy's. As one writer puts is:

> By accepting money, or some other form of remuneration, the volunteer soldiers enters into a contract with the state ... when the nation marches off to war, the soldier would be violating his contract were he to refuse to fight, and perhaps die, in the service of his country.[29]

The key clause of this contract is the one Lt. Gen. Sir John Hackett terms the 'unlimited liability clause' whereby the soldier commits himself to the point of death.[30] A contemporary philosopher who focuses on the justification of consensual killing is Paul Woodruff. He rejects the justification of preventative killing as a basis for killing soldiers (and sparing civilians). In its place he focuses on the claim that soldiers have placed themselves in danger of attack:

> Military actions against military people are excusable on the following grounds: the lives that are taken from soldiers who have chosen to expose themselves to extreme danger – they have taken up arms. Unlike civilians, soldiers go into the danger of war in full knowledge and with the intent to face that danger ... Soldiers who kill soldiers may claim that the people they kill are responsible for their own fates, and this ... is a good excuse.[31]

Consent, of some form, is needed for the rules of this game to be just. Many combatants have agreed to the risk of death in war. Justice permits the non-preventative killing of willing combatants in war. If all combatants have consented to the risk of death in war, war can be just. For war, then, would be between consenting adults. The current laws of war (which permit the killing of regular combatants when they are not engaged in an act of combatancy) would be fully just. In the age before 1789, when European armies were professional, the justification of consensual killing may have covered all killing of combatants in war.[32] With the introduction of conscription, however, this justification was rendered problematic. Combatants may be acting under duress or ignorance if they have been coerced to join armed forces or manipulated by deception and conditioning into volunteering. Does conscription undermine the justification of consensual killing? Or have conscripts who take up arms thereby acquiesced to their risk of death? The question of the degree of consent (or acquiescence) sufficient to render just the non-punitive, non-preventative killing of combatants in war attracts a wide variety of answers. Woodruff himself believes that such conscripts have acquiesced to their treatment:

> That even conscripts take up arms under conscription (which involves a threat) does not undermine the excuse. Even conscripts act, as most civilians do not, to cause danger to themselves in war ... *The responsibility of the victim for his plight* is what differentiates soldiers morally from civilians.[33]

At the other extreme is the claim that few soldiers in the modern world can be said to have made a free choice to go to war.[34] Almost all combatants, it could be claimed, can be described as coerced. Poverty, conditioning, state propaganda and 'patriotic duty' push many to volunteer. This occurs even in liberal democracies where volunteers come disproportionately from the least well off and least educated. One writer goes so far as to claim that

> the experience of life in an open, democratic and generally just state can also prove a coercive factor when it comes to citizens volunteering or consenting to serve in the armed forces. People come to assume that the state is in the right and accept without too much question the cause for war and the obligation to serve the country.[35]

Between the extremes lies a position that accepts that many conscripts may be judged to have consented or acquiesced to their treatment in war as instruments rather than people. On volunteering to join, or acquiescing to conscription, they agree to be the human instruments of war. Some may agree to be treated as such regardless of the justice of their country's cause. Others may feel that the contract no longer binds them because their state is fighting a manifestly unjust war.[36] It is then only in countries where severe pressures are placed on conscripts or where the conscript is too young to consent does the justification of consensual killing run into trouble.

If this is accepted, the relevant distinction is not that between conscripts and volunteers. Rather it is between, on the one hand, volunteers and conscripts with a real chance to refuse military service and, on the other, conscripts on whom unbearable pressure has been placed or who are too young to consent. An example of unbearable pressure may be the threat to execute the unwilling conscript or his family. A conscript who submits to military discipline rather than lose his life (or the lives of his family) can hardly be held to have consented to his non-punitive, non-preventative killing in war. Nor can a child-soldier.

An explanation of the PNCI that seems to contain elements of both consent and prevention is that of Barrie Paskins and Michael Dockrill. They take a Humean approach that starts from the acknowledgment that justice requires people to be treated as ends, rather than as means to an end. They write:

> Some people, in virtue of *what they are doing*, can regard death in battle as, however terrible, neither more nor less than suffering the consequences of their own actions. Some other people who might be killed in war do not have this thought open to them. The distinction coincides pretty closely with that between combatant and non-combatant. For the combatant must recognise that death in war would be a fate internally connected with the activity in virtue of which he is a combatant. But, except in very special circumstances, this does not apply to the non-combatant ... Because of the internal connection between combatancy and being killed, a combatant has the *option and opportunity* to regard the prospect of death in war as meaningful: written into what he is doing is a connection with being killed that gives his own death a meaning ... But the death in war of a noncombatant does not have any such guaranteed meaning.[37]

However, the issue is not whether there is a guarantee of meaning in killing a person but whether there is a guarantee of justice. The issue is not whether the killing of a person in war is 'internally connected' with that person's activities but whether it is a just response to that person's activities. If it is not, then it should not be done. To justify killing people by reference to 'what they are doing' is to try to apply the justification of preventative killing. Such preventative killing, to be just, must be in response to the acts or threats of the person killed. It does not permit killing other than in cases of immediate mortal threat. If Paskins and Dockrill's explanation is one in terms of consent, then it is crucial that the victim have consented (or at least acquiesced) to the risk of death. If Paskins and Dockrill's combatants had the 'option and opportunity' to decline to be combatants in war, then their killing in war may be justified as consensual.[38] They have then consented to be members of armed forces and to be treated in whatever way that the laws of war currently allow. They have knowingly accepted the risk of death in war and cannot complain when it happens. If they did not have the option and opportunity to decline, then they may not be justly killed at any time in war. A forced conscript or child-soldier may justly be killed preventatively (in self- or other-defence) but not consensually. They may justly be killed only when placing the life of another in mortal jeopardy.

The combatant

Different combatants may justly be killed for different reasons at different times. Volunteers and willing conscripts may justly be killed consensually at any time in war within the existing 'rules of the game'. The justification of consensual killing can justify the killing in war of all who consent to wear a military uniform. The justification of preventative killing can justify the killing of those who are combatant, regardless of pressures on them to fight. Any combatant, even an unwilling conscript or child-soldier, may justly be killed preventatively (in strict self- or other-defence). The other justifications, of punitive and charitable killing, have little application in war. However, the laws of war, as they currently stand, are founded on an acceptance that those in the role of combatant may, in war, be treated as instruments. They may be killed with no claim that they as individuals deserve it and they may themselves kill without incurring blame. No distinction is made between willing combatants and unwilling conscripts.

In the Falklands and in Kuwait respectively, British and American troops (who had chosen to join the armed forces of their countries) faced largely conscript armies. Conscription may not raise the issue of consent in a country such as Argentina where men may refuse military service at no risk to their lives. In such countries, conscripts may be thought to have acquiesced in their occupation of the role of combatant and their treatment as instruments. The problem of consent arises with countries such as Iraq and with much contemporary informal war, of which the pressing and abduction of young males into military service has become a feature. Those threatened with death (of themselves or their families) cannot be said to have consented or acquiesced to the role of instrument. Were any of the Iraqi soldiers killed in the 'Highway of Death' massacre at the end of Desert Storm unwilling conscripts? If so, then justice restricts the use of lethal force in such cases to prevention: only those actually engaged in acts of combatancy may be targeted (and then only as a last resort, if no other means are available). It is difficult to justify the 'Highway of Death' killings as preventative. There are other clearer instances in which consent or acquiescence to the role of combatant cannot be construed. Child-soldiers may justly be killed only in situations of the prevention of serious harm by them.

The civilian

Why may civilians not be killed in war? It is justice that requires that innocent civilians should not be killed in war. As innocents, the justification of punitive killing does not apply to them. As non-combatants, the justification of preventative killing does not apply to them. As civilians, the justification of consensual killing does not apply to them. They have not agreed to occupy the role of instrument; they have not consented to be treated as means to a military or political end; they have done, and are doing, nothing that warrants attacks on them. It is then the most fundamental principles of justice which require that civilians be immune from targeting in war. Civilians may not be targeted in war whatever the consequences.[39]

They are the same principles of justice which demand that no one should be punished except for their own crime, that innocent life should never be taken as a means towards an end, and that the individuality of all should be acknowledged and respected. Damage to civilian property can be outweighed by a proportionate good achieved but, if humans are respected as separate individuals, then the loss of a civilian life can never be outweighed by a good end achieved. Death is different to any other harm; it cannot be offset by any good. It is unjust to trade in human life, to balance and trade off innocent human lives against any good. It is wrong to kill an innocent person so that another innocent life may be saved. It is wrong to kill an innocent person even so that an entire nation may be saved (as the Athenians did to Socrates during the Peloppenesian War, as the Jews did to Jesus under Roman occupation). The stories of the trial of Socrates and the crucifixion of Jesus express Western civilization's most fundamental principle of justice that such sacrifice of innocent lives to a good cause is wrong. It fails to treat the individual person as justice demands they should be treated.

Yet innocent civilians are killed in war. Civilians are killed in all wars (and never more so than now). The killing of civilians in war is often neither accidental nor coincidental (it is not accidental as it is not an unforeseen occurrence; it is not coincidental as it is not an event occurring simultaneously with, but causally unconnected to, another event such as the destruction of military targets). Rather, the killing of civilians in war is collateral, that is, it occurs parallel to, or side-by-side with, the destruction of military targets. It may be probable, or even certain, that civilians will die as a result of the military operation. The phrase 'collateral damage' is an admission that civilian deaths were neither unexpected nor arising by chance; rather they were the foreseen effect of certain military acts.

Western thought has developed a method of justifying a foreseen wrong such as the collateral killing of innocent civilians in war. This is the principle of 'double effect' which has its roots in Aquinas's writings and which has recently been the subject of a revival of interest in moral philosophy.[40] The principle is evident in international law's prohibitions on direct attacks on civilians and on indirect attacks which cause 'incidental loss of civilian life ... excessive in relation to the concrete and direct military advantage'.[41] The principle of 'double effect' starts from an acknowledgment that the deliberate taking of innocent human life as a means to an end is always forbidden. To take the life of an innocent human being as a means to an end is never justifiable. However, the principle of 'double effect' suggests that the non-accidental taking of innocent human life can still be morally justified if certain conditions apply. In the case of a military act which leads to two effects (one of which is the killing of innocent civilians), the conditions are four. First, the act itself must be good or at least indifferent (attacks on military objectives in war satisfy this requirement).

Secondly, the evil effect must not be intended or desired (only the good effect of destroying the military objective must be intended).[42] Thirdly, the killing of innocent civilians must not be a means to the end of military victory (it must not contribute to military or political victory, to disheartening the enemy, to increasing public pressure on the leadership). Fourthly, the contribution of the military effect of the action to overall victory must be sufficient to warrant the unintended evil effect of the same action, that is, the killing of innocent civilians (a small or trivial military benefit does not warrant the inflicting of great harm on civilians, even when that harm is unintended).

The principle of 'double effect' then is never thought to justify unlimited collateral damage. It does not permit the disproportionate killing of innocent civilians in order to achieve some military aim. Rather, it permits only the killing of civilians when such killing is thought proportionate to the end achieved (if the deaths of civilians would be too numerous, then the act must not be done). The fourth condition is a vitally necessary prohibition on acts which have passed the test of the first three conditions. It is the fourth condition which prohibits the dropping of a nuclear weapon on a city of one million in order to kill a few thousand combatants or terrorists stationed there. Without that condition, the principle of double effect provides carte blanche to bring about (as a side effect) harm out of all proportion to the good that one seeks.

This fourth condition has been the subject of much debate.[43] Both sides to the debate agree that there must be a proportionately grave reason for the act which has bad as well as good results. The greater the harm done as a side effect, the greater must be the good sought. At issue though is whether the required balancing be precise or rough. On one side is Kaufman who stresses that the fourth condition of the principle of double effect does not take a consequentialist, cost-balancing approach to the good and evil effects. Indeed, such weighing up of good and evil in order to decide how to act is the very approach rejected by the principle of double effect. Instead, says Kaufman, the principle of double effect requires only that 'the harm produced be roughly proportionate to the good ... It is not even required that the good outweigh the bad, only that they be in the same ballpark, of the same proportion'.[44] The balancing of good and evil results, far from being an essential component of the principle of double effect, is the very thing the principle rejects.

The problem with this approach is that it seems callously indifferent to the killing of civilians in war as a foreseen side effect of one's action. Once an act is performed for a proportionately grave reason, then the collateral killing of civilians need not be weighed up and balanced against the expected good outcome. There need be no strict balancing of the harm done to civilians against the good achieved; it is enough that there is a good reason for doing the act. Indeed, Kaufman points out that killing two or three attackers in self-defence has long been held to be permissible by proponents of the principle of double effect. To kill two or three hundred enemy civilians as a side effect of an act to save the lives of a hundred of one's own people is to take a callous and uncaring attitude to the lives of innocent civilians. Whereas justice prohibits the killing of innocent people even if it would maximize the overall good, Kaufman's interpretation of the principle of double effect does the opposite: it sanctions an act which kills innocent people with no requirement that more good than harm come of it. This seems both extraordinary and unjust.

It is no surprise that many philosophers interpret his condition more precisely. They require that the harm done collaterally is matched or exceeded by the good achieved. As Judith Lichtenberg suggests, in assessing whether an act should be done, the number of civilians killed and injured as a (unintended though foreseen) result of it simply must matter.[45] The main problem with this second approach is that it appears calculating in its assessment of whether the foreseen but unintended killing of a certain number of civilians is offset by the goal that it is hoped will be attained. Though the civilian deaths must be unintended, this approach comes close to trading innocent lives off against some other good or right end. This is the very attitude forbidden by the PNCI and by the most fundamental principles of justice which the principle is supposed to strengthen.

There is a further problem with the 'precise' interpretation of the fourth condition (it is not a problem for Kaufman's 'ballpark' approach which remains indifferent to whether more good than harm comes of the military action which kills civilians collaterally). What is the good that comes from an attack on a military objective, a side effect of which is the death of innocent civilians? The good is some tactical advantage: yet this is of instrumental value only. Its worth cannot be assessed without reference to the *ad bellum* end for which the war is waged by that party to the conflict. Yet, if the focus is switched to the strategic level, then the end for which civilians are killed as collateral damage may not be clearly good or right; indeed, one party to the conflict firmly believes that end to be wrong or bad.[46] Not only is the goodness of the ultimate end in doubt, but so too is the probability of attaining it.[47] Chance, as Clauswitz asserted, is essential to the nature of war. In war, no good at all may come from the harm that is done. In fact, no good at all will come from the harm that is done by one side (the side that loses). At least one side sacrifices the lives of innocent civilians for no good or right outcome. From a strategic perspective, civilians killed collaterally by the losing side are, ultimately, killed for nothing.[48]

These then are two interpretations of the proportionality condition of the principle of double effect; one seems callous in its attitude to innocent civilian life, the other calculating. One sanctions the killing of people with no requirement either that death is a just treatment of them as individuals or that more good than harm comes of it. The other weighs up good and evil outcomes in a way that is anathema to the justice-based approach to morality which the principle of double effect is supposed to support. There is also a problem that both approaches share. This time it is a problem of quality and not of quantity.[49] The principle of double effect is held to permit an act to save one's own combatants, even if a side effect of the act is the killing of enemy civilians: saving combatants is a proportionately grave reason, and therefore some harmful side effects are permitted if unintended. This fails to take account of the different status of combatants and civilians. Combatants are treated in international law as instruments; civilians remain persons.[50] Given this, it does not seem right for saving one's own combatants to be the proportionately grave reason for an act that kills civilians collaterally. Yet the usual case in war is that civilian life is lost in an action designed to save combatant life; rarely is civilian life lost in an action designed to save other civilian life. Civilians ought not to be killed as a side effect of an action to save one's own combatants.

The conclusion must be that the principle of double effect is unconvincing in its application to the 'collateral' killing of civilians in war. The attempt to apply it to the collateral killing of civilians in war reveals only the weaknesses of the principle and its openness to abuse. We are responsible not only for that which we directly intend; we are culpable also for our negligence and for the foreseeable avoidable consequences of our acts. To be excusable, the deaths of civilians in war must be accidental. The deaths must be, not only unintended but also unforeseen and reasonably unforeseeable (accidental killing is both unintended and unforeseen; collateral killing is foreseen).[51] Where the deaths of civilians is a near certainty or great probability, it is not accidental. For an attack on a military objective to be just, there must be, not only an intention but also a likelihood of no civilian deaths occurring as a result.

This view is shared by Richard Hull who denies that we can credibly 'not intend' a harmful effect of our action which we foresee *will* happen.[52] There must, he writes, 'be some likelihood that a harm will not occur if foresight is to mean anything other than intention'.[53] In a similar vein, Lichtenberg argues that, for there to be a difference in moral culpability between the collateral killing of civilians and the direct killing of civilians, there must be a difference in the probability and magnitude of civilian deaths between the two cases.[54] If the same number of civilians is just as likely to die in both cases, then the wrongness of the acts is the same. Camillo Bica too concludes that where the death of an innocent person 'is the foreseen though unintended effect of an act and *as probable* an occurrence as is the intended effect', an injustice has been committed.[55] The deaths of civilians in war, he concludes, must be not only unintended but unforeseen. This is the conclusion of this book too; for a military act to be just, it must be reasonably probable that no civilian will be killed.[56] In short, the bold claim made by the British Prime Minister, Tony Blair, which was quoted on p. 1 of this book ('we take every single measure we can to try to avoid civilian casualties'), must be a genuine one. Shifting the focus from the intended/unintended distinction to the foreseen/unforeseen distinction may seem like no improvement in clarity, but this is not so. Standards for culpable negligence in the loss of human life are set and operated by law courts in all countries.

A war, if it cannot be fought justly, must not be fought at all. How then to respond to aggressive and criminal regimes? Many such regimes meet with no belligerent response. It is not always the greatest injustice that provokes the most powerful response. The self-interest of nations must also motivate nations before they resort to war (indeed, the 'just war' approach sets out when war is permissible, not obligatory). War, then, is not the standard response to aggression and injustice. Most unjust acts by states meet with responses of other sorts (from diplomatic pressure to UN sanctions). But when war is chosen as a means to undo injustice, it must be waged justly. Attacks on innocent civilians are a gross injustice; but in combating civilian massacre or ethnic cleansing, further gross injustice must not be committed. Trading the lives of innocent civilians off against some good or just end is wrong regardless of whether that end is the lives of a greater number of innocent civilians or the achievement of a re-integrated Iraq or a Greater Serbia.

Can war be waged justly? Certainly a stricter adherence to the principle of civilian immunity raises problems for war as it is currently waged.[57] In some conflicts, though, genuine civilian immunity could come at the expense of civilian property. A strategy of destroying civilian property may be an effective and technologically feasible way of avoiding the unjust taking of human life. The new technologies of intelligence, guidance and munitions may some day permit the sort of victory of which a senior US Air Force commander dreams:

> Just think if after the first day, the Serbian people had awakened and their refrigerators weren't running, there was no water in their kitchens or bathrooms, no lights, no transportation system to get to work, and five or six military headquarters in Belgrade had disappeared, they would have asked: 'All of this after the first night? What is the rest of this [war] going to be like?'[58]

Currently, however, such attacks on civilian objects are unlawful. During the Kosovo war, it was reported that a NATO plan for a computer-based attack on Serbian leader Slobodan Milošvić's personal bank accounts was aborted for reasons that included the illegality of attacks on civilian objects.[59] Anyone concerned about the loss of civilian life in war must agree with Stauffer that 'hurting a civilian's pocketbook is more ethical than bombing him'.[60] An admirer of Douhet's theory of the decisive airborne blow against civilian morale, Colonel Charles Dunlap of the USAF proposes a strategy of attacks on the 'property of the sentient, adult population ... so long as it is not ... *indispensable* to human survival'.[61] Dunlap includes on the target list banks, financial institutions, 'Factories, plants, stores and shops ... or, indeed, *anything* not absolutely indispensable to noncombatant survival'.[62] Infrastructure providing the necessities of life, such as drinking water, ought not to be attacked. The drawback, as Dunlap notes, is that such a strategy could work only against 'accumulative wealth-oriented nations with assets to lose'.[63] Such attacks on civilian property would be welcome if they were accompanied by a genuine immunity for civilian life in war.

The history of the idea of non-combatant immunity shows how Western thought has struggled for nearly two millenia to reconcile war with its principles of justice. The PNCI has withstood the many challenges put to it in the era of total war. In the past two centuries, civilian immunity has been undermined by the rise of informal combatants and assaulted directly by the strategy, tactics and weapons of total war. Yet the distinction between combatant and non-combatant has remained crucial to modern international humanitarian law. It has been the lynchpin of attempts to limit the waste and cruelty of war. The PNCI has also remained central to Western thinking about the morality of war.

But the evolution of the principle is not yet complete. Justice demands further advances in the PNCI. First, the PNCI must prohibit not only the intentional killing of civilians but also the negligent or non-accidental killing of them. If the death of civilians is a reasonably foreseeable consequence of a military act (whether or not it is intended), then that act is unjust. Only then would civilians be immune in war. Secondly, consent to the occupation of the role of combatant is required. If such consent is absent, then the category of 'combatant' must be defined more precisely and more narrowly than before. In such cases, only those killing, or immediately about to kill, other human beings can be the targets of just lethal force. The ascription of combatant status must then be made on the basis of engagement in military operations. This requires only one judgment to be made: is the person at this moment engaged in a military attack or in a military operation immediately preparatory to an attack? Only if the answer is 'yes' does justice permit that person to be targeted in war.

Such a standard has been set for the Western world by its principles of justice and its focus on the individual. What justice requires in war is primarily discrimination between the combatant and the non-combatant. Such discrimination may be aided by developments in 'real-time' intelligence gathering, information-processing and precision-targeting. But only when such discrimination is achieved can war be just. Only when war is fought without killing innocent civilians can it be justified by Western thought in a manner that satisfies itself. Western thought can never have a convincing justification of the non-accidental killing of innocent civilians in war because only a justification of killing which focuses on the acts and attributes of the individual killed will suffice. As long as it kills innocent civilians non-accidentally, war remains violence against people, not as individuals, but as members of categories, such as nationality, institutional role and territorial location. Such violence can be justified, not on the basis of the guilt or combatancy or consent of those targeted, but only as a means to an end. To treat people as a means to an end, to kill those who have done nothing to deserve it so that some good or right end may come about, is something Western thought has long condemned and sought to prohibit.

Notes

1 Introduction

1. Erich Maria Remarque, *All Quiet on the Western Front*, trans. A. W. Wheen (London, 1970), 224.
2. Cohen quoted in 'NATO acknowledges civilian hit', www.cnn.com (16 April 1999); Blair quoted *Los Angeles Times*, front page, 15 April 1999.
3. Richard Shelly Hartigan, *The Forgotten Victim: a History of the Civilian* (Chicago, 1982), 21.
4. *Protocol Additional to the Geneva Conventions of 12 August 1949, and Relating to the Protection of Victims of International Armed Conflicts*, 1977. While some countries, including the USA, have not ratified this protocol, this portion is considered part of customary international law and therefore binding on all states. AP1 refers to both civilian life and civilian property. Civilian objects, which are to be immune from attack, are all things that are not military objectives (defined as 'those objects which by their nature, purpose, location or use make an effective contribution to military action and whose total or partial destruction, capture and neutralization, in the circumstances ruling at the time, offers a definite military advantage' (AP1, Chapter 3). The concern of this work is with attacks on civilian life in war, not civilian property. Indeed, it would welcome a reduction in the immunity from attack of civilian property if it were accompanied by a simultaneous increase in the immunity of civilian life from destruction as 'collateral damage'; see the concluding chapter.
5. *Convention of the Prohibition of the Use, Stockpiling, Production and Transfer of Anti-Personnel Mines and Their Destruction*, Oslo, 18 September 1997.
6. At least in its American formulation. The principle of military necessity has been defined by an authoritative US military publication as 'the principle which justifies measures *not forbidden* by international law which are indispensable for securing the prompt submission of the enemy' (*International Law – the Conduct of Armed Conflict and Air Operations*, Air Force Pamphlet 110–31, Washington DC: Department of the Air Force, 19 November 1976, 1–5–6; italics added). It continues: 'the principle of military necessity is not the 19th century German doctrine of *Kriegsraeson*, asserting that military necessity could justify any measures – even in violation of the laws of war – when the necessities of the situation purportedly justified it'. The principle of military necessity is clearly not permission to do anything that is militarily useful or even crucial for victory. As direct attacks on civilians are prohibited by international law, the principle of military necessity does not clash with the PNCI.
7. Geoffrey Best, *War and Law since 1945* (Oxford, 1994), 27.

8. 'The Challenge of Peace: God's Promise and Our Response', The Pastoral Letter on War and Peace, 1983, in Jean Bethke Elshtain (ed.), *Just War Theory* (Oxford, 1992), 77–168, esp. 123 and 153.
9. For instance, Richard Norman, *Ethics, Killing and War* (Cambridge, 1995).
10. 'The Challenge of Peace', 150.
11. John C. Ford, 'The Morality of Obliteration Bombing' (1944), reprinted in Richard A. Wasserstrom, *War and Morality* (Belmont, CA, 1970), 23.
12. This moral equality of soldiers is defended by Michael Walzer, *Just and Unjust Wars* (New York, 1977), 34–47.
13. A point made by Norman, 68.
14. Best, 262.
15. Gourvenec, Diana, 'The Combatant/Non-combatant Distinction in Just War Theory: Does It Have a Moral Basis?', M.A. Thesis, University of Essex, 1992, 12–13.
16. Robert H. Thouless, *Straight Thinking in War-time* (London, 1942), 138.
17. That the 'just war' approach must be capable of yielding negative conclusions (criticizing a particular war as unjust and one which must not be fought) is a point forcefully made by the pacifist John H. Yoder, 'Surrender: a Moral Imperative', *The Review of Politics* 48:4 (Fall 1986), 567–95.
18. I believe that Best and Hartigan misinterpret the development of the PNCI when they see the underlying motive as one in terms of 'the good' and not justice. Because of this, they see too much consistency in the development of the principle over the past 2000 years. They also see the principle as a successful representation of its underlying aims, when it is not. If the evolution of the principle is interpreted as motivated largely by concerns of justice then it will be seen that these concerns were never satisfied. Indeed the history of the idea of non-combatant immunity reveals that the Western world has never succeeded in justifying war to its own high standard.

2   Guilt and Punitive War 1

1. *Quaker Faith and Practice* (London, 1995), 24.03.
2. Augustine, *City of God*, ed. David Knowles (Harmondsworth, 1972), xvi.
3. Joan D. Tooke, *The Just War in Aquinas and Grotius* (London, 1965), 1.
4. O. L. Spaulding and H. Nickerton, *Ancient and Medieval Warfare* (London, 1994), 193.
5. Tooke, 3.
6. Tooke, 4; an influential interpretation of the pre-Constantinian Christians as pacifist was forwarded by Roland Bainton, *Christian Attitudes towards War and Peace: a Historical Survey and Critical Re-evaluation* (London, 1961), Ch. 5, 'The Pacifism of the Early Church'; the contrary interpretation is taken by James Turner Johnson, *The Quest for Peace: Three Moral Traditions in Western Cultural History* (Princeton, 1987), Ch. 1.

7. F. H. Russell, *The Just War in the Middle Ages* (Cambridge, 1975), 23.
8. *The Political Writings of St. Augustine*, ed. Henry Paolucci (Chicago, 1962), 1–2.
9. Augustine, *Political Writings*, 60.
10. Augustine, *Quaestiones in Heptateuchum* 6.10, quoted Hartigan, *Forgotten Victim*, 29, italics added.
11. Russell, 18.
12. Augustine, *Political Writings*, 138, quoting Augustine, *City of God*, book XIX ch. 7, italics added.
13. Augustine, *Political Writings*, 164, quoting Augustine, *Contra Faustum* XXII.
14. A point made by R. S. Hartigan, 'St. Augustine on War and Killing: the Problem of the Innocent', *Journal of the History of Ideas* 27:2 (1966), 195–204, esp. 199.
15. Augustine, like many Christian authorities, also justified slavery in the same peculiar manner. Though contrary to the basic equality of all men as human beings, slavery is a consequence of sin and therefore tolerable as an institution (though not necessarily approved by God). Augustine justifies slavery first as a due and proper punishment of the slave for his vice and, secondly, as a benefit to him in that it curbs his vices. Such a justification suffers from the same obvious deficiencies as the attempt to justify war as punishment of wickedness and prevention of further wickedness: not all slaves qualified for such punishment and no attempt is made to distinguish those who do from those who do not. Again, Augustine's ultimate line of defence is the doctrine of original sin: all are wicked and none can complain if targeted in war or enslaved; see Tooke, 83; Knowles in Augustine, *City of God*, xviii.
16. This doctrine was the Christian fathers' most significant contribution to political theory yet, as Tooke writes, 'its theological and metaphysical truth was accounted of rather less importance than its political usefulness to the parties involved'; Tooke, 85.
17. The just war requirement of 'proper authority' rested originally on the doctrine of the divine right of kings (the 'proper' authority is God's authority, delegated to the ruler as his agent on earth). Yet, though the original basis of this 'just war' principle has crumbled, the requirement of proper authority has remained in the 'just war' framework, lacking the immense force of the original.
18. Russell, 21.
19. Russell, 25.
20. Hartigan, *The Forgotten Victim*, 33.
21. Hartigan, *The Forgotten Victim*, 33.
22. Tooke, 12.
23. Russell, 22.
24. Augustine, *City of God*, 32.
25. Russell, 20.
26. James Turner Johnson, *Ideology, Reason and the Limitation of War: Religious and Secular Concepts 1200–1740* (Princeton, 1975), 40–1.

27. Philippe Contamine, *War in the Middle Ages*, trans. Michael Jones (Oxford, 1984), 265.
28. Contamine, 269.
29. Tooke, 2.
30. Contamine, 269.
31. Russell, 12.
32. Russell, 217–18.
33. A point made by Tooke, 115–24.
34. Thomas Head and Richard Landes (eds), *The Peace of God: Social Violence and Religious Response in France around the Year 1000* (Ithaca, 1992), 6.
35. Head and Landes, 1.
36. Head and Landes, 13.
37. Christian Lauranson-Rosaz, 'Peace from the Mountains: the Auvergnat Origins of the Peace of God', in Head and Landes, 104–34, esp. 114.
38. Amy G. Remensnyder, 'Pollution, Purity and Peace: an Aspect of Social Reform between the Late Tenth Century and 1076', in Head and Landes, 280–307, esp. 284.
39. Remensnyder, 280.
40. Remensnyder, 301.
41. R. I. Moore, 'Postscript: the Peace of God and the Social Revolution', in Head and Landes (eds), 308–26, esp. 311.
42. Acts of the Council of Charroux (989), trans Thomas Head, in Head and Landes, 327–8.
43. Hans-Werner Goetz, 'Protection of the Church, Defense of the Law, and Reform: On the Purposes and Character of Peace of God, 989–1038', in Head and Landes, 259–79, esp. 264.
44. Goetz, 264.
45. Goetz, 268.
46. Goetz, 270.
47. Head and Landes, 31.
48. Georges Duby, *The Three Orders: Feudal Society Imagine*, trans. A. Goldhammer (Chicago: 1980).
49. M. H. Keen, *The Laws of War in the Late Middle Ages* (London, 1965), 2–3, 189–90.

3   Guilt and Punitive War 2

1. Russell, 179. The Decretalists were twelfth-century canon lawyers studying the decretals of Pope Gregory.
2. Russell, 84–5.
3. Tooke, 13.
4. Russell, 60.
5. Russell, 58–9.
6. Russell, 87.
7. Russell, 89.
8. Russell, 113.

9. Russell, 215.
10. Russell, 89.
11. Russell, 89–90.
12. Russell, 219.
13. Russell, 106–8.
14. Russell, 155.
15. Russell, 234.
16. Draper sees these penitentials as a lingering relic of the Early Church's more pacifist attitude to war and also as evidence of its persistent 'agony of conscience' over the matter: G. I. A. D. Draper, 'Penitential Disciplines and Public Wars in the Middle Ages', *International Review of the Red Cross* (April and May 1961).
17. Contamine, 266.
18. Contamine, 267.
19. Russell, 34–5.
20. Richard A. Preston, Sydney F. Wise and Herman O. Werner, *Men in Arms: a History of Warfare and Its Interelationship with Western Society* (London, 1962), 48.
21. Preston *et al.*, 66.
22. J. F. Verbruggen, *The Art of Warfare in Western Europe during the Middle Ages: From the Eight Century to 1340*, trans. Sumner Willard and S. C. M. Southern (Oxford, 1977), 23.
23. Contamine, 31.
24. Preston *et al.*, 66.
25. C. W. C. Oman, *The Art of War in the Middle Ages* (Ithaca, 1953), 63–4.
26. *Ordric Vitalis* vi.241, trans. Margaret Chibnall, quoted Contamine, 256.
27. Russell, 179.

4 Social Roles and Feudal War

1. Leo Tolstoy, *The Kingdom of God Is within You*, ed. and trans. Leo Wiener (London, 1905), 41.
2. Anthony Kenny, *Aquinas* (Oxford, 1980), 2.
3. Kenny, 8.
4. Tooke, 27–8.
5. Thomas Aquinas, *Summa Theologiae* Part 2 (Second Part), Question 40, Article 1, trans. Fathers of the English Dominican Province (London: Burns Oates & Washbourne, 1917–22); the *Summa Theologiae* is usually cited by part, question, article, and (if applicable) objection or reply; thus the extract cited becomes II.II Q.40, Art.1.
6. *Summa Theologiae*, II.II Q.40, Art.1.
7. Aquinas's political theory, with its emphasis on the common good, limits the authority of the ruler: law is not law unless it serves the common weal. In this way, Aquinas not only mitigated the bleak pessimism of Augustine's political theory but also foreshadowed modern liberal thought's concern with limits on governmental power.

8. *Summa Theologiae*, II.II Q.40, Art.1.
9. *Summa Theologiae*, II.II Q.83, Art.8, ad.3 (that is, Part 2, Second Part, Question 83 article 8 argument 3).
10. *Summa Theologiae*, II.II Q.64, Art.3.
11. *Summa Theologiae*, II.II Q.64, Art.5.
12. Although Aquinas did mention that war should be fought even for the good of those against whom one fights, there is no attempt by him to relate warfare to the international community as a whole; see Tooke, 27.
13. Russell, 290–1.
14. Aquinas's definition of 'just cause' rules out the possibility of simultaneous justice: 'a just cause is required, namely that those who are attacked should be attacked because they deserve it on account of some fault': *Summa Theologiae*, II.II Q.40 Art. 1.
15. Tooke, 126.
16. Contamine, 275.
17. Contamine, 297–8.
18. Jean de Bueil, *Le Jouvencel* ii.21 quoted in C. T. Allmand (ed.), *War, Literature and Politics in the Late Middle Ages* (Liverpool, 1976), 36.
19. Verbruggen, 60.
20. See Johnson, *Ideology*.
21. Tooke, 100n. 19.
22. Russell, 224–5.
23. Russell, 227–8.
24. Russell, 233.
25. *Summa Theologiae*, II.II Q.40 Art.2.
26. Tooke, 23.
27. Russell, 282.
28. Tooke, 68.
29. *Summa Theologiae*, II.II Q.64 Art.6.
30. *Summa Theologiae*, II.II Q.64 Art.6 ad 2.
31. Though it has its roots in Aquinas, systematic usage of the principle did not occur until the sixteenth century; see Joseph Mangan, 'An Historical Analysis of the Principle of Double Effect', *Theological Studies* 10 (1949), 41–61; James F. Keenan, SJ, 'The Function of the Principle of Double Effect', *Theological Studies* 54 (1993), 294–315.
32. *Summa Theologiae*, II.II Q.64 Art.7.
33. 'The Challenge of Peace', 150.
34. Verbruggen, 26.
35. Contamine, 71.
36. Donald Featherstone, *Warriors and Warfare in Ancient and Medieval Times* (London, 1997), 255.
37. Anna Comnena, *The Alexiad of Princess Anna Comnena* (1148), trans. E. A. S. Dawes (London, 1967), 255–6.
38. Russell, 243.
39. Russell, 241–2.
40. Russell, 156–8.

41. Russell, 243–4.
42. Preston *et al.*, 74.
43. Spaulding and Nickerson, 379.
44. Featherstone, 244–5.
45. Verbruggen, 99.
46. Contamine, 258.
47. J. H. Yoder, *The Original Revolution: Essays on Christian Pacifism* (Scottdale, PA, 1971), 77.

5 Innocence and Modern War

1. Herbert Spencer, *Principles of Ethics* (London, 1892), Book 1 Part 2 Ch. 8 Section 152.
2. Francisco de Vitoria, *Political Writings*, ed. Anthony Pagden and Jeremy Lawrance (Cambridge, 1994); Bernice Hamilton, *Political Thought in the Sixteenth Century* (Oxford, 1963).
3. Hamilton, 184–6.
4. Preston *et al.*, 89.
5. H. W. Koch, *Medieval Warfare* (London, 1978), 182.
6. Koch, *Medieval Warfare*, 188.
7. Johnson, *Ideology* 209.
8. Katherine Nell MacFarlane, 'Isidore of Seville on the Pagan Gods', *Transactions of the American Philosophical Society*, vol. 70 part 3 (1980), 3–10.
9. Hartigan, *Forgotten Victim*, 43.
10. Johnson, *Ideology*, 57.
11. Johnson, *Ideology*, 55.
12. Vitoria, *De jure belli*, 10, 11, in Francisco de Vitoria, *The Principles of Political and International Law in the Work of Francisco de Vitoria*, intro. by Antonio Truyol Serra (Madrid, 1946), 80; Johnson, *Ideology*, 157–63.
13. Vitoria, *De jure belli*, 13, 13 and 44, in *Principles*, 79–81.
14. Hamilton, 142.
15. Johnson, *Ideology*, 55.
16. Vitoria, *De jure belli*, 32, in *Principles*, 86–7.
17. *De indis* sect. III, 7, in Johnson, *Ideology*, 188.
18. Hamilton, 152.
19. Vitoria, *De jure belli*, 59, in *Principles*, 97.
20. Hamilton, 155.
21. Hartigan, *Forgotten Victim*, 95.
22. Vitoria, *De jure belli*, 35, in *Principles*, 88.
23. Hartigan, *Forgotten Victim*, 87.
24. Vitoria, *De jure belli*, 36, in Johnson, *Ideology*, 196.
25. Hartigan, *Forgotten Victim*, 90.
26. Vitoria, *De jure belli*, 37, in J. B. Scott (ed.), *The Classics of International Law* (Washington, DC, 1917), 163–87, esp. 178, italics added.

27. Gabriel Palmer-Fernández, 'Civilian Populations in War, Targeting of', in *Encyclopedia of Applied Ethics*, vol. 1 (San Diego, 1998), 509–25, esp. 515.
28. Vitoria, *De jure belli*, 37, in *Principles*, 88.
29. Vitoria's distinction between standards of conduct in wars of certain justice and in wars of doubtful justice is ironic given that, as he was writing, the Catholic Church was losing its status as the one body with the potential to make authoritative and objective judgments on the justice of a war.
30. Hartigan, *Forgotten Victim*, 84.
31. Hartigan, *Forgotten Victim*, 86.
32. Vitoria, *De jure belli*, 20–1, in *Principles*, 82.
33. Johnson, *Ideology*, 179.
34. Vitoria, *De jure belli*, 23–6, in *Principles*, 83.
35. Suárez, *On War*, sect. VI, 8, in Johnson, *Ideology*, 182.
36. Tooke, 191.
37. Tooke, 186.
38. Tooke, 187.

6   Non-combatancy and Formal War

1. Attributed to the Irish Prime Minister (and economist) by Fergus Finlay, *Snakes and Ladders* (Dublin, 1998), 16.
2. H. W. Koch, *The Rise of Modern Warfare 1618–1815* (London, 1981), 67.
3. Koch, *Rise Of Modern Warfare*, 81.
4. Koch, *Rise Of Modern Warfare*, 18.
5. Preston *et al.*, 129.
6. Vattel's is the first work examined here not to have been written in Latin.
7. Quoted in Palmer-Fernández, 'Civilian Populations in War', 510.
8. Grotius, *De Jure Belli ac Pacis*, trans. L. R. Loomis, with an intro. by P. E. Corbett (Roslyn, NY, 1949), 10–11.
9. Tooke, 202–3.
10. Grotius, Bk 3 Ch. 11 Sect. 7, 353.
11. Tooke, 197–8.
12. Grotius, Bk 3 Ch. 11 Sect. 16, 357.
13. Grotius, Bk 2 Ch. 1 Sect. 2, 72.
14. Grotius, Bk 2 Ch. 1 Sect. 17–18, 77.
15. Emmerich de Vattel, *The Law of Nations, or the Principles of Natural Law applied to the Conduct and to the Affairs of Nations and of Sovereigns*, trans. Charles G. Fenwick (Washington, 1916), Bk. 3 Sects 1, 26, pp. 235, 243.
16. Grotius, Bk 2 Ch. 23 Sect. 13, 253–4.
17. Grotius, Bk 2 Ch. 23 Sect. 13, 254.
18. Vattel, Bk 3 Sect. 40, 247.
19. Grotius, Bk 2 Ch. 1 Sect. 3–4, 73.
20. Grotius, Bk 1 Ch. 5 Sect. 3, 69; Augustine has used this metaphor in connection with both executioners and warriors ('one who owes a duty of obedience to the giver of the command does not himself "kill" – he is an

instrument, a sword in its user's hand': *City of God*, 32). Aquinas uses it to illustrate that the judge, and not the executioner, is to blame for the killing of an innocent man ('nor is it he who slays the innocent man but the judge whose minister he is': *Summa Theologiae* II.II Q.64 Art.6). Neither Augustine nor Aquinas, however, made the notion of instrumentality central to their characterization of the combatant or to their justification of killing in war, as Vattel was to do.

21. Vattel, Bk 3 Sect. 6, 237.
22. Vattel, Bk 3 Sects. 184, 187, pp. 302–3.
23. Grotius, Bk 2 Ch. 26 Sect. 3, 264.
24. Grotius, Bk 2 Ch. 26 Sect. 6, 267.
25. Grotius, Bk 2 Ch. 26 Sect. 4, 267.
26. Grotius, Bk 2 Ch. 24, Sect. 2, 255–6.
27. It is odd that a teaching of Jesus on such a serious matter as the taking of human life is treated as optional when teachings on less serious matters are regarded as binding.
28. Grotius, Bk 1 Ch. 2 Sect. 9, 36.
29. Vattel, Bk 3 Sect. 8, 237.
30. Vattel, Bk 3 Sects 9, 10, p. 238.
31. John Yoder points out how US law favours the general conscientious objector (often a member of a historic peace church) over the selective conscientious objector, who may be a Catholic or Lutheran honestly applying his own church's 'just war' principles and reaching a negative conclusion on a particular war or particular tactic; see Yoder 'How Many Ways Are There to Think Morally about War?' *Journal of Law and Religion* 11:1 (1994), 83–107. For the case of a non-religious selective conscientious objector refused conscientious objector status, see for instance Archibald Baxter, *We Will Not Cease* (Christchurch, 1968). Baxter was as keen as any political theorist to demarcate the combatant from the noncombatant, in his case because he was adamant that he would not serve militarily (though willing to grow food on his own farm in New Zealand, he refused to sow potatoes on the grounds of a British army camp in Belgium).
32. Vattel, Bk 3 Sect. 13, 240.
33. Grotius, Bk 3 Ch. 11 Sects 10–12, 355.
34. Grotius, Bk 2 Ch. 26 Sect. 6, 267, italics added.
35. Grotius, Bk 3 Ch. 1 Sect. 4, 271.
36. Grotius, Bk 3 Ch. 1 Sect. 4, 271.
37. Grotius, Bk 3 Ch. 25 Sect. 5, 443.
38. Grotius, Bk 3 Ch. 12 Sect. 8, 364–5.
39. Vattel, Bk 3 Sect. 168, 293.
40. Vattel, Bk 3 Ch. 8 Sects 145–6, pp. 282–3.
41. Vattel, Bk 3 Sects 136, 138, pp. 279–80.
42. Hartigan, *Forgotten Victim*, 104.
43. Jean-Jacques Rousseau, *The Social Contract*, trans. Maurice Cranston (Harmondsworth, 1968), 56; the lines come from the section, 'On Slavery',

in which Rousseau argues against Grotius as regards the liberties lost to a ruler through contracts.

7   Involvement and Total War

1. John Le Carré, *The Russia House* (Sevenoaks, 1990), 256.
2. Quoted in Hoffman Nickerson, *The Armed Horde: 1793–1939: the Rise, Survival and Decline of the Mass Army* (New York, 1940), 64.
3. Koch, *Rise of Modern Warfare*, 229–30.
4. H. W. Koch, *Modern Warfare 1815–Present* (London, 1985), 110.
5. Koch, *Modern Warfare 1815–Present*, 157.
6. Koch, *Modern Warfare 1815–Present*, 36.
7. Chris Hables Gray, *Postmodern War: the New Politics of Conflict* (London, 1997), 130.
8. Guilio Douhet, *The Command of the Air*, trans. D. Ferrari (New York, 1942), 195.
9. In 1938, US Secretary of State Cordell Hull declared of the German bombing of Guernica and Barcelona during the Spanish Civil War that 'No theory of war can justify such conduct.' On 1 September 1939, US President Franklin D. Roosevelt described as 'inhuman barbarism' the bombing of unfortified cities from the air and appealed for all sides to avoid it; see Gray, 131.
10. Archer Jones, *The Art of War in the Western World* (New York, 1987), 579.
11. Though President Reagan proposed, in March 1983, a 'Strategic Defence Initiative' aimed at intercepting nuclear warheads, no such system has yet been developed. Research and development continues under President George W. Bush into the proposal, now renamed National Missile Defense.
12. For example, William Temple, Archbishop of Canterbury from 1942 to 1944, defended the bombing of German cities with the claim that citizens of a modern state are implicated in the wrongs of their governments; see S. L. Lammers, 'William Temple and the Bombing of Germany: an Explanation in the Just War Tradition', *Journal of Religious Ethics* 19:1 (Spring 1991), 71–92. Another Briton, Robert Thouless, had already pointed out how such claims of national war guilt, and the justification of war as punishment, commonly rely on a deceptive use of language. To say 'John has done wrong therefore John may be punished' makes some sense as long as we are referring to the same person. If, however, the first is John Smith and the second John Jones, then an injustice is committed in punishing someone who has done no wrong. Likewise, a country's name can be used twice in the same sentence but with different meanings. The word that is the name of a country may mean a particular part of earth's surface, a people, a culture, all the inhabitants of that territory, most of the inhabitants, the country's past or present political leadership, its past or present military leadership, or its past or present armed forces. To say 'Iraq refuses to abide by Security Council resolutions and Iraq will

be subjected to punitive airstrikes' or 'Serbia has treated Kosovo unjustly so Serbia must now suffer the consequences' is to commit a similar confusion. Rarely is any serious claim made of the collective guilt of the whole population on the basis of act or omission; see Thouless, 27.

13. In his speech on 16 January 1991, then-President George Bush appeared to threaten the people of Iraq unless they somehow changed their government or its policies: 'It is my hope that somehow the Iraqi people can, even now, convince their dictator that he must lay down his arms, leave Kuwait, and let Iraq itself rejoin the family of peace-loving nations' (quoted in Laurie Calhoun, 'Violence and Hypocrisy', *Dissent* 48:1 (Winter 2001), 79–85(85)). Any hint of punishment in the justifications of the strikes on Iraq would have been unjust in that most Iraqis played no role in Saddam's accession to power (some may even have tried to prevent it). As Vattel wrote in 1758: 'The threat of unjust punishment is itself unjust; it is both an insult and an injury. But to carry it into effect would be barbarously cruel': Vattel, Bk 3 Ch. 8, 282.

14. Jenny Teichman, *Pacifism and the Just War* (Oxford, 1986), 94–5.

15. Maurice Pearton, *The Knowledgeable State: Diplomacy, War and Technology since 1830* (London, 1982), 186.

16. Hartigan, *Forgotten Victim*, 115.

17. Best, 120–1.

18. *Protocol Additional to the Geneva Conventions of 12 August 1949, and Relating to the Protection of Victims of International Armed Conflicts (Protocol 1)*. The first three sections of Article 51 are repeated verbatim in the second Additional Protocol (dealing with non-international armed conflicts) as Article 13, sections 1, 2 and 4.

19. Best, 255.

20. *Annex to Hague Convention IV, 1907: Regulations Respecting the Laws and Customs of War on Land*.

21. Best, 127.

22. *Protocol Additional to the Geneva Conventions of 12 August 1949, and Relating to the Protection of Victims of International Armed Conflicts (Protocol 1)*. Intriguingly, AP1 refuses to give to mercenaries the status of lawful combatant. In Article 47, it denies the right to combatant or prisoner-of-war status to fighters who are not nationals of a party to a conflict, not members of its armed forces, and 'motivated to take part in the hostilities essentially by the desire for private gain'. This attitude to mercenarism is a remnant of the old Augustinian model's view of the combatant as 'just warrior' and its concern that the just warrior be motivated by the 'right intention'. This attitude does not fit with the modern era's view of the combatant as a depersonalized instrument who attracts no guilt by killing and who need not be guilty to be himself killed.

23. Best, 255.

24. Best, 255.

25. Barry Buzan and Eric Herring, *The Arms Dynamic in World Politics* (London, 1998), 150.

26. Palmer-Fernández, 'Civilian Populations in War', 510n.
27. Buzan and Herring, 141; Michael Sirak, 'US DoD Considers Testing Non-Lethal Energy Weapons', *Jane's Defence Weekly* 35:10 (7 March 2001), 15; Don Stauffer, 'Electronic Warfare: Battles without Bloodshed', *The Futurist* (January–February 2000), 23–6.
28. Though not without qualms: President Nixon, in his 1971 report to Congress, declared, 'I must not be – and my successors must not be – limited to the indiscriminate mass destruction of enemy civilians as the sole possible response to challenges' (*U.S. Foreign Policy for the 1970s: Building for Peace*, Washington, 25 February 1971, 58). More nuclear options ('counterforce' or military-targeting ones as well as 'countervalue' or civilian-targeting ones) were the result of these qualms.
29. This view has been questioned e.g. Andrew Erdmann, 'The U.S. Presumption of Quick, Costless Wars', *Orbis* 43:3 (Summer 1999), 363–82.

8 Conclusion

1. Gavin Lyall, *The Most Dangerous Game* (London, 1966), 223.
2. It is true that liberals who are consequentialists can value human life as simply one good among others, to be weighed and traded against other goods. However, something of the characteristic liberal focus on the individual is lost in a purely consequentialist approach to the taking of human life.
3. As the previous chapter pointed out, it is true that, as that century progressed, soldiers' humanity and individuality came to be more and more acknowledged. By the end of the twentieth century, it was no longer acceptable in many countries to treat soldiers like cannon fodder, as happened in the First World War. However, it is still the case that soldiers (during war and until they become *hors de combat*) are treated as instruments. Their lives may be taken as means to an end and not as a response to their acts.
4. Death is a sortal concept: one either is or is not dead.
5. Baldness is a scalar concept: one can be more bald or less bald.
6. G. I. Mavrodes, 'Conventions and the Morality of War', *Philosophy and Public Affairs* 4:2 (1974–75), 117–31. Mavrodes's stance is one sort of 'conventionalist' moral theory. Such theories hold that moral rules are justifiable because they have emerged as conventions in society, or because they are socially useful, or because it would be in our rational self-interest to accept them. The content of moral rules, according to these theories, cannot be justified independently of their acceptance or the effects of their acceptance. Examples of conventionalist moral theories include rule-consequentialism and contractualism. See Jeff McMahan, 'Self-Defence and the Problem of the Innocent Attacker', *Ethics* 104 (January 1994), 252–90(289).
7. Mavrodes, 127.

8. Gabriel Palmer-Fernández, 'Innocence in War', *International Journal of Applied Philosophy* 14:2 (Fall 2000), 161–74(170), italics added.
9. Palmer-Fernández, 'Innocence in War', 170.
10. Mavrodes, 128. .
11. Thomas Nagel, 'War and Massacre', *Mortal Questions* (Cambridge, 1979), 66, italics in original
12. The justice of capital punishment is a matter of continuing debate. My concern here is solely to dismiss the justification of killing in war on the basis of guilt, desert or punishment. Advocates of the 'just war' approach may believe that capital punishment is permissible only as a 'last resort' when other punitive options, such as long-term imprisonment, are not available.
13. Given the historical influence of the Church of Rome on Western moral thought on war, and the focus on Catholic formulations of 'just war' issues which persists regardless of the religious affiliations of the scholars, it is interesting then to note the stance taken by the supreme authorities within the Catholic Church of late. War has changed fundamentally since Augustine sought to justify it; so too have the alternatives to war. Pope Pius XII, in his 1944 Christmas message declared: 'The theory of war as an apt and proportionate means of solving international conflict is now out of date' (quoted in Ramsey, *War and the Christian Conscience* (Durham, NC, 1961), 84). On 1 January 1993, Pope John Paul II took a similar stance: 'After so many unnecessary massacres, it is in the final analysis of fundamental importance to recognise, once and for all, that war never helps the human community, that violence destroys and never builds up, that the wounds it causes remain long unhealed and that as a result of conflicts the already grim condition of the poor deteriorates still further and new forms of poverty appear' (quoted in Brian Kane, *Just War and the Common Good: Jus ad Bellum Principles in Twentieth Century Papal Thought* (San Francisco, 1997), 70). The only exception to this prohibition on war permitted by John Paul is self-defence; the only example he has cited of a just war was the resistance by East European countries to Nazi aggression.
14. E. Anscombe, 'War and Murder', in Richard A. Wasserstrom (ed.), *War and Morality* (Belmont, 1970), 42–53, esp. 49.
15. Anscombe, 'War and Murder', 45, italics added.
16. A Jesuit priest, writing in 1996, claims precisely this; see Richard J. Regan SJ, *Just War: Principles and Cases* (Washington, DC, 1996), 87.
17. John C. Ford, 'The Hydrogen Bombing of Cities', in W. J. Nagle (ed.), *Morality and Modern Warfare* (Baltimore, 1960), 98–103, esp. 98.
18. A point made by Laurie Calhoun, 'Violence and Hypocrisy'. To the usual deaths by blast, bullet, burns, blood loss, shock, asphyxiation and exposure were added deaths by live burial for those Iraqi soldiers in Desert Storm whose emplacements were overrun by allied tanks fitted with bulldozer blades.
19. In fact, capital punishment is excluded by the Charters of the International Criminal Tribunal for the former Yugoslavia, the International Criminal Tribunal for Rwanda and the proposed International Criminal Court.

20. Mark Osiel, *Obeying Orders: Atrocity, Military Discipline and the Law of War* (New Brunswick, NJ, 1999), 66.
21. But to kill their aged mother in order to distract them from killing you (or someone else) is to fail to treat that woman as a person; Jeff McMahan investigates the issues of innocent bystanders, culpable attackers and innocent attackers in 'Self-Defence and the Problem of the Innocent Attacker'.
22. See Seumas Miller, 'Killing in Self-Defense', *Public Affairs Quarterly* 7:4 (October 1993), 325–39; D. Wasserman, 'Justifying Self-Defence', *Philosophy and Public Affairs* 16:4 (1987), 356–78.
23. Kenneth W. Kemp, 'Punishment as a Just Cause for War', *Public Affairs Quarterly* 10:4 (October 1996), 335–53 (338). For a discussion of the differences between self-defence and self-preservation, see Jeff McMahan, 'Self-Defence and the Problem of the Innocent Attacker'.
24. See P. Woodruff, 'Justification or Excuse: Saving Soldiers at the Expense of Civilians', in K. Nielsen and S. C. Patten (eds), *New Essays in Ethics and Public Policy (Canadian Journal of Philosophy,* Supplementary Volume VIII, 1982), 159–76.
25. Anscombe, 45.
26. M. Cohen, T. Nagel and T. Scanlon, *War and Moral Responsibility* (Princeton, 1974), 20.
27. R. K. Fullinwider, 'War and Innocence', *Philosophy and Public Affairs* 5:1 (1975–76), 90–7(94).
28. *The Sunday Times* (London, 8 August 1999).
29. Jeffrey P. Whitman, 'The Soldier as Conscientious Objector', *Public Affairs Quarterly* 9:1 (January 1995), 87–100(94).
30. Lt. Gen. Sir John Hackett, *The Profession of Arms* (London, 1962), 40.
31. Woodruff, 175.
32. As noted above, due to the nature of warfare then most were also killed preventatively. In most cases of the killing of combatants in war then there was more than one reason why it was just.
33. Woodruff, 175, 176; italics in original.
34. Gourvenic, 4; see also Walzer, *Just and Unjust Wars*, 25–9.
35. Gourvenic, 4.
36. E.g. 'The war in Vietnam is unjust and immoral and, if ordered to do so, I shall refuse to fight in that war. I should prefer ... that this resignation be accepted': Cpt. Dale E. Noyd, USAF, quoted in Whitman, 'The Soldier as Conscientious Objector', 87.
37. Barrie Paskins and Michael Dockrill, *The Ethics of War* (London, 1979), 224–5, italics added.
38. For an account of the extent to which a conscientious objector had to go to refuse military service in a Western democracy (and the punishments he suffered), see Baxter, *We Will Not Cease.*
39. Punitive attacks on the civilian population are illegal and wrong. Attacks on civilian or civilian property with the aim of reducing civilian morale are illegal and wrong. So too are attacks on civilians or civilian property

in order to put pressure on the enemy government to change its policies. Indeed, any direct attack on civilians or civilian property with the aim of bringing about any outcome at all from that attack is absolutely prohibited. These are all prohibited regardless of one's attitude to the 'principle of double effect'; even proponents of that principle condemn also any collateral killing of civilians in numbers wholly disproportionate to the intended good effect.

40. The principle's placing of great moral significance on the distinction between what a person brings about intentionally and what he foresees will result from his act but which he does not intend is controversial. The interest stems from an attempt to strengthen absolutist-deontological morality in the face of the dominant consequentialist approaches. The principle of double effect operates to redefine the scope of an absolutist moral prohibition (such as that on ever killing an innocent person). It is thought crucial to absolutist morality which can otherwise prove inflexible and yields results that seem intuitively wrong; Anscombe writes: 'These absolute prohibitions of Christianity ... are bedrock and without them the Christian ethic goes to pieces. Hence the necessity of the notion of double effect', (50–1); see Nagel, 'War and Massacre'; Frances Kamm, 'Non-Consequentialism and the Person as an End-in-Itself and the Significance of Status', *Philosophy and Public Affairs* 21:4 (Fall 1992), 354–89; Warren Quinn, 'Actions, Intentions and Consequences: the Doctrine of Double Effect', *Philosophy and Public Affairs* 18:4 (Fall, 1989), 334–51; Sophia Reibetanz, 'A Problem for the Problem of Double Effect', *Proceedings of the Aristotelian Society* 98 (1998), 217–23.

41. AP1 Article 51.5; see Chapter 7, n. 18.

42. To many philosophers, the primary feature of the principle of double effect is the great moral significance it attaches to the distinction between killing that is intended and killing that is foreseen but unintended. However, intentions may be less than clear in war. When a doctor performs a hysterectomy in pregnancy, he clearly does not intend the death of the unborn child (he bears the child no malice; he does not benefit from its death). In the case of the collateral killing of civilians, there may often be a clear benefit to one side of decreasing civilian morale and increasing popular pressure on the government to end the war. The claim not to intend a result which one foresees, and which one knows will be beneficial to oneself or one's cause, may be a difficult one to make credibly in the heated and desperate circumstances of war. Some philosophers argue that it is in any case difficult to provide convincing and practical criteria that distinguish between intended means and foreseen-but-unintended side-effects; see Jeff McMahan, 'Revising the Doctrine of Double Effect', *Journal of Applied Philosophy* 11:2 (1994), 201–12.

43. See Sophie Botros, 'An Error about the Doctrine of Double Effect', *Philosophy* 74:1 (January 1999), 71–83; Whitley R. P. Kaufman, 'On a Purported Error about the Doctrine of Double Effect: a Reply to Sophie Botros', *Philosophy* 75:2 (April 2000), 283–95; and Quinn.

44. Kaufman, 292.
45. Judith Lichtenberg, 'War, Innocence and the Doctrine of Double Effect', *Philosophical Studies* 74:3 (June 1994), 347–68.
46. In other cases to which the principle of double effect is applied, the good end is clear. In the performance of a craniotomy or a hysterectomy in pregnancy, it is the saving of a woman's life. So too when a bystander pulls a lever to divert a run-away trolley bus onto a track where it will kill only one person rather than five: five lives are saved and only one lost; the 'trolley bus' is a widely discussed case in recent philosophic literature; see Judith Jarvis Thompson, 'The Trolley Problem', in her *Rights, Restitution and Risk* (Cambridge, MA, 1986); see also Kamm, 'Non-Consequentialism, the Person as an End-in-Itself', and 'The Doctrine of Triple Effect and Why a Rational Agent Need Not Intend the Means to His End', *Proceedings of the Aristotelian Society*, Supplementary Volume LXXIV (2000), 21–39.
47. Again, this distinguishes war from other cases. In the craniotomy, hysterectomy and trolley bus cases, the good or right end that is sought can be attained. The surgical intervention will save the woman's life at the cost of her pregnancy; pulling the lever will save five lives and lose one. The probability of attaining the good end is much lower in war.
48. There is also an issue concerning alternative means to the same end. The act, which results in the collateral killing of civilians, should not be performed if other options are available which would achieve the end without killing civilians. But the act which kills civilians in war is rarely a genuine 'last resort' (any more than war itself). In the craniotomy and hysterectomy cases, one is presented with a stark and horrible choice. Someone will die, whatever one chooses to do, but one can act so as to ensure the survival of more rather than a few, or of a woman rather than an unborn baby. In the case of attacks on military objectives which will also kill civilians, one is rarely presented with this choice so starkly, especially when a strategic perspective is taken.
49. This is a problem particularly for the 'precise' interpretation of the fourth condition.
50. A status of combatants which, this chapter has argued, is just as long as the combatants have consented to occupy that role.
51. The death in the trolley bus case is wrong as it is not an accidental (unforeseen) death. One innocent human life cannot be justly traded for five. The death is certain to occur if one pulls the lever, and it occurs because of one action. That action should therefore not be done.
52. Richard Hull, 'Deconstructing the Doctrine of Double Effect', *Ethical Theory and Moral Practice* 3:2 (2000), 195–207.
53. Hull, 203.
54. Lichtenberg, 'War, Innocence and the Doctrine of Double Effect'.
55. Camillo C. Bica, 'Another Perspective on the Doctrine of Double Effect', *Public Affairs Quarterly* 13:2 (April 1999), 131–9(138).
56. Civilians who consent or acquiesce to be 'civilian shields' at a military target are a separate issue. They may be judged to have consented to

being targeted in war. For further on the problem of 'innocent shields', see McMahan, 'Self-defence and the Problem of the Innocent Attacker'.

57. Take, for example, an aggressor state that has invaded and occupied a country and now defends it with coerced conscripts or child-soldiers. They cannot be killed consensually, only preventatively. The usual strategy, bombardment by air or artillery prior to an invasion, is unjust. It is only when they constitute an imminent threat to the life of another that they may be attacked. Yet, as the 'yellow card' instructions for Northern Ireland make clear, one may not have to give the adversary first shot when killing them preventatively.

58. Quoted by Tim Barela, 'To Win a War', *Airman* 43:9 (September 1999), 2–3, esp. 3.

59. Charles J. Dunlap Jnr., 'The End of Innocence: Rethinking Noncombatancy in the Post-Kosovo Era', *Strategic Review* (Summer 2000), 9–17(12).

60. Stauffer, 26.

61. Dunlap, 14; italics in original.

62. Dunlap, 14.

63. Dunlap, 16.

Bibliography

Alexander, Lawrence A., 'Self-Defence and the Killing of Noncombatants: a Reply to Fullinwider', *Philosophy and Public Affairs* 5:1 (Fall 1975), 408–15.

Allmand, C. T. (ed.), *War, Literature and Politics in the Late Middle Ages* (Liverpool: Liverpool University Press, 1976).

Anscombe, G. E. M., 'War and Murder', in Richard A. Wasserstrom (ed.), *War and Morality* (Belmont: Wadsworth, 1970), 42–53.

Augustine, *City of God*, ed. David Knowles (Harmondsworth: Pelican Classics, 1972).

Augustine, *The Political Writings of St. Augustine*, ed. Henry Paolucci (Chicago: Gateway, 1962).

Bainton, Roland, *Christian Attitudes towards War and Peace: a Historical Survey and Critical Re-evaluation* (London: Hodder & Stoughton, 1961).

Barela, Tim, 'To Win a War', *Airman* 43:9 (September 1999), 2–3.

Baxter, Archibald, *We Will Not Cease* (Christchurch: Caxton Press, 1968).

Best, Geoffrey, *War and Law since 1945* (Oxford: Clarendon Press, 1994).

Bica, Camillo C., 'Another Perspective on the Doctrine of Double Effect', *Public Affairs Quarterly* 13:2 (April 1999), 131–9.

Bica, Camillo C., 'Collateral Violence and the Doctrine of Double Effect', *Public Affairs Quarterly* 11:1 (January 1997), 87–92.

Botros, Sophie, 'An Error about the Doctrine of Double Effect', *Philosophy* 74:1 (January 1999), 71–83.

Buzan, B., and Herring, E., *The Arms Dynamic in World Politics* (London: Lynne Rienner, 1998).

Calhoun, Laurie, 'Violence and Hypocrisy', *Dissent* 48:1 (Winter 2001), 79–85.

Cohen, M., Nagel, T., and Scanlon, T., *War and Moral Responsibility* (Princeton: Princeton University Press, 1974).

Comnena, Anna, *The Alexiad of Princess Anna Comnena*, trans. E. A. S. Dawes (London: Routledge & Kegan Paul, 1967).

Contamine, Philippe, *War in the Middle Ages*, trans. Michael Jones (Oxford: Basil Blackwell, 1984).

Douhet, Guilio, *The Command of the Air*, trans. D. Ferrari (New York: Coward McCann, 1942).

Draper, G. I. A. D., 'Penitential Disciplines and Public Wars in the Middle Ages', *International Review of the Red Cross* (April and May 1961).

Duby, G., *The Three Orders: Feudal Society Imagined*, trans. A. Goldhammer (Chicago: University of Chicago Press, 1980).

Dunlap, Charles J. Jnr., 'The End of Innocence: Rethinking Noncombatancy in the Post-Kosovo Era', *Strategic Review* (Summer 2000), 9–17.

Elshtain, Jean Bethke (ed.), *Just War Theory* (Oxford: Basil Blackwell, 1992).

Erdmann, Andrew, 'The U.S. Presumption of Quick, Costless Wars', *Orbis* 43:3 (Summer 1999), 363–82.

Featherstone, Donald, *Warriors and Warfare in Ancient and Medieval Times* (London: Constable, 1997).

Finlay, Fergus, *Snakes and Ladders* (Dublin: New Island Books, 1998).

Ford, John C., 'The Hydrogen Bombing of Cities', in W. J. Nagle (ed.), *Morality and Modern Warfare* (Baltimore: Helicon Press, 1960), 98–103.

Ford, John C., 'The Morality of Obliteration Bombing', in Richard A. Wasserstrom (ed.), *War and Morality* (Belmont: Wadsworth, 1970), 15–41.

Fullinwider, R. K., 'War and Innocence', *Philosophy and Public Affairs* 5:1 (1975–76), 90–7.

Goetz, Hans-Werner, 'Protection of the Church, Defence of the Law, and Reform: On the Purposes and Character of Peace of God, 989–1038', in Head and Landes, *Peace of God*, 259–79.

Gourvenec, Diana, 'The Combatant/Non-combatant Distinction in Just War Theory: Does It Have a Moral Basis?', M.A. Thesis, University of Essex, 1992.

Gray, Chris Hables, *Postmodern War: the New Politics of Conflict* (London: Routledge, 1997).

Green, Michael, 'War, Innocence and Theories of Sovereignty', *Social Theory and Practice* 18:1 (Spring 1992), 39–62.

Grotius, Hugo, *De Jure Belli ac Pacis* (The Law of War and Peace), trans. L. R. Loomis, with an intro. by P. E. Corbett (Roslyn, NY: Walter J. Black, 1949).

Hackett, Lt. Gen. Sir John, *The Profession of Arms* (London: Times, 1962).

Hamilton, Bernice, *Political Thought in the Sixteenth Century* (Oxford: Clarendon Press, 1963).

Hartigan, Richard Shelley, *The Forgotten Victim: a History of the Civilian* (Chicago: Precedent Publishing, 1982).

Hartigan, Richard Shelley, 'St. Augustine on War and Killing: the Problem of the Innocent', *Journal of the History of Ideas* 27:2 (1966), 195–204.

Head, Thomas, and Landes, Richard (eds), *The Peace of God: Social Violence and Religious Response in France around the Year 1000* (Ithaca: Cornell University Press, 1992).

Holmes, Robert, *On War and Morality* (Princeton: Princeton University Press, 1989).

Hull, Richard, 'Deconstructing the Doctrine of Double Effect', *Ethical Theory and Moral Practice* 3:2 (2000), 195–207.

Johnson, James Turner, *Ideology, Reason and the Limitation of War: Religious and Secular Concepts 1200–1740* (Princeton: Princeton University Press, 1975).

Johnson, James Turner, *Just War Tradition and the Restraint of War a Moral and Historical Enquiry* (Princeton: Princeton University Press, 1981).

Johnson, James Turner, 'The Meaning of Non-Combatant Immunity in the Just War/Immunity War Tradition', *Journal of the American Academy of Religion* 39:2 (June 1971), 151–70.

Johnson, James Turner, *The Quest for Peace: Three Moral Traditions in Western Cultural History* (Princeton: Princeton University Press, 1987).

Jones, Archer, *The Art of War in the Western World* (New York: Barnes & Noble, 1987).

Kamm, Frances M., 'The Doctrine of Triple Effect and Why a Rational Agent Need Not Intend the Means to His End', *Proceedings of the Aristotelian Society*, Supplementary Volume LXXIV (2000), 21–39.

Kamm, Frances M., *Morality and Mortality*, vol. 1 *Death and Whom to Save from It* (Oxford: Oxford University Press, 1993).

Kamm, Frances M., 'Non-Consequentialism and the Person as an End-in-Itself and the Significance of Status', *Philosophy and Public Affairs* 21:4 (Fall 1992), 354–89.

Kane, Brian, *Just War and the Common Good: Jus ad Bellum Principles in Twentieth Century Papal Thought* (San Francisco: Catholic Scholars Press, 1997).

Kaufman, Whitley R. P., 'On a Purported Error about the Doctrine of Double Effect', *Philosophy* 75:2 (April 2000), 283–95.

Keen, M. H., *The Laws of War in the Late Middle Ages* (London: Routledge & Kegan Paul, 1965).

Keenan, James F., SJ, 'The Function of the Principle of Double Effect', *Theological Studies* 54 (1993), 294–315.

Kemp, Kenneth W., 'Just-War Theory: a Reconceptualization', *Public Affairs Quarterly* 2:2 (April 1988), 57–74.

Kemp, Kenneth W., 'Punishment as a Just Cause for War', *Public Affairs Quarterly* 10:4 (October 1996), 335–53.

Kenny, Anthony, *Aquinas* (Oxford: Oxford University Press, 1980).

Koch, H. W., *Medieval Warfare* (London: Bison, 1978).

Koch, H. W., *Modern Warfare 1815–Present* (London: Bison Books, 1985).

Koch, H. W., *The Rise of Modern Warfare 1618–1815* (London: Bison, 1981).

Lammers, S. L., 'William Temple and the Bombing of Germany: an Explanation in the Just War Tradition', *Journal of Religious Ethics* 19:1 (Spring 1991), 71–92.

Lauranson-Rosaz, Christina, 'Peace from the Mountains: the Auvergnat Origins of the Peace of God', in Head and Landes, *Peace of God*, 104–34.

Le Carré, John, *The Russia House* (Sevenoaks: Coronet, 1990).

Lichtenberg, Judith, 'War, Innocence and the Doctrine of Double Effect', *Philosophical Studies* 74:3 (June 1994), 347–68.

Lyall, Gavin, *The Most Dangerous Game* (London: Pan Books, 1966).

MacFarlane, Katherine Nell, 'Isidore of Seville on the Pagan Gods', *Transactions of the American Philosophical Society*, vol. 70 part 3 (1980), 3–10.

McMahan, Jeff, 'Revising the Doctrine of Double Effect', *Journal of Applied Philosophy* 11:2 (1994), 201–12.

McMahan, Jeff, 'Self-defence and the Problem of the Innocent Attacker', *Ethics* 104 (January 1994), 252–90.

Mangan, Joseph, 'An Historical Analysis of the Principle of Double Effect', *Theological Studies* 10 (1949), 41–61.

Mavrodes, G. I., 'Conventions and the Morality of War', *Philosophy and Public Affairs* 4:2 (1974–75), 117–31.

Miller, Seumas, 'Killing in Self-Defence', *Public Affairs Quarterly* 7:4 (October 1993), 325–39.

Moore, R. I., 'Postscript: the Peace of God and the Social Revolution', in Head and Landes, *Peace of God*, 308–26.

Murphy, Jeffrie G., 'The Killing of the Innocent', *The Monist* 57:4 (October 1973), 527–50.

Nagel, Thomas, 'War and Massacre', *Mortal Questions* (Cambridge: Cambridge University Press, 1979).

Nagle, W. J. (ed.), *Morality and Modern Warfare* (Baltimore: Helicon Press, 1960).

Nickerson, Hoffman, *The Armed Horde: 1793–1939: the Rise, Survival and Decline of the Mass Army* (New York: Putnam's Sons, 1940).

Norman, Richard, *Ethics, Killing and War* (Cambridge: Cambridge University Press, 1995).

O'Brien, William V., *The Conduct of Just and Limited Wars* (New York: Praeger, 1981).

Oman, C. W. C., *The Art of War in the Middle Ages* (Ithaca: Cornell University Press, 1953).

Osiel, Mark, *Obeying Orders: Atrocity, Military Discipline and the Law of War* (New Brunswick, NJ: Transaction Publishers, 1999).

Palmer-Fernández, Gabriel, 'Civilian Populations in War, Targeting of', in *Encyclopedia of Applied Ethics*, vol. 1 (San Diego: Academic Press, 1998), 509–25.

Palmer-Fernández, Gabriel, 'Innocence in War', *International Journal of Applied Philosophy* 14:2 (Fall 2000), 161–74.

Paskins, Barrie, and Dockrill, Michael, *The Ethics of War* (London: Duckworth, 1979).

Pearton, Maurice, *The Knowledgeable State: Diplomacy, War and Technology since 1830* (London: Burnett Books Ltd., 1982).

Preston, Richard A., Wise, Sydney F., and Werner, Herman O., *Men in Arms: a History of Warfare and Its Interrelationship with Western Society* (London: Thames and Hudson, 1962).

Quaker Faith and Practice (London: Yearly Meeting of the Religious Society of Friends (Quakers) in Britain, 1995).

Quinn, Warren, 'Actions, Intentions and Consequences: the Doctrine of Double Effect', *Philosophy and Public Affairs* 18:4 (Fall 1989), 334–51.

Ramsey, Paul, *The Just War* (Lanham, MD: University Press of America, 1968).

Regan, Richard J., *Just War: Principles and Cases* (Washington, DC: Catholic University of America Press, 1996).

Reibetanz, Sophia, 'A Problem for the Problem of Double Effect', *Proceedings of the Aristotelian Society* 98 (1998), 217–23.

Remarque, E. M., *All Quiet on the Western Front*, trans. A. W. Wheen (London: Putnam, 1970).

Remensnyder, Amy G., 'Pollution, Purity and Peace: an Aspect of Social Reform between the Late Tenth Century and 1076', in Head and Landes, *Peace of God*, 280–307.

Rousseau, Jean-Jacques, *The Social Contract*, trans. Maurice Cranston (Harmondsworth: Penguin, 1968).

Russell, F. H., *The Just War in the Middle Ages* (Cambridge: Cambridge University Press, 1975).

Scott, J. B. (ed.), *The Classics of International Law* (Washington, DC: Carnegie Institute of Washington, 1917).

Sirak, Michael, 'US DoD Considers Testing Non-Lethal Energy Weapons', *Jane's Defence Weekly* 35:10 (7 March 2001), 15.

Spaulding, O. L., and Nickerson, H., *Ancient and Medieval Warfare* (London: Constable, 1994).

Spencer, Herbert, *Principles of Ethics* (London: Williams & Norgate, 1892).

Stauffer, Don, 'Electronic Warfare: Battles without Bloodshed', *The Futurist* (January–February 2000), 23–6.

Teichman, Jenny, *Pacifism and the Just War* (Oxford: Basil Blackwell, 1986).

Thomas Aquinas, *Summa Theologiae*, trans. Fathers of the English Dominican Province (London: Burns Oates & Washbourne, 1917–22).

Thompson, Judith Jarvis, *Rights, Restitution and Risk* (Cambridge, MA: Harvard University Press, 1986).

Thouless, Robert H., *Straight Thinking in War-time* (London: Hodder & Stoughton, 1942).

Tolstoy, Leo, *The Kingdom of God Is within You*, ed. and trans. Leo Wiener (London: G. J. Howell & Co., 1905).

Tooke, Joan D., *The Just War in Aquinas and Grotius* (London: SPCK, 1965).

United States Catholic Bishops, 'The Challenge of Peace: God's Promise and Our Response', The Pastoral Letter on War and Peace, 1983, in Elshtain, *Just War Theory*, 77–168.

Vattel, Emmerich de, *The Law of Nations, or the Principles of Natural Law applied to the Conduct and to the Affairs of Nations and of Sovereigns* (1758), trans. Charles G. Fenwick (Washington, DC: Carnegie Institute, 1916).

Verbruggen, J. F., *The Art of Warfare in Western Europe during the Middle Ages: From the Eighth Century to 1340*, trans. Sumner Willard and S. C. M. Southern (Oxford: North-Holland Publishing Co., 1977).

Vitoria, Francisco de, *De jure belli*, in J. B. Scott (ed.), *The Classics of International Law* (Washington, DC: Carnegie Institute of Washington, 1917), 163–87.

Vitoria, Francisco de, *Political Writings*, ed. Anthony Pagden and Jeremy Lawrence (Cambridge: Cambridge University Press, 1994).

Vitoria, Francisco de, *The Principles of Political and International Law in the Work of Francisco de Vitoria*, intro. by Antonio Truyol Serra (Madrid: Ediciones Cultura Hispanica, 1946).

Walzer, Michael, *Just and Unjust Wars* (New York: Basic Books, 1977).

Wasserman, D., 'Justifying Self-Defence', *Philosophy and Public Affairs* 16:4 (1987), 356–78.

Wasserstrom, Richard A. (ed.), *War and Morality* (Belmont: Wadsworth, 1970).

Whitman, Jeffrey P., 'The Soldier as Conscientious Objector', *Public Affairs Quarterly* 9:1 (January 1995), 87–100.

Woodruff, P., 'Justification or Excuse: Saving Soldiers at the Expense of Civilians', in K. Nielsen and S. C. Patten (eds), *New Essays in Ethics and Public Policy* (*Canadian Journal of Philosophy*, Supplementary Volume VIII, 1982), 159–76.

Yoder, J. H., *He Came Preaching Peace* (Scottdale, PA: Herald Press, 1985).

Yoder, J. H., 'How Many Ways Are There to Think Morally about War?' *Journal of Law and Religion* 11:1 (1994), 83–107.

Yoder, J. H., *The Original Revolution: Essays on Christian Pacifism* (Scottdale, PA: Herald Press, 1971).

Yoder, John H., 'Surrender: a Moral Imperative', *The Review of Politics* 48:4 (Fall 1986), 567–95.

Index

Printed in the United States
19578LVS00001BA/9

9 780333 972373